# ON DEVELOPMENT AND EDUCATION
## OF YOUNG CHILDREN

Lili Peller with Dr. Montessori, Vienna, 1924
—Photo by Elli Weisz

Lili E. Peller

# ON DEVELOPMENT AND EDUCATION OF YOUNG CHILDREN

Selected Papers

Edited by Emma N. Plank

Philosophical Library
New York

301.4314
P360
107225
Nw.1978

# Contents

Introduction                                          vii
    by Emma N. Plank

List of Publications by Lili E. Peller            xxiv

Acknowledgments                                     xxix

*Section I: The Child's Living Environment*
Editor's Comments                                       3
  1. Educational Remarks                      11
  2. The Children's House                     19

*Section II: Child Development and Educational*
*       Practice*
Editor's Comments                                      39
  1. Incentives to Development and Means of Early
     Education                  41
  2. The Development of the Child's Self       55
  3. Language and its Pre-Stages              72
  4. Character Development in Nursery School   76
  5. The School's Role in Promoting Sublimation 89
  6. Psychoanalysis and Public Education      108

*Section III: Children's Play*
Editor's Comments                                     123
  1. Theories of Play                         128
  2. Survey of Development and Types          145

3. Play and the Theory of Learning   194

*Section IV: Language - From Children's Books to Language Theory*

Editor's Comments   205
1. From "Language and its Pre-Stages"   208
2. Daydreams and Children's Favorite Books   210
3. Reading and Daydreams in Latency, Boy-Girl Differences   236
4. Freud's Contribution to Language Theory   252
5. From "Affective and Cognitive Development of the Child"   278

*Section V: Thoughts on Adoption*

Editor's Comments   283
1. About "Telling the Child" of His Adoption   286
2. Further Comments on Adoption   300
Index   319

# INTRODUCTION

By Emma N. Plank

It may come unexpected to find a close connection between those two breakers of tradition in the early part of our century—Sigmund Freud, the founder of psychoanalysis, and Maria Montessori, the originator of a method of education. Yet Professor Freud wrote the following to Dr. Montessori:

December 20, 1917.

It gave me great pleasure to receive a letter from you. Since I have been preoccupied for years with the study of the child's psyche, I am in deep sympathy with your humanitarian and understanding endeavors, and my daughter, who is an analytical pedagogue, considers herself one of your disciples.

I would be very pleased to sign my name beside yours on the appeal for the foundation of a little institute . . . The resistance my name may arouse among the public will have to be conquered by the brilliance that radiates from yours.[1]

Now the psychoanalytic movement and the Montessori movement have gone different ways. Each has its role in the America of today, but the areas and nature of their influence are separate. Psychoanalysts and all others who work the ground first cultivated by Freud, and on the other hand those who have brought the Montessori method to new life and bloom in this country are different groups of people. The two systems of thought do not connect.

Almost alone among writers on either of the two subjects, Lili Peller had the double background of knowledge and experience in both. The papers assembled here, selected from her writings over four decades, deal with psychoanalytic ideas and with the science and practice of education. If the towering figure of Freud embodied for her all that was most important and valuable in psychology, Montessori similarly represented what was original and forward-looking in education.

That was the horizon, these were the lode stars. Their guiding beam was perceived early. The word "disciples" in Freud's letter, as I quoted it, may be a bit strong—the German original has *Anhaengerinnen* (adherents, followers, supporters)—but be this as it may, Freud's "disciple"- daughter helped us young Montessori teachers, through a bi-weekly seminar she led, to better understand children's behavior and our response to it. This was initiated and facilitated by Lili Peller's active study of psychoanalysis, which she began in the Mid-'Twenties—but more about this later. In a letter to Dr. Rudolf Ekstein, written after Lili Peller's untimely death, Anna Freud said:

> The first meetings of my colleagues and myself with Lili Peller were most exciting ones. This was in Vienna, in the 1930's, i.e., when we were intent on forging links between psychoanalysis and education. At that time Lili Peller had already built up a model nursery school which combined the best elements of the Montessori method with the application of the most important principles of psychoanalytic child-psychology. Her work in that setting was admirable and acted as an inspiration. We formed contacts then which continued

Lili Peller as a Young Girl

Lili Peller in the 1920s

on a different level after she had become a psychoanalyst herself, and which did not cease to exist until her death.[2]

There is something special about Lili Peller's writings. I think that as readers work themselves through this book, they will feel her highly individual tone. There is scholarship, of course, there is a certain immediacy, honesty, and clarity, and there is her unwavering feeling for children. There is caution as well: Her papers deal with carefully limited subjects, and she proceeds like a mountain climber, who goes one measured step at a time, probing for a foothold and putting his weight on his foot only after he has assured himself that the ground is firm. I believe that these characteristics of her writing flow from her personality and from the role that writing played in her career.

Publishing papers was part of her professional work, but she never wrote for a living. It would be trite to say that she only wrote when she had something to say, but in the context of her life it means that she only put on paper what she thought were secure conclusions, that she only wrote when she had puzzled out something, when she was convinced she had found a solution to one of the never ending riddles of childhood, and wanted to share her findings with her colleagues; or, when she had carefully evaluated a prevailing practice, found it wanting, and thought the time was ripe to submit an alternative solution to the scrutiny of those concerned like herself.

In one of her papers she quotes with evident approval the saying that a person's reach should exceed his grasp. Creating a synthesis of the Montessori system and psychoanalysis in her writing as well as in her daily work, she reached far. She utilized such divergent disciplines as biology, modern art, dance, human ecology, and linguistics, for an enriched understanding of child development, the reactions of the educator, and the theory and practice of education in general. Her papers deal with reality and observations, addressing themselves to workers with children, teachers, therapists, and at the same time they add a significant challenge to a number of professions ranging from architecture to social work.

The causes Lili Peller embraced have had their ups and downs in public favor. She was too independent for that to faze her. When she had weighed the evidence and the arguments and had arrived at a definite point of view, she simply sent her paper out, for people to allow themselves to be influenced by it, be it sooner or later.

While over the years she tied and untied bonds of allegiance, her thoughts were always her own. Where she built on Maria Montessori's ideas, she did so in the most undoctrinaire fashion. Her psychoanalytic studies penetrated into border zones that had not been preempted. Anna Freud's simple comment on the continuing contacts covers a multifaceted development that can best be understood by considering LP's life history.

* * * *

She was born Lili E. Roubiczek, in 1898, in Prague, the daughter of an upper middle class family where the role expectation for her included to be well educated, but not independent. Following the pattern of their time and class, the real care of the child was given to a "Fraeulein," a warm and dedicated woman. Lili learned Czech from her, and they remained close to each other throughout their lives.

Prague at the turn of the century was prosperous but tense. It was the city where Rainer Maria Rilke was raised, where Franz Kafka was an adolescent when Lili Roubiczek was born. The German-speaking minority formed the top layer, though the independent history of Prague until the 17th century had been as distinguished or indeed grander than Vienna's. Formerly a seat of empire, Prague has the oldest Central European university—which Lili entered, to study biology. She did not finish her studies, but biology as a background supported much of her later work, though it only re-emerged as an overt interest much later—one of her last papers, not included in this collection, was on "Biological Foundations of Psychology: Freud vs. Darwin."

In her university years her interest in the exploration of life became more specific: She turned to the study of the child and of its tool, education. Could it be that her concern sprang from her wish to have been better understood as a child herself? She left home to be independent, and went to Vienna where she studied psychology with Karl Buehler who stimulated her interest in the development of language—this again, as we shall see, an interest that kept flowing on as an undercurrent to well up to the surface much later—see our Section IV. The real opportunity came when Lili decided in 1920 to study with Dr. Montessori in London.

After her return, then 23 years old, she started the "Haus der Kinder" (the Vienna Montessori School) and the "Arbeitsgemeinschaft" (working group) of five of us, sixteen to eighteen years old, who helped in running it.

This was a peculiar beginning of an educational movement—in one of the drabbest working class districts of the city impoverished by World War I, but full of the hopes for the young republic. It was for us a time of serious dedication, but also of hilarious incidents which still seem to give the real flavor of Lili Peller at the time; all that in a place that operated as a day care center for young children, open eleven hours a day, in one of the poorest parts of the city that had lost a war and an empire.

A day care center built during the war for children whose mothers worked in nearby factories had been remodeled by two English people who—as so often with relief workers after a war—had fallen in love with Vienna and its potentialities. They and Lili had attended the Montessori course in London and planned to open the new school together. Not merely in my eyes, but for anybody who cared to look, this new school offered a splendid setting.

It opened for 25 children—and without money to run it. The only income was a monthly allowance from Prague for Lili. I do not know whether the idea of the "Arbeits-gemeinschaft" would have developed had there been money to pay salaries to workers; but it emerged as the plan that those of us who wanted to train as Montessori teachers should first serve a year of practice in some area needed to maintain the school; I started in the kitchen. We all lived at the school. We slept on the children's cots, though within a year we graduated to a small apartment (with water and toilet outside in the hallway, as typical in a proletarian neighborhood of that time).

It was what would now be called a commune (in the eyes of our mothers a life of "senseless self-degradation"), one devoted to a purpose, in our case services to under-privileged children, though the term had not yet been invented. The way we lived and our dedication is very reminiscent of some Peace Corps workers of recent years; the same hope that what we did really mattered and should help build a better world.

The School was to be a center of training as well as service. From the beginning there was the interest not only in setting up the best possible environment for the growth of spontaneous activities in children, but also in training young people for such work. This training could be com-pared to a "co-op" program of two years' duration for a selected group of students who from the start worked on anything necessary to run the place and who became an integral part of the educational community. For instance, I, then seventeen, was responsible for running the kitchen for the 25 children during my first year, but at the same time I could initiate our six weeks living in the country where I lived with four two-year-olds and a few wild mice.

We spent evenings studying psychology, sociology, Montessori's books, and especially Italian so we would be prepared to understand her lectures when our turn came to go to one of the international training courses. After about two years of practice each of us went abroad to study directly under Dr. Montessori, who visited our school repeatedly and was deeply interested in our program, and to return home for new responsibilities. LP accompanied her often on her travels, as catalyst and interpreter and as a trusted friend. Her dedication to Dr. Montessori was limitless at that time. And I think she was the only one of her students who could experiment and broaden the system.

The group of us young people grew; but something more important occurred: educators and social workers in Vienna had taken notice of our work. Seminars began for kindergarten teachers in the day care centers run by the City. A year or two later they were formalized into a two-year training course in the Montessori method which culminated in four months of study with Dr. Montessori herself. Students came from many parts of Central Europe (incidentally, Erik H. Erikson was one of our students). Lili Peller became a consultant to the Child Welfare Department of the City of Vienna, which planned for more than ten thousand children.

An even more helpful sign of recognition came when the City Welfare Department gave us a subsidy to operate the school. It is almost incomprehensible how Lili achieved the recognition and active support from public sources within a short time. None of us had any of the official credentials then; as a matter of fact, we despised the formality of prescribed training. But the exposure to learning, though within our own group, was tremendous. Biology, dance, graphic art, architectural planning were integrated into our learning through Lili Peller's intoxication with them.

The most fruitful exposure, though, for most of us came in the late 'Twenties when psychoanalysis and its meaning for educators and education opened up for us through Lili Peller's vision. In the seminar with Anna Freud we learned how to observe children and to report for consultation. Some of us took the sequence of training for teachers at the Vienna Psychoanalytic Institute and had the good fortune to have the foremost analysts (they later emigrated to England and the U.S.) lecture to us or lead reading and other seminars. Psychoanalysis, first as it clarified the role of the educator and later as a therpeutic tool, became Lili's consuming interest. She was invited to participate in the seminar on child analysis which Anna Freud started as the training platform for the first child analysts. Her hope to interest Dr. Montessori in psychoanalysis did not succeed, though; this probably was the beginning of the loosening of their bond.

Lili E. Peller's original school in the working class district was bombed out of existence in World War II. The much grander Haus der Kinder which is referred to in the Section on the environment still stands, but alterations in Nazi times have changed its character. The City commemorated her work in Vienna by naming a street for Lili Peller near the original building.

* * * *

We trained not as child therapists but as psychoanalytically oriented educators. Lili went further and when she came to this country in 1938 began to work as a psychoanalyst. But her interest in education and educators did not stop. Many of the earlier American papers in this collection, those from the years 1946 to 1958, deal with problems she originally discussed with a seminar of teachers at New York City College. Her eagerness to bring insights of analytic psychology to teachers in practice had found an outlet.

She had meanwhile, in 1933, married Dr. Sigismund Peller, a physician and medical researcher. Her dedication to him and his work were the core of her life from then on. Still, her own interests and professional pursuits remained as vital as ever. When the first wave of Fascism hit Austria, the Pellers left for Jerusalem, where Lili soon established an elementary school. Later Dr. Peller accepted a research professorship in human biology at Johns Hopkins, and his wife joined him in Baltimore in 1937. In 1940 they moved to New York, which remained their home for the next quarter of a century.

Lili Peller could not duplicate here the breadth of influence that she had built up in Vienna; but those she did influence—mostly through her role in professional training, her outstanding activity in her American career, felt the impact. Her teaching branched into the psychiatric field when she became a lecturer at Albert Einstein College of Medicine and at the Philadelphia Institute for Psychoanalysis where she lectured regularly to candidates in training and where she was elected to honorary membership. Some of her later writings appeared in the Bulletin of that Association. One of the residents in psychiatry at that time (1964-1966) at Albert Einstein's Jacobi Hospital spoke of her influence:

> I had the opportunity to work with Mrs. Peller for two years as a resident in child psychiatry. She supervised me both individually and at a continuous case seminar made up of my peers from Jacobi Hospital. As an individual supervisor she was quite firm, successfully dealing with my attempts to avoid facing my personal areas of difficulty which might have interfered with my learning therapeutic techniques. She supervised me with several therapy cases other than the case I was presenting to the conference and when she dis-

Lili Peller in 1966

covered that I had a special interest in the culturally restricted child, she was able to call upon her knowledge both of children in institutions and in such neighborhood pre-school groups as Headstart. Not content to hear my description, she actually accompanied me to the orphanage at which I was consulting and spent the day seeing it for herself as well as conducting a case conference for the staff. There I had an opportunity to see her with children. They were captivated by her and she respected them.

She never said I was a good doctor. She never critically undermined my confidence in myself. She helped me to understand my own special abilities and to begin to develop them. I thought my relationship with her was unique—but while I was preparing this little talk, I spoke with my colleagues who had also been supervised by Mrs. Peller and learned that they felt the same way.[3]

In her paper "The Children's House," written in 1950, published posthumously in 1972, Lili Peller returned to her first love, architecture for children's group living. The last area of her great interest in the 1960s was the development of language and literature. She enlarged her sizeable collection of children's books begun in Vienna and she became an active member of the language seminar at the New York Psychoanalytic Institute. Two papers in Section IV show her involvement. Her overwhelming interest in the rights of children led her in her later years also to the study of problems of adoption and the two publications we are including in this collection.

*   *   *   *

English was not Lili Peller's mother tongue. She had grown up in a German language environment, to some extent bilingually (German-Czech). She used Italian as a disciple of Montessori. Later English became the working language of the second part of her adult life.

In preparing this collection I had to translate several papers which exist only in German. I encountered some minor difficulties. The word for "child" for instance is neuter in German, and the grammatically corresponding pronoun would be "it." I have mostly rendered it by "he," though I wish there were a "neutral" way. Nevertheless I hope the articles transmit the warmth and understanding of children that permeates them all.

I could not have accomplished the excerpting from widely different papers in trying to form a whole while showing Peller's development, and the translating of many passages, all by myself. The loyal cooperation and critical insights of my husband, Robert Plank, made it possible. We are also very grateful to our friend Rosemary McKinnon, now of the Child Study Center at Yale University, who encouraged us in the belief that Peller's writings were as valuable to today's workers in the field as they were when first written. She also edited some of the unpublished material.

We have naturally reprinted the bibliographical references as they were in the original papers. Where I felt that more recent works should in addition be brought to the readers' attention, I have occasionally mentioned this in the Editor's Comments to the Section.

I hope that this book will not merely serve as a memorial to a unique human being, but will enrich the thinking of those who try to give stability to children in this troubled world: to social workers and educators, to students of psychology and psychiatry, to all those who have the power to plan for children and to stand for their rights and opportunities.

## NOTES:

[1]Freud, Ernst L., ed. *The Letters of Sigmund Freud*. New York: Basic Books, 1960. p. 319.

[2] *The Reiss-Davis Clinic Bulletin*, Spring 1967, 4:10.

[3]Harrison, Phyllis Anne. *Speech at Lili E. Peller Memorial Meeting*, New York, December 17, 1966.

# List of Publications by Lili E. Peller

* denotes papers included, in whole or in part, in this book.
(R) = published under maiden name, Lili E. Roubiczek.
(P-R) = published under name Lili E. Peller-Roubiczek.
Some early papers, book reviews and articles in popular magazines have been omitted.

1924 (R) "Die Arbeitsgemeinschaft der Montessori-Schule, Wien X" (The Cooperative of the Montessori School, Vienna X), *Call of Education*, 3.
*1926 (R) "Das Kinderhaus" (The Children's House), *Der Aufbau* (Vienna), No. 8/9.
1926 (R) "Montessori-Methode und Kindergartenreform" (The Montessori Method and the Reform of the Kindergarten), *Neue Erziehung*.
1926? (transl.) (anonymous) Maria Montessori. *Das Kind in der Familie* (The Child in the Family). Vienna: Montessori-Schule.
1927 (R) "Die Grundsaetze der Montessori-Erziehung" (The Principles of Montessori Education), *Zeitschrift fuer psychoanalytische Paedagogik*, 2.
1929 (R) (ed. and contributor) *Aus dem Arbeitskreis der Wiener Montessori-Schule* (From the Scope of Work of the Vienna Montessori School). Vienna: Montessori-Schule.

*1932 (R) "Die wichtigsten Theorien des Spieles," (The Most Important Theories of Play), *Zeitschrift fuer psychoanalytische Paedagogik*, 6.

*1933 (P-R) "Gruppenerziehung des Kleinkindes vom Standpunkt der Montessori-Paedagogik und der Psychoanalyse" (Education of Young Children in Groups, from the Viewpoints of Montessori Pedagogy and of Psychoanalysis), *Zeitschrift fuer psychoanalytische Paedagogik*, 7.

1934 (P-R) (with Hilde Fischer) "Eingewoehnungsschwierigkeiten im Kindergarten" (Difficulties of Adjustment in Kindergarten), *Zeitschrift fuer psychoanalytische Paedagogik*, 8.

*1935 (P-R) "Paedagogische Bemerkungen" (Educational Remarks), in: "Ein 'Haus der Kinder' " (A Children's House), *Moderne Bauformen* (Stuttgart).

1936 (P-R) "Zur Kenntnis der Selbstmordhandlung" (On Understanding the Suicidal Act), *Imago*, 22.

1939 "Psychological Implications of Institutional Life for Children," *The Family*, 20.

1939 "The Child's Approach to Reality," *American Journal of Orthopsychiatry*, 9.

1941 "Some of the Needs of Children," *Children's Institutions*.

1942 "The Roots of Discipline," *Child Study*, 19.

1942 "Institutions Must Be Good," *Survey Graphic*.

1943 "Eating in Groups in Wartimes," *Mental Hygiene*, 27.

1943 "For Better Institutions," *Survey Midmonthly*.

1944 "Early Conflicts and Triumphs," *Child Study*, 21.

1946 "Nursery School Readiness," *Childhood Education*, 23.

1946 "Significant Symptoms in the Behavior of Young Children: A Check List for Teachers," *Mental Hygiene*, 30.

*1946 "Incentives to Development and Means of Early Education," *The Psychoanalytic Study of the Child*, II. Reprinted in: *Studying Psychology and Teaching* (publ. by Scott Foresman, 1957).

1947 "The Child's Need to Anticipate," *Childhood Education*, 23.

*1948 "Character Development in Nursery School," *Mental Hygiene*, 32.

*1952 "Models of Children's Play," *Mental Hygiene*, 36. Reprinted in: R.E. Herron & B. Sutton-Smith. *Child's Play* (New York: Wiley, 1971).

*1954 "Libidinal Phases, Ego Development, and Play," *The Psychoanalytic Study of the Child*, IX. German transl. in: G. Bittner and E. Schmid-Cords. *Erziehung in frueher Kindheit*. 6. ed. Munich: Piper, 1976.

1954 "He Learns Through Activities and Toys," *Your Young Child (Childcraft)*. Chicago: Field Enterprises.

1955 "Libidinal Development as Reflected in Play," *Psychoanalysis*, 3. Reprinted in: M. Hayworth. *Child Psychotherapy*. New York: Basic Books, 1964. German transl. in: G. Biermann, ed. *Handbuch der Kinder-psychotherapie*. Munich: Reinhardt, 1969 (Spanish transl., 1974).

*1956 "The School's Role in Promoting Sublimation," *The Psychoanalytic Study of the Child*, XI.

*1958 "Reading and Daydreams in Latency: Boy-Girl Differences," *Journal of the American Psychoanalytic Association*, 6.

*1958 *The Development of the Child's Self*. New York: Early Childhood Education Council.

*1959 "Daydreams and Children's Favorite Books," *The Psychoanalytic Study of the Child*, XIV.

*1961 "About 'Telling the Child' of His Adoption," *Bulletin of the Philadelphia Association for Psychoanalysis*, 11.

*1963 "Further Comments on Adoption," *Bulletin of the Philadelphia Association for Psychoanalysis*, 13.

*1964 "Language and Its Pre-Stages," *Bulletin of the Philadelphia Association for Psychoanalysis*, 14. Modified version in: P. B. Neubauer, ed. *Concepts of Development in Early Childhood Education*. Springfield, Ill.: Chas. C. Thomas, 1965.

1965 "Sex Education of the Young Child," *Journal of Sex Research*, 1.

1965 "Comments on Libidinal Organization and Child Development," *Journal of the American Psychoanalytic Association*, 13.

1965 "Biological Foundations of Psychology: Freud versus Darwin," *Bulletin of the Philadelphia Association for Psychoanalysis*, 15.

*1966 "Freud's Contribution to Language Theory," *The Psychoanalytic Study of the Child*, XXI.

*1967 "Psychoanalysis and Public Education," *Reiss-Davis Clinic Bulletin*, 4.

*1972 "The Children's House," *Man-Environment Systems*, 2.

# ACKNOWLEDGMENTS

Permission to reprint papers by Lili E. Peller, whole or in part, from several journals and a yearbook where they originally appeared, is gratefully acknowledged: *Bulletin* (now *Journal*) *of the Philadelphia Association for Psychoanalysis* ("About 'Telling the Child' of His Adoption." "Further Comments on Adoption." "Language and Its Pre-Stages"). *Bulletin of the Reiss-Davis Clinic* ("Psychoanalysis and Public Education"). *Journal of the American Psychoanalytic Association* ("Reading and Daydreams in Latency, Boy-Girl Differences"). *Man-Environment Systems* ("The Children's House"). *Mental Hygiene* (now *Mental Health*) ("Character Development in Nursery School." "Models of Children's Play"). *The Psychoanalytic Study of the Child* ("Incentives to Development and Means of Early Education." "Libidinal Phases, Ego Development, and Play." "The School's Role in Promoting Sublimation." "Daydreams and Children's Favorite Books." "Freud's Contribution to Language Theory").

This book also contains Lili Peller's lecture "The Development of the Child's Self," originally published by the Early Childhood Education Council, and parts of "Das Kinderhaus" (from *Aufbau*), "Paedagogische Bemerkungen" (from *Moderne Bauformen*), "Die wichtigsten Theorien des

Spieles" (from *Zeitschrift fuer psychoanalytische Paedagogik*), and "Gruppenerziehung des Kleinkindes" (from *ibid.*). These papers, written in German, were translated by Emma N. Plank. Parts of Lili Peller's manuscript *Affective and Cognitive Development of the Child* are here published for the first time by courtesy of her husband, S. Peller, M.D. Thanks are likewise due to the following for permission to quote: Rudolf Ekstein, Ph.D. (letter to him from Anna Freud); Phyllis Harrison Ross, M.D. (from her speech at Lili E. Peller Memorial Meeting). Suhrkamp Verlag (from a letter by Hermann Hesse). Letter 178 in LETTERS OF SIGMUND FREUD, selected and edited by Ernest L. Freud, (C) 1960 by Sigmund Freud Copyrights Ltd., London, Basic Books, Inc., Publishers, New York.

# Section I.
# The Child's Living Environment

# Editor's Comments

Lili Peller's interest in creating the right environment as a decisive factor in child development goes back to her early days as an educator when she had become a disciple of Maria Montessori. It was the outgrowth of many intellectual and artistic stimuli of Central Europe in the 1920s. The unique fusion of the understanding of developmental needs and the ambiance in which they can unfold and move to the next "level" are, in this writer's opinion, perhaps Peller's most enduring contribution to the literature on early childhood. It stands in direct contrast to the tenets of behavior modification where changes in personality growth are predicted to occur through a system of rewards rather than through the stimulation of children to take these steps on their own, encouraged by the environment and by their eagerness to please adults and to identify with them.

Peller writes in an early paper, published in *Der Aufbau* (Vienna), 1926:

> Man alone among all creatures attempts to adapt his environment to himself rather than himself to his environment. But to what extent he can succeed depends in turn largely on the environment. Confined within four blank walls and without tools he would be as unable to act as when he is confronted with such a mass of objects that any orientation becomes impossible. This is, of

course, even more true of the child's still undeveloped abilities. His environment should therefore be clear and comprehensible, but at the same time it must lend itself to being modified and molded. If we meet these needs, we will have created a unique field of action for the child's intelligence, his energy, and his will.

We begin to realize that the task we have set ourselves—to design and equip buildings for children—is not an easy one. The environment has much more power over the individual who is not yet fully grown than over the mature one. This is a general biological fact. If we deny it we merely make our children grow up in an environment that is unfavorable to them and hampers their development. What a senseless waste of the vitality of the coming generation!

. . . We know that every room we enter communicates its "mood" to us. This goes for the concert hall as well as for the tavern. This mood causes us to adjust our entire behavior, our gestures, the way we move, our voice. The room's "atmosphere" affects us, mostly unconsciously. We should use this potential purposely and extensively in equipping rooms for children. In other words, we should assign psychological functions to the room, functions that heretofore have mostly been vested in the educator.

This brings us to the core of the problem. We adults are content with a room that provides us with a frame for our work and social life, that at most sets a basic mood. For the child the room has to be more: an intellectual and emotional guide. Yet it can only give what it has received. Thus a new task opens: The educator has to prepare the rooms that provide this type of guidance.

This involvement with the environment of early childhood led to planning, with the late architect Franz Schuster,

4

to build the Vienna "Haus der Kinder." An extensively illustrated monograph, written by him and Lili Peller, on the plan for the building (see illustration) and its utilization, was published in *Moderne Bauformen* (Stuttgart) in 1935. I quote from Professor Schuster's introduction:

> We can only show photographs here, which entails the risk that one might look at the building and its rooms as "architecture," though they don't mean to be anything but a simple, unpretentious frame for the children's own small world.
>
> The child develops his skills and forms his relationships to the children's community through his spontaneous interaction with his environment—people and objects. The adult gives the necessary guidance and instruction as inconspicuously as possible. Everything conforms to the child's measurements and is accessible without assistance, so he can grasp everything ("grasp" in both its meanings!). Door knobs, light switches, shelves and cupboards, all are low enough to be reached. Utensils and toys are arranged in special clusters for free choice.
>
> Window sills are low, the windows are large, but there are no glass walls. The room should be equally homey in winter and summer. There is to be an inside and an outside. Each group—the "Haus der Kinder" has three groups of up to thirty children each—is a unit in itself, with its separate entrance from the street. The rooms it consists of—large activity room, niches for cooking and other domestic work, garderobe, wash room—are restricted to use by the one group. The three groups are connected by corridors. The central part has an upper story—a large room used for free movement and dance, for naps for some children, and also for parent meetings and occasional lectures.
>
> The house is kept as simple as possible. Special atten-

View from the garden (from the South).

GROUND PLAN Scale 1:400. The arrow points to the North. 1 Main entrance, 2 Entrance hall with Dutch door to office, 3 Foyer, 4 Stairs to upper story (see Editor's Comments), 5 Stairs to basement.

*Group A:* 6 Entrance to 7 Cloak room, 8 Washroom and toilets, 9 Activity room, 10 Housekeeping corner, 11 Terrace.

*Group B:* 12 Group entrance, 13 Entrance hall, 14 Hall, 15 Entrance to 16 Cloak room, 17 Washroom and toilets, 18 Activity

room, 19 Housekeeping corner, 20 Quiet corner, also usable as observation booth with entrance from hall, 21 Storage closet, 22 Terrace.

*Group C:* 23 Group entrance, 24 Entrance hall, 25 Hall, 26 Entrance to 27 Cloak room, 28 Washroom and toilets, 29 Activity room, 30 Shop and kitchen corner, 31 Quiet corner, 32 Terrace.

*Administration:* 33 Secretary's office, 34 Director's office, 35 and 39 Connecting hallway, 36 Cloak room and toilets for staff, 37

Janitor's quarters, 38 Kitchen with entrance from street, 40 Service kitchen (with cabinets accessible from kitchen and children's housekeeping corner).

*Bath:* 41 Dressing room, 42 showers.

*Garden:* 43 Playground, 44 Gym equipment, 45 Carrousel, 46 Balancing beam, 47 Teeter toter, 48 Tool and animal shed, 49 Quiet shady corner with table and benches, 50 Wading pool and shower, 51 Sundial, 52 Area for children's plantings, 53 Loading zone.

# Floor plan of "Haus der Kinder"

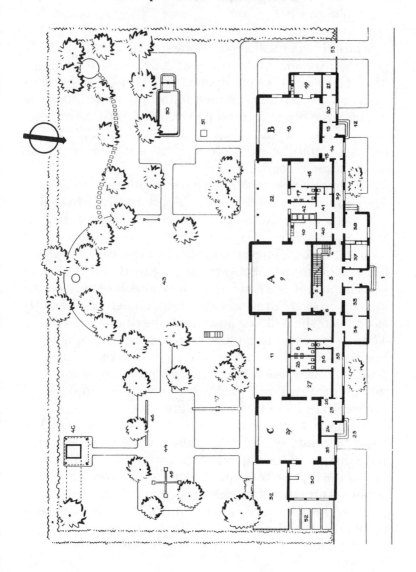

tion to halls, additional rooms, and decoration, such as we often see in school buildings, has been intentionally avoided. It is neither school nor institution: it is a children's house.

Schuster here speaks both of one special building and of a general program. At the time these ideas were formulated (the "Haus der Kinder" opened in 1930) Peller's understanding had already widened to include in the planning not only the optimal environment for the growth of independent physical and intellectual functioning and interaction in a group of children: she had put their emotional needs in the foreground.

This is very clear in the first paper reprinted here, *Educational Remarks* (in the original publication of 1935 following Schuster's architectural ones). The second paper, written about twenty-five years later, shows how the idea of the "children's house" never left Peller's imagination. Applying her insights to the then wide opening field of child care in this country, it is a condensation of a larger study on the interaction of children and their environment, particularly as it affects the building and equipping of nursery schools. Though it was written more than twenty years ago, it still holds some basic and unobserved truths for today. *The Children's House* is a solid texture, a synthesis of progressive thought from different fields and therefore stimulating to professionals from various backgrounds.

The great upswing in centers for young children, like Head Start and similar programs, and the ever increasing yet unmet need for day care facilities have raised the question of the right setting on a broad basis. Unfortunately the public sector has not yet seized the opportunity to provide the best possible environment for children. No noticeable number of "children's houses" has been built.

Peller's ideas are of crucial value for any attempt to improve the situation, but they are also capable of wider application. I personally am particularly interested in applying them to work with hospitalized children or in children's institutions. Some of her basic ideas can be and have been translated into setting up an environment for child patients that allows many children to grow rather than to regress during hospitalization.

# 1.

# EDUCATIONAL REMARKS

*The Vital Needs of the Young Child*

If the young child is to live and to develop into a normal adult, that is into a person who fits into the community and who is productive and leads a full emotional life, certain basic requirements have to be met.

Adults must provide nutrition, bodily care, and safety for the young child. The child also needs loving interest and the personal involvement of his mother or a person who in her place provides for his needs. That this is a vital problem and not just a sentimentality has been seen in young children who were permanently placed in institutions: In spite of excellent physical care, they remained backward in their physical and mental development (hospitalism).

A third developmental requirement is less easily understood. Indeed, it seems to be contradicted by the infant's complete helplessness: The child needs opportunities for activity which call for the full commitment of his abilities. He must find objects and arrangements in his environment that elicit all the abilities he can muster at the stage of his physical and mental development, and that strengthen them. We therefore consider it an overriding task of a children's house to provide such arrangements.

*The Child at Work*

The work must be freely chosen by the child. Only this will bring out in full force his enjoyment of activity. If the

11

child performs some work only because of external pressure, he will try to discharge it in a superficial and perfunctory manner.

Are we speaking of *work* in talking about small children? First of all, the concept of work as used here is a biological, not a social concept. We call "work" any activity of the young child in which he engages with his deepest interest. We are doing this because any such activity is of decisive value for the building of his personality, regardless of whether in the world of the adults it is of some utility or appears useless. It is customary to call an activity work or play, depending on the external result. It is not rare either that work is distinguished from play depending on whether something is done with pleasure, or without pleasure and merely from a sense of duty. We reject such criteria for the concept of work. We consider many activities as serious work which colloquially are called child's play.

### The Definite Spatial Order

Tools and other objects for the child's use should be so arranged that he can see them at a glance. Then he can choose activities without first telling the adult what he wants—which in many cases he wouldn't even be able to do, since he only gradually develops a clear, verbally expressible understanding of what he wants. This is why the child's immediate contact with the things he may use is so important, and this is what the children's house facilitates.

There is still another reason for clear spatial arrangements: Just as the child feels more secure in a house where all objects correspond to his own size, so he also feels more secure where an order prevails that he can understand. We expect of the child, however, that he will return every object to its place after use. This is one of the rules of the children's house, and newcomers learn to follow it quickly and usually without friction.

12

## The Loose Temporal Order

While the spatial order is strict, the temporal order is loose. This seems to be a contradiction. But it results from the child's special relationship to time. Children's life is timeless.

The child should feel secure and as master of his situation. He should not be forever interrupted in his activity because this or that is on the schedule. The course of the day in the life of an adult city dweller runs from one point fixed in time to another. He has learned to keep to a schedule without extra expenditure of energy. There should, however, be as few points fixed in time as possible in a child's life. These, on the other hand, have to be faithfully observed; both to let them become automatic more easily.

The educator must know that children do many things more slowly, others faster, than adults. This is caused by the particular nature of childhood. It gradually subsides, even without an adult engaging in exhausting guerilla warfare against it (Hurry up! Stop dreaming! Don't just stand there and look!). There are many useful skills which the child tries to acquire because he could thereby reduce his feeling of dependence. His home may block him in some such attempts (concerning eating, dressing, cleaning up), but he can acquire and cultivate them in the children's house, simply because the tempo is left to the child.

## The Floor Plan

The "modern" school and the "modern" nursery school differ from the old-style school in their better hygienic equipment—ventilation, heating, bathrooms, showers, etc. These improvements are most welcome, but it is a cause for regret that this is considered sufficient and that the barracks-type floor plan is retained. There is a more or less wide hall, a cluster of bathrooms and dressing rooms, and a row of class rooms or play rooms. Now of course it is

13

cheaper to cluster the bathrooms, to place the class rooms in a row, etc.—but it would be even cheaper to cram more children into one class, to lay off teachers, and all in all to spend as little as possible for education. What we aimed at in our children's house was to create for every group of children an adequate and clearly defined area. The floor plan was governed by the educational task. The essential point is to group all principal and auxiliary rooms of each section into one independent unit with a separate entrance from the street.

## Number of Children per Group

The psychological considerations which make such a separation of the groups of a nursery school desirable, even necessary, can be outlined briefly. It is one thing for a child to live in a community of twenty to thirty, another thing to become part of a crowd of a hundred several times a day (in dressing rooms, toilets, etc.). He can find relationships— albeit loose ones—to thirty other children; but a hundred remains a confusing, alien, and therefore hostile crowd. To feel responsible for a room or for a wash stand that is used by twenty to thirty children is possible. But when rooms are used by a hundred children, the individual child will feel as little relationship to them and as little responsibility as adults in a bus depot.

Within the group, the direct connection of the various rooms to each other is important. The activity room has glass doors to the terrace. When they are open some of the children can be active in the room, some outdoors, this does not have to be "organized," the adult does not have to take over or to raise her voice. It is important for preschool children that as much as possible they find all they need in adjacent rooms connected by glass doors. A workshop or a washroom accessible only by way of a long corridor or a staircase thereby practically loses its value. These are every-

14

day experiences of educational practice which the architect must consider. When the child goes from one room to the other, he remains under the educator's supervision. Each group is a clear unit in itself, where all rooms and utensils have a purpose that the child can clearly grasp.

*Terraces and Gardens*

The connection of playroom and garden is on purpose not too free and open. The terraces (positioned to be protected from wind) are extensions of the room. Being spatially defined they are themselves in a sense rooms. Their further extension is the wide open yard, where a separation of units no longer prevails. Smaller or larger groups form naturally outdoors. In the warm season all the children's work takes place on the terraces and in the garden. But the door to the room remains always open, so a child can at any time return indoors. For children, like adults, feel a need to spend some time in a closed room even in summer. Our generation has out of opposition to the previous one formulated various "ideals," which the adult, however, does not always practice consistently, so we should not force them on children either. Outdoor living is one of them. True, until a short time ago outdoor living was underestimated, but we must not now overestimate its possibilities and significance.

*The Various Opportunities for Activity*

Variety of materials for children's activities seems to us as important as careful selection to eliminate the noxious and the superfluous. Of the play materials which have long been used in nurseries we have selected those which serve as *raw material*. They give the child a wealth of the most elementary—and just for that reason most important—knowledge of material and at the same time take his ability into account to form things (clay, paper, sand, building blocks, paint). The Montessori material is there—including those parts that lead toward the intellectual conquest of reading, writing, and arithmetic—and there are *functional games* which, similar to the Montessori material, elicit the child's independent activity and stimulate his intelligence.

We attribute special significance to the simple activities of daily living. In Vienna's children's house we have made a number of them accessible to the children. In all stages of planning we were intent on arranging everything in the house in such a way that the children could participate helpfully in the needed daily work.

*Practical Work in Daily Living*

Domestic work—preparing meals, kitchen work, cleaning the rooms, the utensils, the child's own body—offers, in my opinion, educational advantages which no teaching material in the narrower sense of the word can replace. First of all these activities make possible the release of energy, since for the most part sweeping movements are required, rarely small and accurate ones. The process of the work as such is uniform—no sequences of different stages—and it repeats itself daily, in many cases several times a day, in its simple entirety. The child therefore can see it as a whole and easily grasps its intent and purpose; he can choose it on his own.

Where there is no sequence of different stages of the work, there is furthermore no need for the constant supervision by the adult that can so easily become oppressive. This distinguishes house work from crafts, where one wrong move can destroy the result of the entire effort so that here the constant supervision, assistance and advice of the adult is needed throughout the activity.

Also, the child can more easily see the connection between his efforts and their effect. The result of his work is the measure of his effort. The evaluation and classification

16

Cutting Vegetables in the Children's Kitchen.
—Photo by Elli Weisz

by the adult can be dispensed with as reality itself is the judge. Small or awkward efforts will yield an acceptable, but meagre result. The child can observe how with better work the result improves, too. He soon gains insight into the use of his work for the children's community of which he is a part. Not only his hands are active, but also his will, his intelligence, his inventiveness. So domestic work becomes also mentally the child's own.

Various tendencies within the child that press for expression can be acted out here: e.g., the enjoyment of all activity involving water or dirty work, such as shining shoes or brass, where hands get good and black. These drives do not simply spill over, senselessly and destructively, in domestic work; they are integrated into meaningful work sequences. The ultimate goal steers the child's work, giving it direction and meaning. But this steering is relaxed, it is inherent in the work, it does not have to be put into words. Therefore it does not restrain the child as much as all the advising and correcting on the part of the adult.

A simple example will make this clear. A swimming pool for dolls, a toy that it has been fashionable to give to children, caters to the enjoyment of playing with water. But here the drive merely finds an *outlet*, while in our domestic work it is poured into an activity that has its significance in reality. In the one case, the value for the child is that he can release, abreact a drive; in the other case his effort does not evaporate, it returns to the child as perceptible result. A tendency toward pleasurable action was utilized to create a chance for activity which enables the child not merely to release his drives but also to establish contact with his environment on a higher level. And this is in our opinion the core of education: *so to direct the child's life and actions that what he does out of innermost joy, out of deepest need, will also be accepted and positively judged in the social world in which he lives.*

# 2.

## THE CHILDREN'S HOUSE

"We need in every part of the city units in which intelligent and co-operative behavior can take the place of mass regulations, mass decisions, mass actions, imposed by ever remoter leaders and administrators. Small groups: small classes: small communities; institutions framed to the human scale, are essential to the purposive behavior in modern society."

(Lewis Mumford: *The Culture of Cities*)

*Introduction*

We take it for granted today that "form follows function," as Louis Sullivan has said, or, rather that good form crystallizes from use. The planner of a home should know well the kind of people who will live and work in the house he is to build. Our concern here is with the house where groups of active children will spend a large part of their day.

The house is a powerful agent contributing to the happiness or the strain of its inhabitants. There is no doubt that the teacher is the most important factor in nursery school. Yet even the most devoted teacher has a limited amount of energy and resilience. It depends largely upon the layout and the equipment of the house whether her working day is a long chain of drudgery and repetitious toil, or a sensible sequence of things which can be done with dispatch and ease.

Before there can be improvements in nursery school

19

housing in a community, people with imagination and courage must visualize them. To achieve better schoolhouses all the teachers who are professionally alert must become interested in housing. Then it may well be that ten years from now photographs of today's nursery schools will be shown with a smile, just as today we smile at grandmother's kitchen.

Looking at some photographs hence, it will seem unbelievable that the houses had been especially adapted and planned for children, and that groups of active youngsters were brought to these buildings and lived in them for eight or more hours daily. Indifference, pessimism, and inertia are our real enemies, not discontent with present conditions.

Modern engineering can help nursery school teachers. This means that we who work with young children must state comprehensively and in detail what group care of young children requires in a building. We, the teachers, cannot do it without the architect, the technician, the builder. Neither can they do it without us and our experience.

It is desirable that nursery schools develop in a direction that will fully preserve private initiative and personal responsibility. Kindergartens in public schools are today too often schoolish and regimented. They are more concerned with readiness for academic work than with the children's need for vigorous play. If cities would provide a number of buildings for nursery schools—possibly scattered over our city parks and along city river banks—and rent them to qualified persons or organizations, this would help tremendously toward improving standards without choking personal leadership. This plan is not revolutionary or unprecedented. Cities have long provided playgrounds for children. Recently these playgrounds have become more numerous and elaborate including large sand boxes, wading and swimming pools (and many, often quite creative opportunities for climbing, sliding, etc.), and simple rain shelters. In this way the community has recognized its responsibility to provide for children's play activities.

Today most nursery schools are housed in rooms, yet we speak here about "houses." This term is not a figure of speech. We hope that in the future many nursery schools will be in detached units, in pavilions. However, even in our Utopia many nurseries will be in rooms in larger buildings. These rooms will take their pattern, their standards, from the houses built for children.

### Children's Needs Determine the Plan of the House

We want the children's houses to be small, unpretentious, and semi-permanent structures. The young child's needs are our guide in planning his house. He has the great urge to play; in order to play well he needs protection from danger as well as from unnecessary interference, and he needs judicious help. The young child should have surroundings which he can explore, understand, and use. He needs an environment which is a compliment to his intelligence, permitting him to be self-steered, to use his abilities, to make a choice, and to make mistakes without endangering himself or others. At home the emphasis is necessarily on the things he cannot do for himself, in the children's house the burden of being small in size, weak, and impotent can be effectively lessened.

Visiting a children's house in the evening after its daytime inhabitants have gone home, we can read "off the walls" the educational philosophy of the teachers. Some schools seem to acknowledge the two main functions of the nursery school as protecting young children from danger and giving them an opportunity to play with peers. Such a school needs shelves for toys and space for play and that is all. The children are not supposed to move freely among the rooms. The adult will call them to the door when it is

21

time to go to the toilet or to go outdoors; she will tell them when it is time to rest and when to go from one room to the next. Thus, the knobs on the doors can be high. It is even advantageous to have them out of the children's reach. The teacher can give her attention to studying, observing, and recording the children's imaginative play. She need not worry about a child wandering away. The adult "takes" the children outdoors as a group and they come back as a group. The basic principle underlying this type of nursery school is: children should enjoy the maximum freedom in their play using materials and toys as they please. In issues pertaining to their physical welfare, the adult knows the child's needs far better and bids him what to do.

A nursery school centering its program around the children's need to play, as well as their need to gain an intelligent use of their environment, should have a building which enables the child to move from one room to another without asking the adult's help. All the rooms used by the children are connected by doors which the children can open. A cluster arrangement with a main room in the center gives direct access to all satellite rooms such as lavatories, workshop, cloakroom, kitchen, and quiet room. This arrangement also has the advantage of doing away with long corridors. Two, three, or four units can be housed under one roof. The rooms for the adults—office, kitchen, and staffroom—serve the whole school. The outdoor play space should also be directly connected with the play room. French or sliding doors connect the play room with the play space outside (be it yard or roof) giving the teacher and children an unobstructed view from the inside out and vice versa. The plan of the house should be so simple and so compact that a child can quickly gain a sense of orientation and the teacher can give unobtrusive supervision to all rooms while being in one.

The children whose nursery day is longer than three or four hours need several rooms. For the child who comes for a half-day only, the company of others is the main need; but if he comes for a longer period, privacy is as important as company. Both are needed for social and emotional balance by children no less than by adults. It seems hardly necessary to say that the seclusion must be self-sought in order to give the child relaxation and serenity. The main room may have alcoves or nooks which can be partitioned off with a sliding door disappearing into the wall when not in use, or with a door of transparent plastic. Transparent doors do not cut off the child from the group yet give him quiet if he wants to look at picture books, to rest, or to play with only one or two children. Or an alcove can be used the other way around— to protect the majority from the noise of a minority. With the carpenter bench in there, the lusty hammering and sawing need not disturb the other children. There is a notion that young children are mob minded and that when given a chance, they will always flock together into a big noisy crowd. Observation of children, for whom the company of other children is nothing new, disproves this; they often like to play in very small groups.

*The Young Child's Adventures in Space*
    The qualities of space—the feeling of spaciousness or of nestling in a small enclosure, the sensation of being high up and looking down—are a source of delight for the young child. Children love a wide open place where they can run with abandon; they like to huddle in a corner or under a table covered with a blanket, or to sit squeezed in a dolls' house. The more cramped and crowded the quarters, the greater the enjoyment can be. The adults' attitude toward space is usually quite utilitarian. They cannot derive from spatial perceptions, as does the young child, the joy and the whole gamut of sensations. If children were studying adults they would put into the textbooks that most adults are "color blind" in regard to space.
    Children like to be high up and look down on objects and

places which are familiar. Every nursery should have a kind of balcony, or as we like to call it, a "treehouse" in the play room. The young child enjoys climbing, and he should have ample opportunity for it inside the nursery as well as outdoors. The raised balcony also gives a chance to get away from the group and, last but not least, it adds a number of square feet of play space.

Good treehouses can be reached in various ways: by a ladder, a rope ladder, or notches cut into the wall. The child can leave his treehouse also by means of a slide. Each approach presents a different hurdle to the child. He may have to crawl into the treehouse through a narrow opening or to climb over a couple of rungs. Children are so taken with this "adventure in space" that they will take the trip many times in succession.

There are other spatial experiences the young child cherishes. The nursery school can offer many as the average home cannot. One school has on one side of the stairway a slide instead of a bannister. It seems superfluous to describe the delight of the youngsters, but we might mention the skill they acquire and point to the clever principle of making legitimate a pleasure which generations of children could obtain only by stealth. Of course, the stair must have a certain incline and the landing at the bottom should not interfere with other traffic in the house. Swinging up and down, gliding down a slide, climbing on the jungle gym and ladders or on a tree with low branches, constitute the more thrilling "adventures in space." The physical exertion, the sense of daring, add to the experience of space as a medium.

### The Room
*Floor*. Today the usual arrangement is to leave one side of the room free or to keep the center part of the room unencumbered. It would seem better to provide several

decentralized floor areas. A part of the room can be elevated with one or two steps. The very young child loves to practice walking up and down and all children love to sit on steps. Besides the steps leading to the platform, there might be a step leading up or down to one of the alcoves; or an alcove might be separated from the main room by a doorsill high enough to serve as a seat for a child. A good place for stationary steps is underneath a window. The children enjoy standing or kneeling there and looking out. Platforms, balconies, steps, and ladders are variations of the theme "floor." At this point, we might suggest the use of a soundproof ceiling to reduce the noise level.

*Walls.* No matter how one plans a room, one will always desire more wall space. The main nursery room is simultaneously a workshop and a display room, so wall space is needed for a number of purposes. Low screens and protruding shelves, variations on the theme "wall," help to subdivide the room and give a certain degree of privacy to groups of playing children. If many children eat in one room, screens may serve as partitions to form a number of booths. They can also be placed to help direct the traffic of children who carry plates and food back and forth. Encouraging children to help in this way allows them a legitimate opportunity to break the strain of sitting at the table throughout the entire meal. At rest time the setting up of enclosures giving privacy is even more essential than at meal times. At play time the children will soon discover that screens can create various enclosures or may even become part of their play equipment on occasion.

*Windows and Doors.* Windows admit light and their coverings (blinds, curtains, or shutters) diffuse it. Both are needed at different times of the day. The room will usually be darkened for rest period. Occasionally a darkened room may set a better stage for a story period or for the game of "listening to all the little noises." A southern exposure and a

25

bright orange or blue curtain will, when the curtain is drawn, fill a room with color and subdued light—a pleasant and quieting effect. In a one-story building a skylight of plain or colored plastic will admit additional light. Children love to look out of the window. This function of windows is as important as the admission of light and air. We must remember that the motionless child who is listening or gazing with all his might is mentally a very active person.

Children like the experience of opening and closing a window. In homes this is usually a privilege reserved for adults. A nursery school window may have one or two small panes for the child to open without endangering himself.

With little expense a door can be inserted in the doll corner or a gate can be installed on the playground or indoors. One door can be constructed as a Dutch door, i.e. it is divided and the upper and lower parts open separately. The amount of experimentation, that is the alternate opening and shutting of the upper and lower part, indicates how much learning goes on in relation to "open" and "closed," or "connected" and "separated." After a time the playful repetitious handling gives way to an intelligent use at the appropriate occasion.

Children also love to pass things through an opening in the wall which can be closed with a door sliding sideways or upwards. Such a counter window with a shelf on both sides may be permanently useful in connecting the children's room with kitchen or workshop. The child who manipulates the Dutch door or the counter window establishes contact or withdrawal between himself and others. Here the perception of spatial relations and of social relations intertwine. This may explain the fascination which these gadgets hold for the young child.

In planning the house we also should remember that water is an essential plastic material. There should be at least one low faucet with sink and drainboard in the main room.

*Indoor Furnishings.* Several nursery school manuals give good detailed descriptions of the sizes and proportions of chairs, tables, and shelves, the main pieces of furniture. Usually chairs and tables in a nursery group are of two different sizes. This is a commendable practice although it does not always lead to our goal, namely to provide each child with a comfortable seat. Children will draw a higher chair to a lower table, and some children will always hunt for the larger sized furniture, although they cannot put their feet down on the floor when seated. The prestige of being taller apparently more than compensates for the discomfort. As the children do not remain seated for long periods, this does not matter and the teacher need not interfere. It is not advisable to use different colors for the different size chairs and tables. This will only make the larger furniture more conspicuous and more coveted. The light weight of a chair is important, for the child likes to carry a chair to different parts of the room or outside.

A nursery for 20 children requires 20 seats, but not all the seats need to be identical. Straight chairs, rocking chairs, armchairs, small stools, straddle-seats, a bench, and floor cushions (hard cushions covered with oilcloth or plastic) give variety. Some chairs will be more appealing than others. The variety will lead to little squabbles among the children. A child who never would have cared for the armchair will become eager to sit in it when he sees how much another child treasures its "possession." The ensuing negotiations, pleading, or violence are important social experiences and necessary in group adjustment. Chairs may be painted in two or three pastel shades or some may be polished wood or aluminum (plastic chairs have excellent contours and are less heavy than wooden ones).

Only in our western culture have we given up squatting or kneeling positions which bring us nearer to the floor than the average chair. Children like to sit tailor fashion on the floor, or to kneel on a flat cushion, sitting on their heels

27

as the Chinese do. Both positions are healthful for the child. Flat floor-cushions match low tables, some of which may have hinged tops to prop up for painting or drawing.

Tables, too, should not be uniform. The majority will be the rectangular type seating two children. In addition, there can be a large table for 8 to 10 children. Large and small tables have their specific advantages and disadvantages. Large tables facilitate supervision. A group of children, each one working with the same material (clay, fingerpaints, paper) or on a joint project, is better off seated at one table. Interest is contagious and the enthusiasm of one child spurs the others. Individual tables discourage copying a design or a clay figure. Round or half round tables are practical for meals. They take up more space but the number of children seated at one table is more flexible. One table may be a dropleaf table, or a small table can be hinged to the wall and dropped when not in use. Incidentally, silence domes on all table and chair legs are an asset.

The variety of chairs and tables plus the fact that some may be taken apart or folded instigate the child's interest in these parts of his daily environment. His attention is drawn to those qualities which constitute the "chairness" of a chair or which are indispensable in a table. The child's discovery is a source of great joy. Soon he tries his hand at making a table or a chair out of large blocks or empty boxes. This shows initiative and intelligence.

The youngster who takes two pieces of wood, nails them together and calls them an airplane can be sure to get recognition from his teacher. Yet his intellectual accomplishment may be very small. Few teachers are equipped to see this. Their perceptiveness is geared to achievement resembling the work of an adult artisan or artist. There are glimpses of intelligence of another order. The child observes, compares, and by some kind of short circuit, discov-

28

ers that things can be put to a different and new use. The more children are accusomed to help themselves and not wait for adult assistance, the greater the probability of such discoveries.

We stop here to assert that educators who want the younger generation to accept conventions without questioning have no reason to foster an experimental attitude towards chairs and tables in early childhood. If we consider it the task of education to fit children into existing molds, then it is logical to expect the child to use each piece of equipment in the conventional way and to make it clear that any other use is a misuse.

Our goal though is a flexible and sensible use of all equipment. Most pieces of furniture can be used in several ways; they also can be abused. The child who is encouraged to observe and to experiment will soon be able to differentiate between use and abuse. All furniture for young children should be sturdy and well built and a certain amount of breakage must be expected. Children who are with well liked adults and who take an intelligent and active interest in their surroundings will rarely be deliberately destructive even when they are on their own.

All material and toys should be accessible to the children without their asking the adult's help. Here again is the recurring theme: the nursery school should lessen the discouraging burden of dependency which in our culture is heavier than in others. The primary purpose of all equipment, toys and furniture is to provide an arena for the child to build intelligence, imagination, initiative, perseverance. Another important reason for making tools and play materials directly accessible to the child is: a young child's intentions or plans are not well defined or fully conscious. He cannot put them into words with ease or precision. The layout of the nursery school enables him to translate into action impulses which are vague and fleeting. This, too, is part of the "self expression" offered in nursery school. To emphasize this point, we make a corollary statement: a child, for whom verbalization of what he wants to do no longer presents a hurdle, has passed the stage where he belongs in a "nursery."

The order of the room should be simple and easy to remember. The child has a feeling of ease and competence when he knows where to look for a thing. Our direct guidance is a burden for him; our subtle indirect guidance gives wings to his conquering steps. Thus, we will take as much effort to display things attractively as a good storekeeper takes with his wares. The color of the open shelves should be neutral and unobtrusive in order not to distract attention from the bright colored toys.

Too many things are confusing. The child cannot find quickly what he wants so gives up and turns to the adult for help. He feels the burden of his own inadequacy. Only functional things have a place on the shelves in a room of active children. Toys or materials which have not been used for some time by any child should be removed. It may be advisable to remove them permanently, or to bring them back after a few weeks, placing them in a different spot.

Some teachers follow a definite "hands off" policy. They ignore youngsters who mill around obviously bored and mentally undernourished. Other teachers are quick to spy an idle child and make alternate suggestions. We believe that a good deal of idleness is a prerequisite for plunging with whole-hearted interest into the next enterprise. If we interfere with the valleys, we will have no peaks. Before resorting to a verbal and direct proposal, the teacher should try an indirect appeal through a piece of equipment.

For children who are accustomed to find their materials in plain sight, things which have to be taken from a closed cabinet or from behind a curtain have a special attraction. Toys kept in a cabinet locked with a key have a particular appeal. Most young children are fascinated with a key which they can insert in a keyhole and afterwards return to its hook on the wall. Of course, a key which is so freely accessible to a group of youngsters will sometimes get lost, or be taken home by a child. One may argue: why should the teacher add another concern to her full day? There are so many things children like to play with, would not the teacher do better to concentrate her effort on satisfying the children's emotional needs? We do not say that a pre-school child who has no chance of handling a key is deprived of an essential experience. Yet he does miss something. The more all "perishable" items, anything that can be lost, soiled, or pocketed, are removed from the children's reach, the more grows their destructiveness. The teacher who looks for help in stemming the tide of carelessness which requires "eternal vigilance" on her part, will usually try to eliminate more and more things which can be broken, swallowed, taken home, or ruined in some way. But some times the opposite approach is more helpful; children are delighted when trusted with "special" things.

It should be possible to move almost everything out-doors—chairs, tables, shelves, screens, and easels. Often the children are glad to do most of the moving; after acquiring a certain amount of experience, the planning can be theirs, too.

The teacher needs some place where she can keep things not intended for the children. A regular desk takes up too much precious floorspace. We have found a cupboard re-ceding unobtrusively into the wall a very good solution. In a room for a group of active children, an adult's furniture should not take up space. While we feel this way about a desk, we would like the teacher to have a comfortable chair where she can sit without cramping her knees. Her work is physically tiring. She is on her feet for many hours. A few minutes relaxation in an easy chair can do much to restore her resilience. When she leans back in her easy chair, her eyes are at the level of the children's eyes. She has a better vantage point for observing the active community than when she stands up and "looks down" on them. But the teacher's big chair is even more important as a haven for the children. It is a special treat to be invited to sit there and look at a picture book, or an upset child will snuggle into the chair and watch the others for awhile from a safe distance. As a rule, at first a child is fascinated with all the furniture which is just his own size, but the sight of so many other children may be frightening. In this case the big chair carries the message that there is a comforting adult in the room. A comfortable chair should be part of the standard equipment in a place where children and an adult live so closely together. Of course the teacher will take on her lap a child who asks for this either by word or deed. However, when she is too busy with the group, then sitting in her chair is the next best "Ersatz."

The room can become the teacher's most valuable assistant. The teacher who wants to give her group a great deal of freedom yet does not want this freedom to degenerate into chaos, and one who wants to make her guidance more and more subtle, will find that time spent with the room and equipment pays ample dividends in improving her work. The teacher has to feel comfortable in her room and it has to satisfy her aesthetic sense. The color scheme makes the room pleasant and cheerful for children and adults. We think that children's color preferences should be carefully studied. Colors certainly stimulate or have a quieting effect. (The effect of colors would be a worthwhile study in an experimental situation where the set-up would allow comparison undisturbed by other factors). Strong colors should be reserved for those things which we want the children to pick up and manipulate, e.g. toys and tools. For tabletops, walls, shelves, and other large surfaces neutral colors are more advisable.

Activity on the Terrace and in the Garden.
—Photo Gesellschafts-und Wirtschaftsmuseum, Vienna.

In arranging the room one will, as a rule, put all the materials used at one time in one corner or along one wall; under some conditions a certain amount of decentralization might be preferable. Frequently all the children's lockers for wraps will be in one part of the room. Yet there may be less general rushing and pushing if the lockers are in two places. Experience shows this may also be true for building blocks. When blocks are stored in two distant parts of the room, groups of children playing independently will be less disturbed by one another.

*Outdoor Equipment.* As mentioned before, the playground should be directly connected with the main rooms. The ideal schoolyard offers not only space for running and apparatus for climbing, swinging, and sliding, but also several areas or, as we may call them, "rooms," with varying degrees of openness. The yard itself should either be partly hardsurfaced or girded by a paved walk for tricycles, roller skates, and other wheel toys. The hard surface has the advantage of drying quickly after a rain. It has the disadvantage of harder falls. The ideal surfacing for children's play yards remains to be invented (though rubberized concrete and tanbark are good solutions under climbing equipment). Part of the yard should be shaded by trees. A pavement of bricks of hardwood or rubber is good, but the expense is prohibitive. Children spend long hours at the sandbox and it is desirable to have it shaded in the hottest part of the summer, yet every sand pile must at intervals be exposed to direct sunlight.

In warm weather an area for water play is indispensable. A tube for crawling through and a jumping board are both desirable. New pieces of outdoor equipment are being tested in various housing developments. Some lend themselves to imaginative play. Although a good selection of outdoor equipment is available today, an observant teacher will be able to pass along valuable tips to the manufacturer.

Blocks, pegs, planks, and tricycles are heavy and cumbersome and should be stored directly on the playground. A simple large bin with a padlock will do, yet a child-sized playhouse which the children can use in their play with a storage space on one side is better. The flat roof, surrounded by railings, can be accessible with a ladder.

*Concluding Observations*

It seems that the public takes more interest in nursery education than formerly. If true, this may be ascribed to a kind of escapism. That is to say, an audience may be more eager to listen to problems concerning little children to escape temporarily from problems of a badly muddled adult world. We have seen evidence of this interest and we should not let it dribble away in sentimentalities. We must channel it into concrete action to achieve the well planned modern school which can provide an environment which is a complement to the child's intelligence (whether he is three or thirteen) and which can give him the opportunity to develop the independence so needed in our society today.

# Section II.

## Child Development and Educational Practice

# Editor's Comments

It seems logical that the papers assembled in this Section should follow those on the influence of the physical environment on children's physical and cognitive growth. Learning and development are driven by internal as well as external factors. The papers presented in this Section stress the human interaction: first with the mother, and then within a group or with the teacher.

The title "Child Development and Educational Practice" would actually fit this book as a whole. It is used here as title for a section of it, because this Section contains the papers of general scope while the more specialized ones are grouped in the other Sections. The arrangement is not chronological, but according to the emphasis on different aspects of the overall subject.

We see how Montessori's recognition of "sensitive periods" in learning and the respect for children's spontaneous interest got broadened by the recognition of the importance of human interaction, and by the theories of play (which will be more fully explored in Section III).

Again we notice Lili Peller's wide range in writing; it moves from observation of children, from which she draws original but practical conclusions, to highly theoretical papers. The theory prevails in the papers addressed to a psychoanalytically trained audience, while Lili Peller's warmth in the description of children and their needs comes through in those addressed to teachers of young children. Though educational practice has changed for the better in the thirty years since the first of these papers was written, we are still haunted by many deficiencies in planning.

"Incentives to Development and Means of Early Education" is reprinted here only partially (its chapters I, IV, and V). After the introductory chapter (I) Lili Peller described in detail (in her chapters II and III) the "school of habit training"—mainly referring to Blatz's writing (see the Bibliography at the end of the paper) and the "school of developmentalism," bringing Gesell's views (see Bibliography) to the reader. Since the theories of development of these two writers are not any more in the foreground of educational discussion, and Gesell's books on older children had not yet been published when this paper was conceived and written (1945), it seemed wiser to bring only the "school of psychoanalysis," as seen in 1945, in order not to burden the reader with an outdated critique.

The second paper, "The Development of the Child's Self," is here reprinted in its entirety.

Of the third paper in this Section we again print here merely a part. The paper is not in its entirety relevant to this Section. A smaller part of it appears in Section IV.

The paper that follows it, "Character Development in Nursery School," an outgrowth of a seminar for teachers, is also reprinted only partially. I felt that of the three topics treated in this paper, two—"Tattling" and "Siblings in School"—were of less interest for today's teachers, while the third, "Segregation According to Age," anticipates what today we call, and cherish as, the "open classroom"; it demonstrates its value for the pre-school child.

The fourth paper is again reprinted in its entirety.

The last paper in this Section, "Psychoanalysis and Public Education," originated in a lecture to teachers and analysts at the Reiss-Davis Child Study Center in Los Angeles. Lili Peller died before she could prepare it for publication. This was completed by her friend and colleague Dr. Rudolf Ekstein, co-editor of the Reiss-Davis Clinic Bulletin.

# 1.

# INCENTIVES TO DEVELOPMENT AND MEANS OF EARLY EDUCATION

"Hitherto education has only set itself the task of controlling, or, it would be more proper to say, of suppressing the instincts. The results have been by no means gratifying, . . . Nor has any one inquired by what means and at what cost the suppression of the inconvenient instincts has been achieved. Supposing now that we substitute another task for this one, and aim instead at making the individual capable of becoming a civilized and useful member of society with the least possible sacrifice of his own activity."[5]

What are the effective means of early education? Wide disagreement as to the answer will be found among different schools of thought. Education is emerging from an empirical to a scientific discipline. When we find it hard to define basic concepts in education, we may turn to parallel areas in medicine in order to gain a frame of reference.

The function of therapy is to initiate, support and/or accelerate the healing process. As medical science progresses, the means of therapy necessarily change. In his diaries, kept during the epidemic of yellow fever towards the close of the eighteenth century in Philadelphia, Benjamin Rush accuses himself because he is unable to make the rounds of all afflicted who need blood-letting. Today we know that his qualms of conscience were unnecessary, because the blood-letting actually undermined the resistance of patients. If Dr. Rush had smoked his pipe with greater leisure, or slept

41

an hour longer, more people might have had a chance to survive the fever.

The function of early education is to initiate, support and/or accelerate developmental processes leading from child- to adult-hood. Means of education considered of central importance yesterday, may be considered unnecessary or harmful today.

A specific educational measure or experience is frequently considered all-important in causing adjustment or maladjustment. As our case material broadens, emphasis may shift from a specific incident to a general condition. The father who remembers the spanking he incurred after stealing apples as a young lad attributes his development into a law-abiding citizen to this well-remembered incident. It may not be easy to persuade him of the possibility that he grew up to be honest mainly because he lived with, and was loved and cared for by honest parents. The corporal punishment which was comparatively harmless in his case may have under changed social conditions a humiliating effect that makes it dangerous.

In the early days of psychoanalysis the psychic trauma occurring once and suddenly was considered the cause of neurotic development. The search for the spectacular trauma has today been replaced by a patient and undramatic unravelling of early tensions and unbearable deprivations. Other changes in causal thinking are just appearing on the horizon. In many case histories of neurotic or delinquent maladjustment the emphasis is still placed on what the neurotic parents *did*. Yet we know that even if parents have insight on an intellectual level and do not *do* anything harmful to the child, but are highly neurotic, the child has but a small chance of normal development.

A historical perspective of changes in educational theory enables us to see in what direction we are moving today.

The child's physical growth is determined by inner factors. He himself indicates his need for food, exercise, rest, etc., and modern child care considers it its main task to answer these requests. Looking back only twenty or thirty years we realize that child care then tried much more to *shape* the child; this trend becomes even clearer if we go back a hundred years. The occasional cutting of the sublingual ligament to facilitate speech, tight swaddling clothes to force the child to stretch his knees, a contraption on wheels in which he was suspended by his arms and forced to "walk" when crawling was his desire, daily painful "cleaning" of the tender and easily injured inner tissue of his mouth—all these preceded the rigid habit training. These are examples picked at random. Their common denominator is to change the child, to accelerate his development.

In modern child care our foremost goal is to interfere as little as possible with developmental trends. A recent attempt to do so concerns the skin of the neonate: since the days of antiquity midwives have carefully removed the vernix caseosa. Aldrich suggests that it be left untouched. The whitish smear is absorbed within forty-eight hours. Nature's handiwork sometimes appears sloppy and in need of improvment, yet when we step back and observe instead of rushing into action, the rather unpleasant-looking paste disappears without our help, leaving the skin excellently soft and clean.

While the main current in modern child care is to study the child's natural development and to follow along with ancillary measures, there are aspects of child care which certainly cannot be brought under this heading. Take the numerous inoculations against children's diseases: they have no counterpart in nature, they cause discomfort and real suffering to the baby—yet they are considered essential to good child care.

A good deal of the child's early intellectual and emotional progress as well as his physical development is maturational. Yet the greater part of his swift intellectual growth and of his ethical development does not follow the same model as his physical growth.

According to the psychoanalytic view powerful stimuli from the social world come into alliance with his innate tendency to develop. There is nothing automatic about the child's emotional, intellectual and ethical progress. The main factors in his early development are his early attachment to his mother, his oedipal attachment to his parents, and the sequelae of this bond.

The child relinquishes childish satisfactions in order to please his mother. ". . . all (the children's) play is influenced by the dominant wish of their time of life: viz., to be grown-up and to be able to do what grown-ups do."[6] This wish is present in every child, but its power rises and falls with the depth of the child's attachment to an adult. In our culture the incentive to give up certain forms of behavior comes from the adult—and from him comes the image which the child wants to resemble, but the metamorphosis itself is carried through by the child; no one else can do it for him. It is not true that the child is inert, while the adult is active, pulling out the weeds and implanting sundry virtues instead.

The simile of the gardener who "bends the twig" is not just a romantic phrase, old-fashioned and innocuous. It stands for a philosophy of education that is still widespread. It should be replaced by attitudes more in agreement with newer insight into the child's development. The gardener cares for an organism inferior to himself. Parent and child need deeply to realize that though separated by age, maturity and experience, *they are peers*. The parent who lacks this conviction will either be despotic or will treat the child as a toy or puppy. The latter is more likely to happen in our

44

enlightened era, yet it is almost equally harmful. The child who fails to anticipate his future role has no motivation to identify with the adult.

The child's early attachment to his mother or mother-figure provides a powerful leverage for his education. In comparison with the child's later oedipal attachment its effect is limited. The baby's attachment to his mother changes but little. He might be compared to a person who likes to go about in an old, torn, and dirty garment, but has learned to throw a clean garment over it when visitors come, and moreover has acquired increasing skill in looking out for the approach of the visitors.

The conflicting emotions of the later oedipal attachment stir the child far more deeply. He goes through many storms, yet we should not be sorry for him, for without this apprenticeship in human relations he could never join the adult group. From these conflicts results the ardent wish to grow up and the first vague outline of his moral self. Their outcome determines his ability to form lasting and sincere attachments and spurs his intellectual development. In short, the oedipal passions, the structural changes which they initiate in the child's mind and their personal variables set the compass for his development in the next years, and, to a certain extent, for all his life. All the other known incentives of development seem small when compared with the oedipal attachment.

According to psychoanalytic thinking the individual undergoes several deep-reaching reorganizations before maturity is reached. The Sturm and Drang of puberty has been well known since Stanley Hall's studies. It took psychoanalysis to discover that the turmoil of early childhood surpasses it. The child experiences love, hate, jealousy, hope, despair, triumph and guilt in great intensity and rapid succession. Intellectually he wrestles with the riddles of sex, birth and death, although he is in no way

45

equipped to understand them, even if the correct information is supplied. In the myth Oedipus solves the riddle of the sphinx, but the child can neither solve nor bypass it.

At the climax of the oedipal phase he strives for physical love satisfaction, for insight far beyond his years and for the exclusive possession of his love object. He attempts the downright impossible with the uniqueness of purpose characteristic of his age—and he fails.

The attachment to his parents survives this collapse and his desire to be like them is tremendously strengthened. So also is his interest in intellectual pursuits. He has tried a short-cut and failed. He is now eager to travel the long road and thus he is now ready for education in the academic sense of the word. He wants to learn and to acquire skills and is highly sensitive to prestige and status. A large share of his energy goes to pursuits unrelated to instinctual satisfactions. Emotional problems continue to hold a priority on his energy over intellectual concerns, but under favorable circumstances the most stirring emotional problems are temporarily solved as he enters latency.

To put it very simply: part of his early aspirations must fail, while the other part must be preserved. For his favorable development one is as indispensable as the other. His oedipal aspirations must collapse, but he must salvage his tender attachment to his parents, his admiration for them. He must be certain that they are fond of him and that he is a needed member of the family. It is highly desirable that he continue to live with them, day in day out, and that there is a wide range of shared interests. All these are incentives and aids to his development. The directly sexual part of his ambitions crashes—to this blow (in reality, it is a long series of blows) the child can adjust. But because this frustration and because confused feelings of guilt are inescapable, we, his educators, should keep other tensions and deprivations at a minimum. He cannot adjust to repeated changes in his parental figures.

In regard to the control of instincts the difference between his person three years ago and his present self is greater than the difference between a member of a primitive tribe and highly civilized man. This change was effected not by punishments and rewards. Cruelty has partly been transformed into concern for others, love of dirt into appreciation of cleanliness, the desire to exhibit his naked body into a sense of modesty. If one may use a simile, one may say that the fervor and passion of the oedipal conflicts has melted his early ego and forged a new structure. In these deeply revolutionary processes the child needs all the help which his attachment to stable and loving elders can provide.

Judging from the current literature of child welfare, the policy of preserving the child's emotional tie to his parents or parent-substitutes even under most trying circumstances, is being widely accepted. But how do we account for the fact that this need is more imperative than all the other needs of childhood? Outside the psychoanalytic school it can be explained only with the view that family ties are sacred. But as the child grows older a rupture of family ties becomes less harmful to him. Does this mean that family bonds become less sacred as the child approaches adolescence? If we take the oedipal situation for more than a figure of speech, then we have the explanation for his inability to advance in his education if his early attachment is broken several times: under normal conditions he already loses so much that he cannot bear losing more.

Leniency in early education is in various degrees practised by all pre-industrial societies and was postulated in our society long before psychoanalytic teaching was widespread, by educators such as Pestalozzi, Froebel, and Dewey. Permissiveness should be the keynote of early education, not because the young child cannot stand strain and frustrations, but because *inevitable* blows and sacrifices

47

make heavy inroads on his resistance.* It may be said that this argumentation is idle and that only the permissive attitude is valid. However it seems to this writer that sometimes teachers waste their efforts trying to spare the child trials that should not and cannot be put out of his way; and that present day nursery education is honeycombed with sentimentalism. A child may be struggling with a piece of clothing, and the teacher's hands may be itching to help him; yet as long as he asks for no help there is no need to run to his rescue. A physician treats a man whom he knows to be frail in one way and prescribes a different regime to another who is strong and sturdy but recovering from a recent grave illness.

\* \* \*

Fenichel identifies as ". . . the basic means of all education . . . direct threat, a mobilization of the fear of losing love and the promise of special rewards." He defines "what education fundamentally desires . . . good behavior not only through fear of opposition from the grown-ups (who can after all, be deceived) but good behavior for its own sake . . ."3, (p. 285). As indicated above, the present author disagrees here, although she is in agreement with the main thesis of Fenichel's paper. Good behavior is too insignificant a goal of education. Good behavior is possible without initiative, without courage, without intellectual acumen, yet every society must expect these qualities in at least some of its subgroups or individuals. It seems doubtful whether good behavior includes the ability to form deep and lasting attachments, or the ability to enjoy mature sexual relations.

*A similar thought has been expressed by Whitehead[12]: "It is not true that the easier subjects should precede the harder. . . . Some of the hardest must come first because nature so dictates, and because they are essential to life. The first intellectual task that confronts an infant is the acquirement of spoken language. What an appalling task, the correlation of meanings with sounds!"

48

To be kind and courteous, even towards those who cannot report on us, to be clean and industrious, to resist temptations even if there is no one to watch us—this is the essence of good behavior.

Freud defines as the task of edcuation: "to make the individual capable of becoming a civilized and useful member of society with the least possible sacrifice of his own activity"[5]. This purports "what education fundamentally desires" with more vision than Fenichel's statement, and it points to the two basic mistakes education can commit: failure to socialize the child, or the sacrifice of too much of the child's spontaneous drive. Yet "good behavior" seems compatible with such a sacrifice.

For educators of the "old school" good behavior might be acceptable as the goal. Education for them is primarily restraint, achieved by external regulatory means. According to them intelligence is not connected with the fate of the child's emotions. Intellectual abilities are inborn and their development depends upon intellectual stimuli. In the sexual field the main concern is to bring the individual to the point where he will be unlikely to infringe upon moral laws and conventions. Punishments and rewards are regulatory measures and as such are able to bring about an increasing degree of restraint. But restraint, *even internalized restraint, can never be the main goal of education based on a dynamic theory of personality.*

There are limited areas where the child comes to modify his behavior on account of recurrent punishment. To take a time-honored example: he learns not to touch the hot stove because of the pain he has experienced. He learns to substitute caution for unreined curiosity. While such substitution and the prompt, rather mild, consistent displeasure that follows actions which he must learn to avoid, works in issues remote from his instinctual needs, it can never make the child travel the enormous distance he has to cover in order

49

to become an adult. The displeasure which the child experiences may be a "natural" consequence of his action, or the educator may introduce it in order to make him change his behavior, sometimes to protect the child from serious harm[11]. But in matters which lie in the path of direct instinctual satisfaction the punishment would have to be so painful that the child would be more bewildered than warned.

Threats and rewards are regulatory mechanisms effective in bringing about minor adjustments. The view that they can build the character structure which makes an adult out of a child, seems a replica of Lamarckian thinking. Lamarck explained the evolution of species by external, environmental regulation. If an organ is useful in a given environment it is retained and developed, if it is useless or harmful, it atrophies. The environment thus rewards or penalizes actions and their carriers, and thus creates new species. According to modern biology external regulatory influences could never lead to a new species. *Creative* processes, mutations, *are postulated*, although so far mutations producing new species have not been observed. Biology has thrown old concepts overboard, although for the time being there are no observational data supporting the new concept.

In the genesis of the adult from the child external pressure initiates many changes and regroupings within the child, but it cannot enforce them. In this case the *creative* factor is the child's attachment to his parents. It is this attachment, and not external pressure that generates the wish to relinquish childish satisfactions.*

---

*It is tragic that Otto Fenichel cannot counter the above views. I want at least to add one remark, which is in line with his way of thinking. It concerns reaction-formations. The child who is especially fond of exhibiting his naked body may become especially modest; the child who is exceedingly cruel may develop deep and broad sympathies with those

Fenichel also states that "children (need) very deeply . . . love and affection from the persons of their environment."** This is correct but too general. The child's greatest need is for love from the persons to whom he is attached, and not merely from persons who chance to be near him. "Persons of his environment," his teacher or nurse or a kind-hearted aunt may offer this love amply to the child— yet he profits but little. We can assume that many foster-mothers appearing in the history of disturbed children have offered love and affection to no avail.

For the older child emphasis shifts from attachment to identification with the person in authority. The youngster will keep rules if he likes the person who gave them, understands why they are necessary, and is given a chance to support them actively. His intelligence must be stirred, his love and loyalty activated, and whatever helps in this is an important tool of education. This is true according to psychoanalytic thinking. According to traditional education the child who misbehaves should be punished harder and harder until he reforms.

---

who suffer. This reaction-formation is initiated by the disapproval of a beloved adult, but its strength is derived from and will be proportional to the strength of the original drive. This is the classical view. On second thought we may conceive another possibility: it may be that the strength of the reaction-formation is determined by the differential which the child senses between his desire and the wishes of his beloved adults. In this case a child living in a highly prudish group or in a society abhorring uncleanliness would develop stronger reaction-formations than if he were living with the identical instinctual equipment in a less "civilized" group. External factors may have a greater weight than the classical psychoanalytic view assumed.

**In a joking vein we may make the corollary statement: "Adults need love and affection from the young children of their environment." From personal experience I should say that for every child who asks to be kissed or taken on the lap, there are at least three adults who want to invade the reserve of a three-year-old and bestow unsolicited affection upon him. Children are highly selective in their quest for affection.

"What shall I do when I have tried every device that I can think of, and will fail?" (asks the young teacher). There is no explicit formula that will cover each specific case, but one general suggestion may be given: *get order*. Drop everything else, if necessary, until order is secured. . . . Pile penalty upon penalty for misdeamors and let the 'sting' of each penalty be double that of its predecessor. Tire out the recalcitrants if you can gain your end in no other way."([1] p. 96.)

The attitude reflected in this old quotation is hardly found today in our schools, yet it still works great harm in some reform schools. The child without a bond to anyone cannot be reformed by punishment. Its only effect may be that he learns to use more cunning in reaching his goals and that he stores up resentment which may precipitate him into a criminal career. Has the education of the youngsters who fill the reform schools failed because they did not receive enough threats and rewards, or was some other means of education missing in their early history? It is far less harmful for a mature person to have promiscuous and shifting relations than for a young child. The personal bond leads a child towards a socialized existence; there is no "Ersatz" for it.

Anna Freud's work in the residential nurseries provides us with a fitting example. In the beginning all the children (about twenty-four) were cared for by all the nurses (about six). Later it was tried to group children and adults into "families." A very stormy period followed. Fights among the children multiplied, crying became more frequent, far more jealousy was observed; yet soon ". . . the state of frenzy subsided and gave way to a quieter, more stable and comforting attachment. At the same time the children began to *develop in leaps and bounds*.* The most gratifying effect was

*Italics of this author.

52

that several children who had seemed hopeless as far as the training for cleanliness was concerned, suddenly started to use the pot regularly and effectively . . . All the children in the group have greatly enlarged their vocabulary . . ."[4], p. 160.)

This may well be called an *experimentum crucis.* The same children, the same physical set-up, the same adults. No doubt they had love and affection for the children before and after the grouping in families. They showed approval and disapproval before and after. Yet after the establishment of the personal tie, the children's education made remarkable progress.

Those who attach greatest relevance to threat and reward make the implicit assumption that the instinct of self-preservation is stronger than any other desire. The child will comply with our demands in order to avert harm to himself. According to psychoanalytic thinking the need for self-preservation, though powerful, does not always rate priority. Under certain constellations a wayward adolescent will not be motivated towards "mending his ways" by increasingly severe and painful punishments. He rather develops an increasing ability to "take it" (plus a number of distorted attitudes like bitterness, masochism, hatred, etc.).

We are all familiar with the young child who is offered good food, yet in spite of his hunger does not eat well because the conflicts with his mother have been shifted to the food she is giving him. He is undernourished although offered tasty food at every meal. Here too emotional conflicts push self-preservation into the background.

Threats and rewards are the main means of education where education is conceived as external restraint. In some areas, such as in habit training, they can be important incentives. However, mechanical training, regardless of the child's understanding of what is being demanded of him, does not lead toward emotional maturity. The child's insight is as much a means of education as his mother's re-

53

warding smile. On each age level a humanized education makes fullest use of the child's critical abilities.

In conclusion we return to the simile of the twig: the elastic young twig is bent into a certain position and held there by a cord and stick; after a year or two this support may be removed; the twig will not snap back, but continue of "its own" to grow as it was bent. External pressure has been "internalized." This well-known process *in horticulture* does not tell us anything about the child. To understand his way of internalizing we must consider his deep and contradicting emotions, his intellectual power, his fears, his ability for keen observation as well as for denying unpleasant facts, his reactions to frustrations, his anticipation of his adult role. Without this complex basis of reaction the child's development would not differ essentially from the results of animal training, and the child would not undergo a transmutation into an ethical and social being.

## BIBLIOGRAPHY

1. Bagley, W. C. *Classroom Management*, New York, 1907.
2. Blatz, W. *Understanding the Young Child*, Morrow, 1944.
3. Fenichel, O. "The Means of Education," *this Annual*, I.
4. Freud, A. and Burlingham, D. T. *War and Children*, Internat. Univ. Press, 1943.
5. Freud, S. "Analysis of a Phobia in a Five-Year-Old Boy," *Coll. Papers*, III.
6. Freud, S. *Beyond the Pleasure Principle*, Hogarth, 1920.
7. Gesell, A., and Ilg, G. *Infant and Child in the Culture of Today*, Harper, 1943.
8. Hilgard, J. R. "Learning and Maturation in Pre-school Children," *J. Gen. Psychol.*, 1932.
9. McGraw, M. *Growth, A Study of Johnny and Jimmy*, Appleton-Century, 1935.
10. Murchison, C. *Handbook of Child Psychology*, Clark University Press, 1933.
11. Spencer, H. *Education*, New York, 1895.
12. Whitehead, A. N. "The Task of Infancy," *Aims of Education*, Macmillan, 1929; and earlier, in *The Rhythm of Education*, London, 1922.

# 2.

# THE DEVELOPMENT OF THE CHILD'S SELF

The "self" is a rather vague term and the various schools of thought give it a variegated interpretation. The beginning of self lies in a child's awareness that he is separate from others, similar to them yet also different. Its development seems to me related to the way the child experiences himself in comparison to others. In order to clarify the concept I turn to observations of children pointing to different stages in its development. Here are a few examples.

Look first at an early infant-mother relationship. The child is still unable to feed himself with a spoon, but well able to hold a cracker and eat it. The mother on whose lap he sits tries to find out whether her child is unselfish—and asks to give her a bite. Willingly he offers the cracker to her and watches with pleasure her mouth and her teeth as she bites a piece off. Then suddenly a disappointed blank expression slips over his face. What has happened? It seems the child was unaware that when his mother would bite a piece off his cracker he wouldn't taste it in his mouth. He had confused her body with his own.

I'd like to mention here some experiments by Piaget. Approaching a 10 or 11 months old infant Piaget opened and closed his own mouth. In answer to this, the watching baby would sometimes open and close his mouth, another time he would close and open his eyes and sometimes he would close and open his little fists. Or Piaget slowly and

·deliberately opened a matchbox in front of the child, and when seeing the void inside the matchbox, the child again opened his mouth. The infant is able to mirror what another person does—or even—what happens with inanimate objects—but in doing so, he sometimes confuses the organ of his body which corresponds with the respective organ of the person whom he observes. He is more likely to get the activity right than its location.

Now to other observers and older children: A three year old had learned to count his fingers. When the proud parents announced this to a visitor he remarked, "Let me see, count mine." And the boy replied, "No—I can count mine—not yours."

Another observation: A two year old girl was wheeling her doll carriage on a garden path and in turning a corner the wheel got caught. The harder she pushed—the firmer the carriage was struck, and finally she cried. Her twin sister, also playing in the yard, looked up, ran over to her, and helped her to lift the doll carriage, so that she could go on wheeling it around. A little later the same afternoon, this twin sister pushing the same doll carriage, got caught at the same corner and cried—and now the first girl came to her rescue and lifted it for her. In other words, each one could see what was wrong with the other, yet had been unable to help herself when she was trapped.

The boy who had learned to count did not realize what could be transferred from his own body to the body of others—and the two sisters, as least the second one, was unaware that a skill which she had used with her sister could also be applied to her own predicament. On the simplest and on all subsequent levels the child learns about others by watching his own actions and vice versa. His learning is always enbedded in social relations.

The very young infant is passive and very gradually comes to be active—to interact with his environment by perception and motor action. At least these are the observable aspects of his behavior and he seems highly selective in his perceptions. Here I may point out a basic difference between academic and psychoanalytic psychology. According to the former, the range of stimuli grows gradually because his body grows and because his perception and his body control improve. There is an inherent growth potential and as time passes an unhampered child will realize more and more of it. In the psychoanalytic view these factors are essential but they are not enough. The child must be motivated to use the apparatus and all along his comfort and discomfort act as motivators. To understand what moves him on each level, we have to be aware of the changing range of pleasure and displeasure within his orbit.

There are several main phases in the child's development, each one with different governing principles, but by no means clearly separated from one another. In the very early days of life the infant seems unaware of the existence of other people. He feels his own body needs keenly and soon responds to those things in his environment which regularly soothe his needs. Within a few months the child becomes attached to his mother. Because she contributes so much to his comfort he conceives her as a very powerful being, willful and arbitrary in coming to his rescue or denying him the relief she can provide. On the next level the child is able to establish relationships with several people. Slowly, slowly he approaches readiness for nursery school. And there is the fourth stage—when the child's wishes have lost the compelling urgency they had in the first years of life. He is able to sit still, to follow what others have to tell him. He's also able to do things which require not only two or three steps, but many, even hundreds for their completion. It is usually said that his attention span has increased. But this is not correct for the attention span of a young child can be quite long, e.g., when he plays with mud or sand and water. What has lengthened is his attention span with activities that make sense to us and entail more than direct instinctual gratification or endless repetition of the same motion.* He is now ready to attend regular school.

Development never happens in a straight line. There's always a shuttling back and forth. An achievement, a sensitivity which is present today, may be blunted tomorrow. We may also think of development as not happening in one single line—but along many avenues and while there is progress along some there may be none in others—and regression in other aspects. A considerable amount of back tracking is part and parcel of all normal development.

In describing the child's growth we would like to find out how he experiences the world, how things look to him. In other words, we would like to attain an inside-out view of development. However, in describing it, we have to use our words, our adult concepts, and thus we unintentionally distort the child's experience. This is especially true of the earliest, the pre-verbal phase of development. The acquisition of language modifies all our perceptions and actions. A verbal label not only makes an experience and its memory image far more clear cut and easier to manipulate; it changes an experience that was private and unique into one that has generalized and socialized elements. Through the acquisition of language the child comes to live in a world which is far more densely populated with stimuli. It is a world with more order, more stability and more nuances. And as he handles the symbols provided by language it

*Anna Freud and Dorothy Burlingham bring the observation of a 21-months-old girl who in her patient efforts to put on her socks was assisted by a boy of 23 months. Both children "were absorbed in their occupation and had an expression of the utmost strain on their faces." Observations of early rapt and prolonged attention offers an interesting project for the nursery school teacher.

58

becomes easier for him to switch places with other people and to see things from their point of view. The acquisition of language does not cause this progress but makes it possible. Again we see the interdependence of intellectual and emotional and social progress.

We also have to be aware that the child's feelings are at least as intense as our own but far less consistent. The sudden shifts in his mood sometimes deceive us as to the intensity of his feelings.

Because the child is in some ways an open book to us we should not overlook that in others his emotions and his reasoning are more tightly closed to our understanding than those of a fellow adult.

There are various schools of thought concerning the forces of development. Some stress environmental factors, the environmental school, while others see the moving forces inside the child—the maturational school of development. Today most of us realize that both play their part; the child's development results from the interplay of both—environmental and maturational factors.

If maturation is essential it follows that the same environmental stimulus may have a very different effect depending upon the period in which the child, or for that matter any organism (animal or plant) finds itself.

This interplay between organism and environment was first described for plants. The biologist De Vries spoke of "sensitive periods" in the plant's life. For instance, intense sunshine may be harmful, yes disastrous, for a very young plant. At a later phase, it may be incidental, harmless—and still later sunshine becomes indispensable for the plant's growth or its fruition. Of course, the reverse is also true—that is, a factor either beneficial or neutral in the organism's infancy may later become detrimental. Maria Montessori in her educational system put great stress on these observations. A sensitivity to certain stimuli or an interest appears, grows to a certain intensity and then declines.

The combination of the maturational view-point with psychoanalytic insight promises the best key to the understanding of the young child's behavior and his needs. Maturation makes motor, sensory and language skills possible but the emotional development determines which pleasure and displeasure he is able to receive, and thus the emotional development determines which ego skills will be used and "pushed" in their development. The child's emotional (libidinal) phase plays the dominant part. It "dials" the anxieties which he can feel and the kind of attachment he can form. In short, the emotional development organizes all behavior—including adaptive behavior. Thus a presentation which concentrates on adaptive behavior, or treats emotional and intellectual development as separate entities, remains on the purely descriptive level.

Let us look at the child shortly after birth. He perceives pleasures and displeasures—he is never too young for that —but they are extremely simple, body comfort and discomfort. At that time, his interaction with the environment is almost nil. Quite possibly many stimuli reach him, but we are unaware of his response to them. As our observational skill, our empathy grows, our description of the infant may change radically. Today we see this: he gets restless, he cries when he is hungry or uncomfortable; the crying is a distress signal from our point of view, from his it's a magic gesture with which he dominates the environment.

Besides, we have reason to assume that in the beginning the child has no awareness where his body ends and where the outer world begins. His crying stops only when the nipple of breast or bottles touches his lips. But soon this will change: the crying will stop when the infant notices preparations for his meal; indeed, his distress may stop as soon as he hears the faint noise of his mother's approaching steps in the adjoining room.

We may say: the child has learned to wait. But I don't

think it explains anything and it sounds moralistic. Let us put it differently: the child has found out that there is a wider range of pleasure. Besides direct gratification, there is the pleasure of anticipating it. (It is predicated on a low intensity of hunger.) There is the pleasant sensation of having something given into your hand and there is the pleasure of "finding a string" with which you can pull something towards you.

And so, the child begins to observe, to listen, to look, and to use his motor apparatus towards gratification. He now may turn his head towards the approaching bottle or breast and he shifts from an uncomfortable position to a more comfortable one. He uses perception and motor behavior, yes and some mental actions, to haul in gratification.

A little while later he looks around and moves and listens even when he is not in any need. Certain sensory and motor skills have become pleasurable in themselves. We call the pleasure derived from the functioning of body parts and without ulterior motives "functional pleasure" (K. Groos). And as the baby grows older by days and weeks the functions which give him pleasure become more diversified and occupy a greater part of his day.

Functional pleasure is a very important aspect not only of early life; indeed, many of the satisfactions offered by the nursery school are functional pleasures.

The young child who builds, paints or handles clay is not primarily steering toward an end product—the building or the painting—but he enjoys the activity as such. In an environment scaled to his abilities, he can be far more active. In nursery school he discovers new dimensions of his self.

We might say the child paints, uses the brush (or other tools) pretty much in the same way as we dance. We do it because we enjoy the movement and so the child enjoys the moving lines which his brush produces on the paper.* He also wants to produce a nice picture, but the act of painting may be so enticing that he finds it hard to stop. Kris speaks of the child's "inner battle against smearing." At times the teacher helps him by stepping in and saving the sheet while it is still a picture and not an overlaid mass of muddy paint, but sometimes it is wiser not to interfere. We shouldn't stress too early the doing for the purpose of achieving an end product. This is also true when he plays with words, with rhythm and cadence. The teacher's offer to write a poem down for him or to play his tunes back to him may encourage him, but it may also deaden his joy. The adult gets puzzled or annoyed because the child, when asked to repeat, brings another version instead. By the way, I remember a bright five year-old who was strangely inhibited in his ability to draw or to paint. I did not know then what the inhibiting force was. Later I learned that a really charming painting produced when he was a little over two (!) had been framed and was hanging prominently in the family living room. This child's development demonstrated that not only criticism but excessive praise too can become a stumbling block.

Let's return to the infant who enjoys moving his hands and fingers and toes. He plays with his voice; he listens to it and also he starts using early toys, a ball, a rattle. At this level, is it the rattle which the child enjoys, or is it the rattling? You may say this is hair splitting or a senseless question. However, my question is related to certain very ingenious experiments by Piaget. To quote just a few out of his long series: the observer plays ball with an infant (five or six months old) and after a while covers the ball with a piece

*As Miriam Lindstrom puts it in a book on children's art: ". . . . the picture seems to be only a byproduct of the main interest, the act of painting."

62

of cloth. The child reacts to this as if the ball had completely disappeared, although the bump underneath the cloth is plainly visible. He looks in different directions, moves his hands away from the covered ball. As far as the child's world is concerned the ball has ceased to exist. Possibly he responds this way because he is unable to remove the cloth? Oh no, says Piaget, if his face were covered, he would attempt to pull it away.

Another experiment with infants a little older, but still well under one year of age: the baby is seated comfortably between two pillows, one to his left and one to his right. Again the observer introduces a ball. After a while he takes it away from the child and hides it under the pillow to the child's left. A few seconds later he takes it out and plainly in view of the baby puts the ball underneath the right pillow. What is now the child's reaction? He searches for the ball under the left pillow. Piaget, whose inventiveness is matched by his patience, repeated these experiments with several children. One of them learned within a few hours where to look for the ball, while another took as long as three weeks.

And here is Piaget's explanation: the child, although able to coordinate hand and eye movement, i.e., prehension and vision, has not yet constructed the concept of a permanent object. The ball exists only as a sort of semi-object. Localization is linked to the place of the child's previously successful action, not yet to the object itself.

The ball which vanished under the left pillow was "the ball-which-gave-pleasure." The ball which the observer takes out from under the pillow and slowly moves over to the right side is a neutral object, one which is indifferent (not cathected, i.e., not covered by the child's interests). To be more precise: the child searches for the pleasurable activity and this has vanished under the left pillow.

It is Piaget's great merit to have captured through his

experimental set-up a phase of play-behavior which is short-lived and quite unexpected and for these reasons has escaped earlier observers.

Actually, the play reactions which he was the first to describe are governed by the same principles as the child's earliest behavior towards basic gratifications which psychoanalysis has studied. The infant uses or tries to use wishes, magic gestures and haphazard motions and perceptions to achieve pleasure and avoid displeasure. And many of his motions have no goal besides the discharge of excitation. We speak of "primary process" behavior, and psychoanalytic study has shown that this prelogical behavior and such drive-governed thought processes continue in adulthood in our dreams, and may come to the surface in situations of great stress.

The infant is able to interact with his environment, to do something in the direction of a goal before his mind has established the framework of space, time and causality which supports our, adult's world and enables us to anticipate events. (Both faculties are basic acquisitions of the self of the human child.)

According to psychoanalytic thinking permanency is granted first to the mother who fulfills the child's needs. The mother who has been with the child, feeding it, playing or talking with it, and leaves the room, and the mother who reenters after a while are experienced as the same object. The child who has had "good enough mothering" (a term coined by the British psychoanalyst Winnicott) begins to recognize the approaching mother also when he is not hungry, when he has no urgent needs. Now he may refuse the bottle offered by a stranger, even when he is hungry. He now perceives that she is different from strangers and this causes the so-called "eight-months anxiety." If a person approaches him, the first faint noise lets him expect his mother and he is disappointed, or frightened, when somebody else comes. The appearance of this anxiety is actually a sign of progress! (I would not have gotten away with this statement a few years ago. Everybody had to be full of courage all the time.) I hasten to add that a few weeks or months later his anxiety lessens and changes into a watchful attitude towards strangers. And this will again be a token of progress.

It is the child's maturation plus the good mothering which makes his attachment possible, but once it has come about it brings tremendous progress. This is the circular character of development. Once a child has developed a true attachment to his mother, and sees her as distinct and different from strangers, the range of pleasure he can receive from her and the intensity of his interaction with her grows considerably. He communicates with her through more and more channels, reserves for her the smile formerly offered indiscriminately to anyone approaching the crib smiling and nodding at him. I'm referring to the studies of Eino Kaila, later amplified by R. Spitz. Kaila and Spitz showed that a child between two and six months of age will smile at practically any one whom he sees en face, he will smile even at a nodding mask!

We can assume that once permanency has been accorded to his mother, permanency may be accorded to those inanimate objects, which are very familiar and give pleasure. Winnicott calls them "transitional objects" and mentions early toys or a blanket. And he adds that if we don't want to destroy this attachment, we must be careful not to change the object in any way, e.g., not to wash the blanket, when it becomes soiled or not to mend it, because this may destroy its value for the child. This shows how much more observant the child has become. At every point we see the interdependence of intellectual (adaptive) and emotional development.

The glaring deficiency which still exists may show up

65

when the period of the child's sole attachment to the mother is compared with later times when several people play a role in his life.

In the early days the child obviously assumes that his mother exists for the sole purpose of caring for him. If at times she does not respond promptly, doesn't relieve his pain or his displeasure, he cannot perceive that she may not be looking after him because other things, too, have a place in her life.

At this time he begins to imitate the mother, but he doesn't compare himself to her. He doesn't identify with her. I know that several of my colleagues would not agree with me, but I am of the opinion that the child imitates, or rather mirrors an increasing number of the mother's activities, but he doesn't make any attempt to put himself in her place; he doesn't perceive the sameness between him and her—and hence can not identify with her. The gulf existing between him and her is taken by the child as granted and as permanent; he is helpless and the mother is powerful. Actually he changes tremendously and learns something new practically every day. Yet he is very conservative—everything must be done in the same way, in the same sequence.

Then comes the time when the child has discovered that other people exist and has come to like father and mother as two separate and different people. One day he finds out that these others have interests among themselves which don't concern him, and more than this, from which he is excluded.

With the urgency which is characteristic of all his early wishes, the child wants to be included, or more correctly, he wants to be right in the midst of what the others are doing and from which the two-and-a-half or three year old finds himself left out.

Now he identifies—and he identifies with both—with father and mother—he wants to be in the place of either one or both of them. Yet he is excluded, relegated to the nursery, treated as a child. The urgency of his wishes prompts him to form fantasies which—from our point of view—are preposterous. And many times a day he wants to take part in everything the grown ups are doing.

At this age, the child is aware of the existence of men and women, boys and girls, and while the boy identifies himself more with the father and the girl more with the mother, both sexes identify with both parents. Please remember this in nursery school and don't get alarmed when a boy dresses up as a girl and vice versa. Only the consistency of such wishes should cause concern, not their occasional occurrence. As long as our observational skill is limited, only the consistent display of such wishes comes to our attention, but as we become keener observers we also need to become more cautious with our conclusions, otherwise we see the spectre of pathology everywhere.

The child notices sex differences and at one time or another a glimpse of the adult's sexual life—but about both he is hopelessly wrong. By this I mean even if the right explanations are provided—and they should be—he will distort it all according to the level of his own development. Most frequently he sees it in terms of romping, hurting, naughtiness and a wild good time.

He wants to be accepted as a full partner by his parents—and this is not possible for biological reasons—not just for social reasons. There is no society which would receive a five year old as a full member (although there are societies accepting thirteen and fourteen year olds). In many mammals the second dentition (development of permanent teeth) and ovulation in the female occur within a short interval; in the human child, however, the two events are separated by a number of years. The young child senses and shares sexual genital excitement but it will be at least another decade before his body is ready for the task of reproduction. He wants desperately to be his parents' part-

67

ner, to do what they do and feel the same feelings—and in this central instinctual wish he is defeated.

But he has a tremendous potential for growth—and this brings about a new development. He does not give up in spite of all his frustrated efforts. The recurring urgency of his wishes leads to a development specific for the human child. It bounces him out of his home in search of images and symbols of grownupness, images and symbols of masculinity; or of being a mother. He uses his fantasy to achieve some degree of gratification of his urgent wishes; he plays, he enters into make-believe activities. Play, which goes beyond sensory-motor elements and uses symbols, implies a great change in the self and the self image.

What is the child's fantasy so often mentioned by poets and writers? Can we define it, single out its essential elements? Fantasy implies the use of symbols for wish-fulfillment, plus the ability not to see what interferes with wish-fulfillment. Denial combines with the use of colorful symbols in the service of wishes.

This ability not to see what interferes with pleasure is characteristic of the young child. Formerly we said that perceptions are admitted when they bring pleasure. And here is the corollary statement: perceptions producing intense displeasure are cast out, denied existence. The child uses denial and repression to keep displeasure at a bearable minimum.

We grown-ups have various techniques at our disposal when encountering displeasure. We can fight it directly; reason about it; can make plans how to deal with it later and if we can't do anything else, we usually can run away from it. In most instances none of these techniques are available to the young child. He's far too dependent, far too weak. Without the techniques of denial and repression displeasure would loom large in his world.

Let's look at the following example: The mother of a child between one and two years old is hospitalized for about ten days. When she returns—the child acts as if he didn't recognize her—looks at her with a blank expression—and it may take her a couple of days to establish the old relationship. It seems, the child has "forgotten" the mother, as you and I forget historical data we have learned in school and which gradually dwindle from our memory.

Yet it isn't this kind of intellectual forgetting, because he is able to remember things for a much longer spell of time. For instance, the same child who seemingly has forgotten his mother runs directly for his favorite rocking chair at his grandmother's even after an absence of two or three weeks. He has not forgotten where it stood.

Therefore, what has really happened is that the child has—on account of the shock of disappointment—cast away a chunk of the outer world which he has had established for himself.

The child of nursery school age—three to five—uses denial and fantasy a great deal in his play. By means of play he digests and assimilates experiences which were overpowering or painful or anxiety arousing; or he reproduces events where he had been the passive, the suffering party—repeating them in play he becomes the active one, he is the instigator.

He needs a broader environment where he can play, where he can get away from the limitations and frustrations of his home. Under primitive conditions he might simply stroll away from his mother and thus attain some independence although there is no planning for it. Things are different in our society and this is where the nursery school has its important function: It offers a more spacious environment —in the physical sense of the word as well as figuratively speaking—a place where he can be active and thus organize his abilities, where he finds playmates and play materials. There is one more essential factor: the teacher's willingness to stand by but to refrain from interfering with his play. The playing out, the realistic activities offered, the give and take with the others, the relationship with his teacher—all these change him and his self-image.

A few words about the teacher. A nursery school teacher should not try to imitate the mother—this is not her function. There are many reasons for this and one is very practical: you can not be a "good mother" to twelve or even to ten young children. It is a good experience for the child to be with a person who is kind and resourceful—yet as a rule—keeps at a certain distance.

Although the nursery school teacher shouldn't duplicate the mother, it is essential for her to be a motherly, a warm person. The child comes to nursery school to have a different experience from what he has at home, yet there are unexpected shifts in his moods and on the level on which he functions and at times he does need a protective, motherly person.

But motherliness is not the only requisite, and if this quality of a teacher is stressed too much then I get a little suspicious about her all-round qualifications for being a good teacher.

One more word—we don't like to hear any one using baby talk with the child. We get annoyed when the mother—or even the grandmother—who brings the child to school uses the child's own idiom to talk to him. Do we always abstain from it ourselves? Well, we don't use verbal baby talk with him, but we may use baby talk in other media. Our endeavors to offer in nursery school stories, music or pictures which are simple, are justified but may go too far, as for instance the rigorous avoidance of words and images he does not know. (Perhaps this is my purely personal opinion. But I would not like my reading restricted to the vocabulary I myself am using.) The best environment for children is one where "his reach can surpass his grasp" a phrase used by Anne C. Moore, the well-known expert on children's literature.

The stories we give to the child should depict not only his personal experience in every-day life, they should include the full range of his emotional experiences—and in order to do this, they must use symbols and images which he understands and appreciates through the world of his own emotions, even though they may not be present in his daily world.

Only by transcending his own sensory experience do we offer to him what art has to offer to us—a broader spectrum, a deeper resonance to his own feelings. A story which goes beyond the limits of the child's own idiom, but which is honest and lively, may present to the child a mirror of his own joys and conflicts, of his self.

Through his sometimes fully and sometimes partially gratified instinctual needs, the child arrives at the first notion of me and non-me. The ego functions of motility and perception get started in the service of his body needs, but they come into full bloom only in response to mothering, not through the child's effort to wrestle his sustenance from an indifferent or hostile surrounding. The growth of adaptive behavior (motility, perception, memory, reasoning, integration) is rooted in and governed by his emotional development.

Through imitating others, through wishful thinking which involves taking the place of others (identifying himself with others), through the acquisition of language, through play, alone and in close give and take with others, and finally through elementary experiences in the arts, the child develops a growing knowledge of his own self.

I have pointed to some of the building materials that form the child's self—by no means to all. As I am deeply interested in current educational trends I could not refrain from referring to some of the practical nursery school problems which you encounter in your daily work with children.

# 3.

## LANGUAGE AND ITS PRE-STAGES

We seem to be at the eve of revolutionary changes in early education and I for one am worried about some trends and developments. To put it simply: until very recently all academic learning was withheld from children under six and often from those nearly seven, although there were children obviously ready and eager to learn. More correctly, the intention of informed educators was to withhold it, but some children learned to read or cipher on their own or with the secret help of a grandparent or a servant.

Suddenly there is complete change. We are treated to films of nursery schools where three-year-olds learn to read and to use typewriters and the public is highly impressed. There is a real danger that the former attitude which tried to postpone academic learning will be replaced by pressuring the young child towards tangible achievements in reading or arithmetic or book-learning.

Achievements considered to be the result of "simple maturation" are in reality the combined outcome of intricate developments in several fields, some of them seemingly far removed from the area where the achievement occurs. We still know very little about the growth of the mind and in our eagerness to bring the "3 R's" into the nursery we may come to neglect or to crowd out activities which are vital for mental growth.

Our ignorance about the earliest phases of child development is appalling. I'll give you a recent example. The doings of the infant in the cradle seem haphazard, a sheer waste of time and energy. He just coos and gurgles and smiles and makes jerky random movements. It sometimes happens that a newborn scratches his face in the first days of life and mother or father when shown their baby get upset. So somebody had an idea and today practically all better grade garments for young infants have flaps at their sleeves and the hands of the infant are put into these pocket-like contraptions. This practice started with newborns but today you can see older infants in hospitals and in homes where they are lovingly cared for whose hands are "protected" in this way, sometimes day and night. The mother or nurse has no idea that she is interfering with an activity which is of vital importance. The infant's fingertips are highly sensitive and should collect a lot of tactile experience and also come to cooperate with the eyes and with one another.

For a trivial hygienic reason we enforce their idleness and mutilate their development. Mittens put on for an outing are harmless, but mittens for many hours destroy an essential pattern of growth. The same mother who routinely puts the flap over the infant's little fist would be shocked to hear that a child is left in the dark for many hours. The sense of vision is so important for us adults that its relevance for the infant is accepted, but being able or not to finger something seems irrelevant.

Early childhood development is at times presented as dominated by two important factors. The one is *maturation* (in the sense of Gesell, i.e. the realization of an innate, prestructured pattern independent of environmental stimulation) and the other is *instruction* or adult planned stimulation. I tried to show that between these two powerful factors are wedged others of equal importance. There is the huge area of contacts with the environment which the child

73

himself initiates and the even larger field of self-stimulation. Spontaneous exploration and *circular stimulation* probably account for most of the learning of the young child.

All early intellectual learning is predicated upon emotional development. A presentation of the young child's cognitive development hangs in mid-air unless we relate it to the development of drives and affects, of his object relations and of the early self-image. We all are aware of the value of the child's play, but our concept of play is often too narrow. I differentiate between the inarticulate archaic play and play on the oedipal level, when the child tries to copy the adults or actually to ursurp the adult's privileges. In the latter type of play he may accompany his doings with a commentary; often he dresses up, assigns roles to other children; his play is colorful and varied. We like to watch it. In contrast the earlier play reminds us at times of a record playing where the needle gets stuck in a groove and there are endless repetitions, so monotonous that we get annoyed. Yet simple, monotonous play forms support archaic fantasies and are not less important than the later make-believe play.

A few words about the role of the nursery school teacher and about the child's playmates. Repeatedly we have referred to the child's tie to his mother. Because the affects binding him to his family are so intense these ties should be kept unbroken, but for the same reason the child also profits by being away from his family for a part of the day. Under certain simple social and economical conditions it is easy enough for him to wander away—while in our society we must usually make special provisions for him, i.e. nursery school, kindergarten. Intense inner and outer conflicts which are unavoidable in growing up, recede in another human environment, in nursery school.

From the above it follows that it is not the nursery school

teacher's function to copy the mother. She should be able to mother, i.e. reassure a child after an upsetting experience, but as a rule a certain distance between her and the child entrusted to her is best for the child and best for the child's relation to other children.*

Because the attachment to the teacher and the identification with her is so important a child should not be moved to another group during a school year. In large nursery school systems this is at times done for administrative reasons, e.g. the child is promoted to another group on the day when he completes his third or fourth year. It is interesting that this is never done in elementary school—but with the young child we are unaware of the damage we may inflict.

The child forms an attachment not only to the teacher but also to the other children in his group. The *narrow age range* which we find today in most nursery schools and kindergartens does not favor attachment and identifications among the playmates. In a group with a broad age range a child can assume a protective role towards others or seek the greater skill, competence of an older child. Skills, attitudes of perseverance or self-control are learned easily and painlessly from older children. The three-year-olds can play with one another, but it seems they cannot carry on even a short dialogue about things not present—but a three and a five-year-old can do so and thereby gain something else than from a talk with a grownup.

*As originally published, this paper had a footnote in which Lili Peller quoted the following from her earlier paper *The School's Role in Promoting Sublimation* (#5 in this Section):

"What is the specific feature of a good teacher-child relationship? The child forms a strong attachment to a person who does not share the intimacies of his home but remains at a certain distance. The fact that there are other children competing with him to be noticed by the teacher arouses his jealousy, but it also intensifies the child's admiration for her and confirms the existing distance." (L. Peller, 17).

# 4.

# CHARACTER DEVELOPMENT IN NURSERY SCHOOL

Psychoanalytic insight not only can help in the treatment of the child who is maladjusted; it has a great deal to offer in the case of the average well-adjusted child. In certain aspects of education, psychoanalytical insight can carry on where progressive education leaves off—or, rather, left off, one or two decades ago. Let us look at the main conceptual tools of progressive education: an attitude of permissiveness toward the young child; consideration of his play interests and concerns as important; the postponement of academic learnings and exacting skills in such a way as to shield the child from frustration, failures, and experiences of inadequacy. In short, the so-called progressives declare a kind of educational moratorium: all pressures should be removed from the young child. This is an excellent beginning, but it is not enough.

The psychoanalytical educator, too, is lenient. However, he sees beyond the gratification of early instinctual needs. *He is lenient in order to win as his ally the full force of the child's own wish to grow up.* As little as possible of the energy of this precious wish should be dissipated in fighting the adult. A severe, suppressive education is as wasteful as one whose only tool is indulgence. The more the child is understood, encouraged and supported in his efforts to grow up, the more external pressure can be reduced.

\* \* \* \*

In large nursery schools, children are placed in such a way that all in one group are of the same age. The range within a group is usually from ten to twelve months. Recently some schools even have groups of "younger fours" and "older fours," and so on. Thus the age range is only about six months. Of course small schools cannot carry out this stratification according to age levels and this is considered a drawback.

The question arises whether this view is borne out by experience. A second question is whether *psychoanalytical* insight into the formation of the ego makes it advisable for a child to spend his school time prevailingly or exclusively with children close to his own age. Grouping according to age levels is an application of the principle of homogeneous grouping. The large elementary and high schools had— and in many instances still have—their pupils divided in such a way as to make each group as homogeneous as possible. That was achieved by combining grouping according to I. Q. with grouping according to age. To-day this seems an inheritance from the days when a high degree of permanency was ascribed to the results of an intelligence test.

In 1931, Alice Keliher took exception to this practice.[1] Among other things she was able to show that friendships as often crossed the lines of these groups as followed them. To the best of my knowledge, the positive value of a narrow age range in nursery school has never been questioned.[2] Only Lois B. Murphy has attempted a comparison of certain features of a group with a wide and one with a narrow age range.[3] Group "W" had 20 children with a range of from thirty-seven to forty-seven months, while group "H" had 19 children of from twenty-eight to fifty-four months.

For the problem that we are considering here, it is unfortunate that the two groups differed also in other respects.

Group "H" had more play space and more equipment and the teachers showed more spontaneous warmth than those in group "W." The main object of Dr. Murphy's study was the children's spontaneous response of sympathy. In group "W" the ratio of sympathetic to unsympathetic responses was 1.63, while in group "H" it was 6.63. This is an enormous difference. However, on account of the peculiar set-up, we are unable to decide which one of the three factors— age range, play space and equipment, and teacher personality—caused it mainly or exclusively. Thus Murphy's study cannot provide an answer to our problem. The amazing difference between the two ratios only increases our curiosity.

How much importance do the children themselves attach to age? (The members of our seminar reported frequent discussions among their children about age.) The following are characteristic discussions:

> Stanley, aged four and a half, stands in the yard and starts a conversation with children from the "Threes" across the fence: "You're a baby."
> Linda: "No, I'm only in the baby group."
> Marsha: "That is not a baby group!"
> Linda: "How big?"
> Marsha: "It's very big, up to the sky."
> Ricky: "This is a baby group, but a very big one."
> Alan: "This is the big baby group because we play on the sliding pond and swings when we go to the big yard."

> A group of four-year-olds discusses the arrival of a new baby in Ileen's family.
> Ileen: "He has brown eyes, black hair, and red cheeks and he rolls around a lot."
> Joan: "Does he drink from a bottle?"

78

Ileen: "Yes, and finishes it all up. But I don't drink from a bottle because I am four years old. When he's four, he won't either."

Judy, three years and seven months, an only child, was very much interested in the babies in the park. One day she rushed up to a baby carriage and peeked in saying: "Oh, look at the little baby! Is not he little? I was a tiny baby once. I drank out of a bottle with a nipple when I was a baby. I am three years old now. I'm a big girl. My mommie does not give me a bottle."

Children in our culture ascribe a great deal of prestige to age. This can be observed even when the adults mention age only occasionally. The importance of being three or five is enhanced when the child's group in school is actually called "The Three's" or "The Fives." Just what makes a child five and another one four is not clearly understood by the child himself. Of course it is impossible to explain to a young child the passage of time, and hence young children fall prey to many misunderstandings, such as the following:

Richard: "I'm six."
Jeff: "Is he six?"
Teacher: "No, Richard is five."
Richard: "No, I'm six now."
Teacher: "Don't you remember your birthday cake had five candles on it? That means you were five years old—one candle for each birthday."
Richard: "Yes, but after my school party on Friday I had one home on Saturday, so that makes me six."

This point is also illustrated in a story by A. A. Milne, who often shows an amazing insight into young children. In his story a little girl, Barbara, finds herself convalescing in the country as her birthday comes along. The birthday party has been postponed, but her nurse arranges an impromptu tea party, and Barbara explains to her guests: "I'm six as soon as I get back. I would have been six to-day if I had been well."[4]

This may be taken as an example of childish realism in Piaget's sense—*e.g.*, mistaking a conspicuous consequence for the cause. However, there may also be another explanation: Not being aware of time, the child takes his respective birthday parties as a kind of initiation ceremony which the adults plan as they time and plan other things for him. At the birthday party the adults bestow upon him the status of being "five" just as a fraternity gives its club membership through an initiation ceremony.

Children have other misconceptions about age. M. had emphasized that he was five while A. was only four. A. retorted: "But next year I'll be five, and then I'll be six, and then I'll be older than you!" Here, again, the child hopes that age is a kind of status in regard to which you can catch up on others or even outdo them, as you can in regard to skills and possessions.

> Ronnie, aged six years and two months, has a cousin aged six years and ten months. The two girls are inseparable friends. To her teacher's question: "How old is your cousin?" Ronnie replied: "She is as old as I am, only she was born a little earlier."

Progressive educators call the lower elementary grades "The Sixes," "The Eights," etc., on the assumption that this will remove pressures from children. It may be a question of merit or demerit whether a child finds himself in the first or the third grade, whereas age is a biological fact and as such neutral. This is adult reasoning. Among children age carries as much status as grade in school. I have observed that most young children tell many more fibs and lies about their ages than they do in order to escape punishment. This indicates the urgency of the wish to be older.

In regard to adults, most children have a vague idea that they stay as they are and that therefore children will eventually catch up with their parents. Thus the typical remark of a little boy to his mother or to a well-liked teacher, "When I grow up, I'll marry you," makes sense to the child. It seems to me that the child's belief that he will catch up with his elders is not entirely mistaken. The numerical difference in years remains, but the difference in status shrinks rapidly. The relationship between a sixteen-year-old and his parents is very different from that of a six-year-old and his parents. Many children also believe that getting old means getting smaller and smaller. There is a vague notion that death is the end of this continued shrinking. A child who passes through a period of acute fear of death will thus be doubly glad if told how much he has grown recently.

Even this quaint idea that adults get smaller may be based on partly correct observations. Grandparents as a rule are considerably smaller than parents in our decades. This is not only because they walk with a slight stoop, but mainly because for about a century, because of more favorable environmental conditions, children have tended to be taller than their parents.

Freud has stated more than once that the wish that dominates childhood is the desire to grow up. From whence does this wish derive its strength? The Oedipal attachments dominate this period, and the three-to-five-year-old suffers minor and major rebukes in his efforts to be taken as the full partner of his parents. His ascribes his lack of success, at least at times, to the fact that he is too small and too young. The boy who fails in competition with his father derives a grain of relief in finding that, nevertheless, other boys who are older than he take him as their equal. Sometimes he

81

needs to know that others look up to him and that he can be their protector. He now can be at times the active party, in a relationship similar to that in which he is the receiving party only at home. Thus the two antithetic situations—"I'm smaller than X, yet he accepts me as his friend; I'm stronger and bigger than Y, and thus I can protect him"—provide relief from the burning wish to grow up. In an environment that is planned for his optimal growth, a child should be able to associate with others who are his own age as well as with older and younger playmates. According to our experience this applies to children of nursery-school and of elementary-school age.

For a comparison of a group with a narrow and one with a wide age range, let us turn to Murphy's forementioned study.[5]

> "The differences in group H were great enough (they were thirty months) to avert constant competition for the same play materials and activities, and to stimulate a protective, 'big-brother' type of response of older towards younger children. There may doubtless have been important imitative factors: when older children set examples of protective and sympathetic behavior, these would be copied by younger children when occasion offered. Group W, on the other hand, consisted of children developmentally close enough together to be interested largely in the same materials and activities; this necessarily resulted in more competition and conflicts over these materials. And the same imitative factors that were present in Group H and which led younger children to pick up coöperative and helpful patterns from the older ones, would result in acquisition of more techniques of conflict in Group W. In this connection it is interesting to note that for three successive years, groups occupying the present quarters of

Group W had shown high conflict scores, as compared with groups in the quarters of Group H."

Murphy describes how feelings of protectiveness in the older children are substituted for competition, aggression, and defense. I should like to supplement her excellent description by pointing to the corollary feelings in the younger children. They look with great admiration toward the older ones and are happy and flattered when drawn into their play projects. And yet in the same children, when with playmates of exactly their own age, the strife for ascendency would be foremost. Each child would want to be the first. There would be the strong urge to outdo the other fellow in physical strength, in cunning, in number of friends, and so on. Consequently there would be a good deal of boasting, quibbling, fighting, and suspicious watching intermingled with their play.

In the *Haus der Kinder* in Vienna, all groups of children—those on the pre-school level as well as the regular school groups—had an age range of two, two and a half, or three years. In contrast to the educational views held in this country, we never questioned the fact that a wider age range is more conducive to the child's emotional, social, and intellectual development and lessens the feelings of inadequacy generated by the Oedipal frustrations. Thus control groups with a narrow age range were never established, and our experience lacks the support of experimental proof.

Often a younger child became attached to an older one and showed distinctly what would be termed hero worship in an adolescent. A child seemed well satisfied when a group of older children who were building or working at the carpenter's bench permitted him to carry blocks or pieces of wood back and forth for them. The school children did their regular school work in self-formed groups, sitting around a table, and here, too, a younger child seemed quite content to be permitted to sit with them and watch them. Precise records are no longer in existence, yet I remember that we were at first uneasy seeing a child assuming for too long periods the rôle of the inactive observer. With a young school child we were worried as to whether he would not fall behind in his own school work. In each instance, however, the period of being an onlooker ended without direct interference on the teacher's part, and the child returned to his own work with a new zeal.

There is no doubt that Dewey's principle of "learning by doing" is correct, yet the interpretation that doing must always be some muscle activity is too narrow. Apparently the child who sat and eagerly watched an older friend was "learning by looking" or, in instances in which the older child's school work was beyond the younger child's technical understanding, he derived from his association with the older friend a heightened incentive to go on with his own work.

In recent years I have worked prevailingly with schools whose groups were strictly stratified according to age. In some instances the school had the practice of "graduating" a child to the next group the very day he turned three or four. The birthday party was at the same time the child's farewell party. The party as such was certainly helpful, yet, with the turn-over of teachers and children in New York City's nursery schools and kindergartens, it often meant that the child severed his attachments to his teacher as well as to the majority of his playmates twice a year—he entered one new group right after his birthday and another in the fall. For children whose family life was of average stability, this had no patent bad consequences. I remember, however, A. C., whose transference to another group on his fourth birthday coincided with his father's leaving for the army. He showed signs of serious disturbance which subsided when he was returned to his former group.

Far more frequent is the reverse case—*e.g.*, a child in need of promotion to an older group. A child finding himself in a group in which everybody is his own age may become so unmanageable that the school considers asking the parents to take him out. When, as a last resort, this youngster is placed in an older group, he may make good.

> Betty, five and a half, and Frankie, three years and five months, had been in nursery school for one year. They were in different groups and met only in the yard. There were three older children in the family. In February Betty entered public school. She called in the afternoon with her mother for Frankie. He became very unhappy, refusing to join in any activity whatsoever. He would sit and sulk for hours or seek trouble with some other child. He ignored his sister completely when they called for him in the afternoon.
>
> For two months his teacher and the director of the school tried everything to help him. As a last resort he was transferred to the older group, although he acted more infantile than he did when he first entered the school. It worked like magic. He became his old self again. In the afternoon he greeted his sister with "I've been promoted. I'm a big boy now." Since then several months have passed and Frankie has been accepted by the older group.

As long as both children attended nursery school they had an almost equal status. Betty's promotion in the middle of the year, however, meant indirectly a demotion for Frankie. That he is the youngest of five siblings may have increased the pressure he felt and his reluctance at being "left behind" while everybody in his family grew up. The fact that the promoted sibling was a girl probably increased the aggravation.

The mechanism underlying such a successful adjustment

is a kind of silent barter. The adult promotes the child, thus increasing his status, and the youngster in return makes a more determined effort to please the adult and restrain himself. In some cases the child had been getting out of bounds because he was the unchallenged leader in his group or because he was the child with the longest group experience and, therefore, the greatest social facility. Joining a group of children who are a better match for his abilities makes him more willing to accept also the adult authority. A healthy child cannot enjoy a placid, static existence. He has to pit his strength against that of another person. If there is no other youngster against whom he can test his abilities, he will test them against the adult.

Some nursery schools have introduced the practice of having children visit older groups, either for special activities or for half days and, in at least one school, the corollary practice is being used—one or two older children may come to a younger group and help the teacher if they want to do so. The visiting is very helpful in overcoming an isolation that in the long run is apt to impoverish the formation of ego ideals. This is of course more true for children attending all-day schools than for those in half-day sessions.

A school that is centered around the principle of the teacher's guiding and supervising each child will simplify the task by striving for uniformity among the pupils in one group. The administrators and attendants of any institution in which people are taken care of aim at homogeneity to simplify their work. This is a sensible policy, whether the charges are newborn infants, physically sick people, or mental patients. A school also "takes care" of children, but this is only preliminary to its focal interest—the children's social and intellectual growth.

A school that capitalizes the influence of one youngster upon another needs interaction between them, and this in turn is predicated on variety among the group members.

Homogeneous grouping is not compatible with the "embryonic society" Dewey wanted each classroom to be.

Assuming at times the rôle of the older, the protecting friend, and at times the rôle of the follower, the receiving party, broadens the development of the child's ego and strengthens his feeling of competence. A wider age range increases the occasions for such relations.

Rewards and punishments meted out by the adult group leader, the teacher, are the main educational tools of an education based on "training"—*e.g.*, enforcing desirable behavior until, by dint of frequent repetition, it becomes a part of the child's character. If we accept the psychoanalytical view of human development, identification becomes the most effective lever for the shaping of character. In a group with a wider age range, such opportunities are increased, and there the child also finds a wider selection of individuals with whom he can identify.

In a homogeneous group, coöperation is mainly on the basis of quantity: "I do this half; you do the other half." If the members of a group *differ* in their abilities, there can be another kind of coöperation: "I do what I can do well; you apply your skill." It is obvious that—*ceteris paribus*—there will be less mutual helping out and more competition, more comparison, in a group all of whose members have about the same abilities. The modern nursery-school teacher avoids comparison between children and avoids arousing feelings of rivalry. Nevertheless, in a homogeneous group a certain norm of performance becomes established and small deviations attain a high visibility. The children themselves, as well as the teacher, are aware of the child who excels in building or painting or of the other child who is more slow or clumsy in dressing or eating.

In a group of differing ages, wide varieties in performance are the order of the day. Within this general diversity, differences between children of equal age disappear or are taken casually. It is well known that in a family in which siblings of the same sex are close in age, competition is far more dominant than in families in which the difference is more than three years.

A large nursery school that could open parallel groups, alike in every respect except that one would have a wide and the other a narrow age range, would be in an ideal position to test the respective advantages and drawbacks of homogeneous *versus* heterogeneous grouping.

## NOTES

[1]See *Critical Study of Homogeneous Grouping; With a Critique of Measurement as the Basis of Classification.* New York: Teachers College, 1931.

[2]At a recent meeting in San Francisco, Dr. Ruth Benedict questioned the tendency to separate children by ages.

[3]See *Social Behavior and Child Personality.* New York: Columbia University Press, 1937.

[4]"Barbara's Birthday" in *A Gallery of Children*, by A. A. Milne. Philadelphia: David McKay, 1925.

[5]*Op. cit.*

# 5.

# THE SCHOOL'S ROLE IN PROMOTING SUBLIMATION

Over the years a number of studies have re-examined the concept of sublimation. These, and particularly the panel discussion (1955), have greatly clarified the theoretical aspects of sublimation. My own interest is far more limited and I shall confine myself to some practical implications of our knowledge of sublimation for education.

With the term sublimation Freud originally referred to the process by which the primary aims of instinctual drives are given up for certain cultural or otherwise highly valued achievements. Repeatedly he points to the gratification, the discharge of tension which sublimation provides. Today, we would add that in sublimation primary and secondary processes interact, with secondary processes prevailing. Activities based on sublimations are, at least to a large extent, communicable, not idiomatic, not part of a person's private world. They may yield pleasure of high intensity as well as lasting contentment.

Bernfeld (1922) at one point suggested to redefine the concept of sublimation in such a way as to eliminate the implied value judgments and to speak of ego-syntonic aims instead. However, there is behavior which has ego-syntonic aims, yet offers no gratification. If we accept Bernfeld's suggestion, then all behavior which comes under the reality principle might be based on sublimation. In my opinion, the term sublimation should be restricted to processes lead-

ing to ego-syntonic actions which retain a libidinal investment and have a discharge value. In this study our attention
will be focused on those ego interests and attitudes which
are highly invested.

Sublimation may serve defense, but is hardly a "mechanism" in the usual sense. Pleasure is yielded also by other
defense reactions but is seldom of comparable intensity, or
not so securely anchored in reality. In sublimation the pleasure is inherent in the process itself, not only in the attainment of the goal. Already en route to it, tension may be
discharged and gratification may be harvested.

Not all processes of sublimation have an adaptive function. They occur also when our essential needs are not
covered. Even in a situation of marginal existence (see, e.g.,
recent reports from detention camps) a prisoner may trade
badly needed food or other essentials for paper scraps and
a pencil, or for chess figures. In this connection, Hartmann's (1948) statement that the id of human beings is
further removed from reality than the instincts of animals is
relevant and could be expanded to include these aspects.
From the point of view of self-preservation or survival the
substituting of chess play for essential food is not adaptive.

A child may take his play—which is his main avenue
toward sublimation—seriously, an adult may invest a
stupendous amount of libido in his work. "Every playing
child behaves like a poet, creating his own world. . . . It
would be wrong to assume that he does not take this world
seriously. To the contrary, he takes his play very seriously."
Freud's phrasing (1908) indicates that he is disputing a
generally accepted view—namely that "taking something
seriously" and "playing" are mutually exclusive or at least
represent contrasts. Everyday psychology considers play
the opposite of serious pursuits. Procuring (directly or indirectly) life's necessities is considered "serious," while activities not connected with useful goals, as play or leisure-
time activities, are rated "not serious."

No doubt, play has a quality of levity, of lightheartedness (I almost said of playfulness) and yet children and adults as well may take their respective play activities very seriously. How can we solve this apparent contradiction? Could we define what is implied by "taking something seriously"? Before attempting this, Freud's comments concerning a completely different field, namely *rational thought*, might be helpful. He considers thinking essentially a trial action with small quantities of energy.

In rational thinking there is less expenditure of physical effort than in action—this is obvious. Moreover, a trial action has no immediate consequences in the world of reality, hence there will be less anxiety than in action (or more correctly: no anxiety). To these signal features of rational thought I may add that the ideas involved in thinking are invested with neutralized energy. (The pleasure inherent in intellectual work, in functioning per se is a different matter.) Rational thought is thus characterized by the absence, or near-absence, of physical *effort*, of *anxiety* and by the cathexis of ideas and images with *neutralized energy*.

We may now examine whether this little excursion can solve the apparent contrast between the levity of play and the fact that it may be often taken seriously. Applying to it the same three criteria we find: great physical and/or mental *effort* can be called forth in play and its *libidinal cathexis* may be high, but only mild degrees of *anxiety* are compatible with play. Mounting anxiety (arising in play) will disrupt it. However, anxiety which is of low intensity, i.e., which is experienced as a challenge and not as a threat to ego organization, adds spice to play.

The absence of anxiety characterizes rational thought. With other aim-inhibited activities, anxiety is compatible as long as the ego is not threatened to be flooded by it. (According to Hartmann [1955], the threat of anxiety eruption characterizes sexualization but is absent in sublimation.)

Sublimation is a kind of hybrid concept in so far as its definition includes both psychological and social elements. Behavior which at one time is socially acceptable in one society may not be so in another. Something similar may be said about activities based on reaction formations.

We have indicated the importance of sublimations for our libidinal balance, because activities so derived bind psychic energy while retaining a high libidinal investment. Another economic aspect concerns *fatigue*. Obviously action demands expenditure of energy and is in the long run tiring. But there is no straight positive correlation between investment of effort and feeling tired, neither for the adult, nor for the child. Expending energy in disliked or indifferent work may lead to exhaustion. Yet the same amount of energy will be spent with little or no fatigue in an activity based on true sublimation. This may be an extension of the truism that sublimations always bring pleasure. In true sublimations great expenditure of effort will result in very little fatigue. The pleasure gain seems to counteract it. Descriptively this is correct, but we would like to put this in psychoanalytic terms.

In sublimation ego, id and superego are on excellent terms. Their actions are synergic, not antagonistic (Hartmann, 1955). When a distasteful task is replaced by well-liked work, the change from fatigue to a surplus of vigor may be dramatic. Here an earlier simile of Freud may help our understanding. He compares ego and id to a rider and a horse. When a rider has difficulties in making his recalcitrant horse trot on the path he has chosen—a short distance will wear out his strength. But if the horse comes along willingly, a long stretch can be covered with but minor exertion.

We return to an already mentioned characteristic of sublimation: the discharge of tension and the gratification attached to the process. In other reality-syntonic activities we try to reach the goal on the shortest route and with the smallest expenditure of energy. In sublimations the pleasure hinges not only on the goal—the acting, the doing, the functioning as such is gratifying and hence the joyful, often lavish expenditure of energy and effort.

We may speak of *functional pleasure* if we keep in mind that this describes the phenomenon without explaining it. In academic psychology, the term has been introduced to obviate the search for other causes, to account for behavior. Waelder (1932) has pointed to its limitations, yet in recent years it has shown up quite often in psychoanalytic literature.

Academic psychology needs the term because it makes the implicit basic assumption that our everyday behavior is rational and instigated by goals. When a person stirs without a strict goal, the needed explanation is found by assuming that the doing, the functioning per se yields pleasure.[1]

In psychoanalysis we see that the pleasure in functioning is related to specific symbols and fantasies, to specific zonal tensions, to the desire for mastery. Not only the choice of an aim-inhibited activity, but also the intensity of the pleasure derived from it, is highly variable. What seems a trifling outer or inner change, may completely destroy the gratification value of an activity.

In sublimation, there is the process and there is a goal. The latter may be a tangible product or it may be a skill, an ability. According to Kris (1952), every sublimation solves a conflict. Kris probably has creative activities in mind; however, his statement is valid for all sublimated activities in the sense that lessening of tension also is a kind of conflict solution.

It is about time to point out which pursuits we consider to be based on sublimation: creative achievements in the arts, in science, philosophy and religion come to our mind first and this large group is mentioned in psychoanalytic literature most often. Well-liked work, even quite humble work, represents another group.[2] Many hobbies, leisure-time pursuits and play activities can be similarly regarded. In characterizing the aforementioned groups of sublimations, we may say: in a creative act the path to the goal seems to lead through territory where nobody set foot before— hence the proverbial toil and pain, the steep joy and anguish of the artist. The person whose sublimations lie in the realm of well-liked work moves on a well-traveled path. And what happens in the area of hobbies and avocations? There is neither a hazardous lonely trail nor a smooth public thoroughfare. The amateur moves through a park-like area, whether he strolls this way or that is of little consequence. Needless to say that these are prototypes. In life situations mixtures of these types will be encountered just as we will meet mixtures of behavior based on sublimations and other processes.

In a highly industrialized society there are fewer jobs entailing hard labor and back-breaking toil, but there are also more and more routine jobs which do not invite libidinal investment. There is in our society a great flowering of all kinds of hobbies, sports and spectator activities which are sometimes seen as related to the longer leisure hours that a growing segment of the population enjoys. I think avocations and leisure-time skills become *a necessity* when bread-earning activities do not yield libidinal gratifications. The less personal fulfillment or challenge there is in a person's daily work, the greater the need for hobbies and amusement. The unexpected does not happen in life, so one turns spectator and identifies oneself with the person in the arena, on the screen, the stage or inside the book covers. Hence, the ever-growing variety of colorful hobbies and sports offered in our society. Whether the mental stability of a society is furthered more by work which carries libidinal investment or by routine jobs combined with a wide range of hobbies is a question which may be raised, but will be hard to answer.

Another aspect may be relevant in the context of the present paper: What becomes of children growing up in such a society? It has been emphasized that in our days children see less of the work of their parents and can understand but little of what goes on in their professional lives. Now we add: What happens to children when the work of their elders is predominantly void of libidinal investment, when it has hardly any sublimative aspects?

### THE SCHOOL'S CONTRIBUTIONS

It is the function of the school to supplement the child's life experiences. Under certain cultural conditions the school's task is very simple: mainly to teach the three "R's." Everything else the child is supposed to acquire outside the school, without formal teaching. As society becomes more complex, as there are more and more compartments in the adult's life in which the child cannot take part, the program of the school grows and grows. And because the adult's work is so often unrelated to his interests and preferences, it becomes especially important that the school provide the child with work which fosters true sublimation.

Every educational system has a central concept to which it adheres. The old-fashioned school stresses discipline, obedience, while some modern schools make the avoidance of frustrations their main concern. Neither type of school emphasized work which is well liked, irrespective of whether or not it requires effort and self-denial. Such work facilitates sublimation and a variety of factors may further or interfere with its development. We will point to a few only.

Which factors determine that a particular activity or interest is chosen as the main goal of drives, thus permitting their sublimation? One among them is certainly natural

95

endowment. Frequently the assumption is made that talent will manifest itself if only the child is well cared for, receives love and intellectual stimulation. Yet psychoanalytic experience indicates that a child may possess many more abilities than actually come to fruition. A chance success, e.g., an unexpected narcissistic gratification may result in the development of a talent. This is obvious, but the opposite experience, i.e., a narcissistic injury may also open the door. Anna Freud (1936) cites the case of a boy who after a frightening dream gave up his beloved football playing and started writing good stories and poetry. Here an ego restriction opened the path to a sublimation.

THE TEACHER

An object libidinal core is seldom or never missing in sublimation. The child's desire to please a teacher or to identify with him may lead to a genuine interest which will outlast the personal tie which started it. New interests are acquired through identification with an ego ideal. And the child entering school is usually eager to identify himself with his teacher. Let us repeat briefly what preceded this development. The infant identifies himself with the *function* of a needed or loved person before he identifies himself with the person. As Ruth Mack Brunswick (1940) put it: "The child attempts to repeat actively every detail of physical care which it has experienced passively. . . . Each bit of activity is based to some extent on an identification with the active mother." Thus the development of identifications parallels the development of object relations: a true object relationship is preceded by the relationship with a need-gratifying object. Earliest attachments as well as early identifications relate to need-gratifying functions or body parts, not to persons.[3]

In the oedipal phase he forms ties of love and of identifications with his parents. While these early intrafamily iden-

96

tifications by far overshadow all later ones, they also pave the way for new ones. Thus, the six-year-old entering school is ready to identify himself with his teacher.

What is the specific feature of a good teacher-child relationship? The child forms a strong attachment to a person who does not share the intimacies of his home but remains at a certain distance. The fact that there are other children competing with him to be noticed by the teacher arouses his jealousy, but it also intensifies the child's admiration for her and it confirms the existing distance. As long as no one receives too much, the child can accept the limited share given to him. Consciously each one in class would ardently like to have a greater part of the teacher's personal attention—and yet in the latency years when the child strives to escape from oedipal entanglements it may relieve him to know that the distance to the admired object is not likely to shrink much.

In progressive schools a teacher sometimes tries to eliminate this distance and to become entirely the child's buddy. In nursery school she may sit on the floor while telling a story, although this is uncomfortable for her, makes her squirm, and makes it harder to hold the attention of her listeners. By eliminating the traditional aura surrounding the function of the teacher, by dispelling the awe and the projections of the young school child, it was hoped to eliminate anxiety and to solicit the child's fuller participation in the school program and a more relaxed use of his abilities. This expectation failed.

The teacher who puts herself on the child's level all the time, who encourages indulgence, who shows lavish admiration for any scribble—this teacher fails to inspire the child's wish to identify himself with her. Much as she tries to captivate the children's interest, she fails to get it. This does not imply that the so-called old-fashioned school has the most effective ways to promote learning and growth; it only

97

indicates that conditions are more complicated than we thought. Basically a school program must be geared to children's abilities and interests. But the latency child also expects the teacher to make demands and is disappointed when he receives no assistance from her in dealing with his instinctual pressures.

It seems that identification depends on an optimal blend of gratification and deprivation and that either extreme disfavors them. The identifications which are most relevant in school may follow the lines indicated by Waelder (1939) in his examination of group processes. He speaks of the type of identification that "contributes to the establishment of an agency which stands back from the ego and watches it critically. What happens in this type of identification is not that the child feels that he is like his father, or that he does really become more like him, but rather that he criticizes and punishes himself just as he was formerly criticized and punished by the father."

If the child's teachers change every year or even every term, or if on the higher school levels a teacher has a "student load" of over one hundred, then the teacher-student relationship is reduced to a mechanical level. The recent development of teaching several hundred students simultaneously through a closed T.V. circuit carries the deficiency, the lack in personal relationship even farther. The detriments to the student are not nearly as drastic as they are to an infant whose mother figure has changed several times. Yet without the mutuality of a personal relationship a teacher can pass on information, but he cannot inspire and thus the development of identifications will be impeded. Indeed, the outstanding book has a better chance to stir the reader than the gesticulating screen teacher.

### THE GROUP

Once we realize the importance of identifications as *catalysts* of development, not only stable identifications, but also a wider choice of them become imperative. This leads to a consideration of the group in which the child finds himself in school.

A child entering school must be ready for a group of age-mates. Without this readiness for a wider circle of friends he will receive custodial care only—even in the best school, i.e., a school offering excellent opportunities for identifications and sublimation. A child needs others who are about his age, but the strict segregation according to age levels which most schools practice today limits his friendships and deprives him.

If a class consists of children of the same age, then ties of affection and admiration toward an older child or a paternal protective attitude toward a younger friend cannot develop. A narrow age range increases competition and comparisons between the members of the group, making the child more conscious of his limitations. It increases the pressures inside the group, and it does so even in a school which has a highly permissive attitude. Ironically some of the most advanced and progressive schools take at present pride in the fact that the age range in their classes has been reduced from twelve to six months! Fortunately a few schools are experimenting with arrangements making the mixing of age groups possible. The advantage of mixed ages are so obvious—especially in these days when families are small and most teachers are women, thus reducing the boys' chances for identifications—one wonders that this problem has received so scant attention. There are several reasons for this. The mutual educational influence of children of different ages is hard to assess. There may be an old puritan view that innocent young children learn "bad things" from older children. Moreover, there are the very real dangers of abuse. Indeed, autobiographical and fictional stories of British public schools can be amply quoted for instances of institutionalized or personal abuse and exploitation of younger boys by older ones.

Among another group of educators we may find the belief that a friendship with a younger child increases the attraction of childish behavior and thus detracts from the child's eagerness to go ahead—in other words, association with a younger child may encourage childish behavior labeled as regressive in the older child. Many modern teachers have learned about the norms for each age level before they ever enter a classroom. These teachers may have a static conception of those norms and be unaware that everyday life normally encompasses considerable fluctuations back and forth. A play interest which, according to the book, is below the child's age is easily seen as indicative of pathology. The close association and even interdependence of growth and regression are overlooked.

Observations by Fraiberg (1952) may be relevant in this context. A child treated by her also attended nursery school and the teacher reported an interesting pattern of growth: "Before Sally took each major step forward in the acquisition of new skills or new relationships, she would regress for a while to thumbsucking and withdrawal or to infantile behavior and speech." It was also typical for Sally that after achieving one level of performance or acquiring certain elementary skills she seemed for some time to have little desire for mastery and moving on to new levels.

With the spread of psychological knowledge the tendency to "observe" a child and to evaluate all his doings has also entered the home, so that now parents get alarmed when their child seems to be intrigued by play material designed primarily for a younger child. Manufacturers cater to this by printing age levels on equipment and toys. Thus, the range of "approved" activities which give pleasure and provide avenues for the discharge of tension becomes narrower.

There are several trends in today's education likely to interfere with the goal set forth in this paper. Modern

100

education wants to integrate the child into the community and exercises gentle or not too gentle pressure on doing things *together*. Teachers with a certain amount of psychoanalytic training are aware that the lonely child is at times queer and that the distance between queerness and schizophrenic trends may be short—hence they reason that solitary play will in turn favor schizophrenic trends. In their thinking cause and effect are reversed. I have seen teachers in progressive schools go to all lengths to prevent a child from playing or working alone—even for a short time. They seem obsessed with the fear that the lonely child may indulge in daydreaming or in fantasies along the lines of primary process thinking. Of course he may, but he may also be absorbed in highly constructive work or thought.

Here I would like to return to the initial proposition of this paper. It is the libidinal charge of an activity which really counts. The child who shares a collective activity with lukewarm interest profits less than the child deriving a deep gratification from a solitary pursuit.

### ANTICIPATION

The dimension of time does not seem to exist for the deepest strata of the id. The meaning of a deprivation remains the same, whether occurring now or later. But for the ego's capacity to deal with it, it makes a great difference whether something occurs suddenly, as a kind of surprise attack, or whether there is the possibility to anticipate it. According to Hartmann (1952), anticipation is one of the most important achievements of early ego development; it is also a prerequisite for the development of action and participates in every action to some degree. The school's setting can give wide scope to this ego development, or it can nip it.

A sudden change or deprivation may harm a child, yet the identical deprivation introduced in a way allowing anticipation, will lead to adjustment. Anna Freud and Dorothy Burlingham (1943) give an example which many of us can duplicate from our everyday experience.

Hetty and Christine were of comparable age and background and both their mothers expected another baby. Both children were placed in a residential nursery. In Hetty's case this was done with foresight and intelligent planning from the mother's side. She entered the nursery as a day child, her mother helped her through a period of adaptation. Christine, on the other hand, was brought in and left at once, though she had never before left her mother's side. In the completely strange surroundings she reacted in a most bewildered way. She did not respond but stood around quietly or crying and would only say at intervals: "Mum Mum." She fell ill a few days after her arrival.

Both children suffered the same deprivation yet Hetty adjusted while Christine developed neurotic symptoms. Hetty had been able to anticipate the changes ahead of her. On her visits to the nursery she had experiences which later were "copied" by reality ("I will eat here, sleep here, like these children do"). Through this preliminary inner rehearsal she had a grip on the situation *before* it occurred (anticipate = *antecapere*).

Here anticipation was used to prevent pathology. But anticipation has a less dramatic, though not less important, function in a child's everyday life. A good deal of a child's play helps him in looking ahead. Many features of a good nursery school come under the heading of making anticipation possible. If dangers are excluded and if—indoors or outdoors—spatial boundaries are well defined, then many choices can be left up to the child, even a very young child. The limits actually increase his freedom by reducing the need for close surveillance.

The young child lives in a world where he is taken by surprise many times a day. To compensate for this a school for young children should provide a place where they can do things for themselves—as has been rightfully stressed for many years—but it also should permit a maximum of anticipation. A stable order and a simple intelligible organization will assist him in looking ahead. Each thing, each tool he uses has its definite place. If he knows where to look for it, he is never quite separated from it; he can command its presence. The area where an inner planning precedes reality action widens.

The young child's ability to *select* is limited, even under very favorable conditions. His schoolroom needs to be uncluttered, simple, serene. Recently Alpert and Krown (1953) suggested that not all drawings of a child should be displayed on the walls of the nursery in order "to avoid reinforcement of the distorted image . . ." Walls covered with the large sheets of children's drawings may add confusion and disorganization to the room. Yet this kind of conspicuous display which makes children the prisoners of their own imperfections is today an accepted practice in many schools. Let us remember, however, that similar attempts have been made earlier; e.g., in the 1920's the very progressive Berthold Otto school in Berlin taught reading by the use of books written by other children of the same age. The readers were printed, with great care to preserve the age-specific punctuation and sentence structure of the child authors. Such an attempt seems rather ridiculous today. Here a school went out of its way in order to prevent the child's exposure to correct grammar and syntax. Yet other practices of isolating children in an artificial child-centered world still occur today.*

*On the other hand, I know from my own experience that stories or poems written by children (though typed by the teacher with correct spelling and punctuation) enrich the reading experience and stimulate creative writing of 6- to 10-year-olds. These stories were made available for individual selection by the children and were enjoyed and re-read by them.

E.N.P.

## CONCLUSION

Freud (1909) postulated as the task of education "to enable the individual to take part in culture and to achieve this with the smallest loss of original energy" (*"das Individuum kulturfähig machen mit der kleinsten Einbusse an Aktivität."* The meaning of the German word *Aktivität* is, in my opinion, not adequately rendered by "activity"). This statement takes the multiple function of education into consideration. Education aims at enabling the child, on the ego level, to participate in cultural pursuits, and on the drive level, to preserve the original energy.

Education fails when too much of the original strength of the instinctual drives becomes invested in rigid reaction formations, repressions, or neurotic symptoms. This energy is then not available for other ego purposes which may be less rigid and more adaptive. But education also fails when the child does not become ready for cultural interests, when he receives too little guidance—in short, when he is neglected. Neglect may be unintentional, for instance, when it is due to poverty, or intentional as in a certain brand of progressive education or in misunderstood psychoanalytic education.

Good education is not characterized by its degree of permissiveness or strictness. A school with inadequate teachers or with a poor program cannot be improved by loosening (or tightening) the reins. There are a few indications that the dominant educational climate may change radically. The pendulum may swing all the way back from overindulgence to strict discipline and still miss the essential. A school may be very permissive, take a very lenient attitude toward some of the child's instinctual needs and consider academic work a necessary evil, something that children naturally dislike. In consequence it will postpone academic learning, reduce the study load, and for the irreducible rest impose passive acceptance upon the child. This is exactly what some schools do today.

In terms of Freud's postulate for education such a school is not successful. The child's cultural activities are fed by a trickle of his energy—they are not effectively connected with the deeper wells of his being.

Activities and interests which are highly cathected and stable may be a better indication of what has been done to enrich the child's life, and to promote his capacity to sublimate. The process of sublimation follows certain laws which are by no means new in psychoanalytic thinking, but have been pronounced with greater emphasis and clarity in recent studies of ego development.

## NOTES

[1]Academic psychology provides us with a number of concepts which are descriptively excellent, e.g., "habit" or "drive to imitate" or, of more recent vintage, "emotional insecurity." They fit so well phenomena we all know and thus seem to explain them. Actually they explain too much. Thus they blur the issue and, far from uncovering the motives, interfere with even a clear statement of the problem. Because these omnibus terms explain too much, they cannot be used to predict when a phenomenon will not occur.

Functional pleasure is a striking phenomenon and easy enough to observe. So is the urge to imitate. But these "concepts" fail to tell us why, in certain situations, the desire to imitate will not show up, no pleasure in functioning will be observable, or why a well-established habit pattern will be broken.

[2]See Freud's footnote in *Civilization and Its Discontents* (1930) about tending a garden.

[3]This is also true of my observations of early play. The very young child who "mothers" a doll or another child does not dress up for his play. His interest is riveted on feeding, caressing, or punishing the doll, on mothering it, not on playing the mother's role, and he plunges into it without wasting time on preliminaries. This changes with the onset of oedipal play. Now the child dresses

up, hunts for scenery and props for his play, he imitates the mother, not only her actions. The character of his play changes, although the content—mothering—may remain the same.

## REFERENCES

Alpert, A. and Krown, S. (1953), Treatment of a Child with Severe Ego Restriction in a Therapeutic Nursery. *This Annual*, VIII.

Bernfeld, S. (1922), Bemerkungen über Sublimierung. *Imago*, VIII.

Brunswick, R. M. (1940), The Preoedipal Phase of the Libido Development. *Psa. Quart.*, IX.

Freud, A. (1936), *The Ego and the Mechanisms of Defence*. New York: International Universities Press, 1946.

—— and Burlingham, D. (1943), *War and Children*. New York: International Universities Press.

Freud, S. (1908), The Relation of the Poet to Day-Dreaming. *Collected Papers*, IV. London: Hogarth Press, 1925.

——(1909) Analysis of a Phobia in a Five-Year-Old Boy. *Collected Papers* III. London: Hogarth Press, 1925.

—— (1930), *Civilization and Its Discontents*. London: Hogarth Press.

Fraiberg, S. (1952), A Critical Neurosis in a Two-and-a-Half-Year-Old Girl. *This Annual*, VII.

Glover, E. (1931), Sublimation, Substitution and Social Anxiety. In: *On the Early Development of Mind*. New York: International Universities Press, 1956.

Harries, M. (1952), Sublimation in a Group of Four-Year-Old Boys. *This Annual*, VII.

Hartmann, H. (1948), Comments on the Psychoanalytic Theory of Instictual Drives. *Psa. Quart.*, XVII.

—— (1952), The Mutual Influences in the Development of Ego and Id. *This Annual*, VII.

——(1955), Notes on the Theory of Sublimation. *This Annual*, X.

Kestenberg, J. S. (1953), Notes on Ego Development. *Int. J. Psa.*, XXXIV.

Kris, E. (1952), *Psychoanalytic Explorations in Art*. New York: International Universities Press.

—— (1955), Neutralization and Sublimation. *This Annual*, X.

Lantos, B. (1955), On the Motivation of Human Relationships, *Int. J. Psa.*, XXXVI.

Panel on Sublimation (1955), reported by J. A. Arlow. *J. Am. Psa. Assoc.*, III.

Peller, L. E. (1954), Libidinal Phases, Ego Development, and Play. *This Annual*, IX.

Sterba, R. (1930), Zur Problematik der Sublimierungslehre. *Int. Ztschr. Psa.*, XVI.

Waelder, R. (1932), The Psychoanalytic Theory of Play. *Psa. Quart.*, II.

—— (1939), Psychological Aspects of War and Peace. *Geneva Studies*, X.

# 6.

# PSYCHOANALYSIS AND PUBLIC EDUCATION

We hear frequently about *the educational crisis of today*. The situation in many schools is tense, indeed, and, in some, even desperate. But many teachers and administrators feel that any help or inquiry offered by an outsider —like a psychoanalyst—may perhaps be helpful in the *long run*, but for the *present* it only increases tension.

Psychoanalysis as an approach, a method for understanding human behavior in *all* its manifestations (normal and pathological), has so far seen its main task as helping children to adjust to school and helping teachers to understand children who have special needs. These are tremendously important, yet psychoanalysis can fulfill a broader task; it can help define the function of the school, specifically as applied to the role of learning in the development of child and adolescent.

A look at the history of education reveals it has fostered both great changes and great conservatism. One special difficulty today is the survival of outmoded practices despite lip service to "new" slogans. Compare today's incessant talk about "motivating the child to learn" with how little is actually being done about it.

When living conditions as well as psychological insights are fairly stable, then we may confine ourselves to thinking of minor improvements. When societal changes are as radical as present ones, however, my opinion is that a thoroughgoing analysis is the primary need. But this is not a unanimous opinion, as James B. Conant, e.g., demonstrates in *The Child, the Parent, the State* (Cambridge: Harvard Univ. Press, 1959):

> When someone writes or says, that what we need today in the United States is to decide first what we mean by "education," a sense of distasteful weariness overtakes me. I feel as though I were starting to see a badly scratched film of a poor movie for the second or third time. In such a mood, I am ready to define education as what goes on in schools and colleges. I am more inclined to examine the present and past practices of teachers than attempt to deduce pedagogical precepts from a set of premises.

Though I disagree completely with Conant, his sarcastic statement can be helpful as a warning. "Eternal vigilance" is needed in many areas, including the use of technical or idealistic terms as a means of avoiding the necessity of solving real problems. I do not agree with him that any discussion of principles must be sterile.

Schools are set up to teach *content* (information, and its organization; skills; development of specific abilities and talents); they also invariably convey and implant *attitudes*. The latter function is at least of equal importance with the former.

Formal education, as we know it today, had its start after the industrial revolution. The principal tasks were to teach the skills of literacy to all young children—not because the children needed these skills, but because experience had shown that the skills needed in adult life were more easily taught to children than to adults. Justifiably, it was taken for granted that children were unwilling to take in what the school offered, and would, therefore, have to be forced to

109

go to school and to learn. It was expected that the great majority of pupils would leave school after a few years. This was the situation in Western society, roughly up to 1900.

And these were the *attitudes* such a school implanted: the ability to work with regularity, punctuality, reliability in details; deferring to rules; keeping order. These attitudes must rank high in an industrial society and the schools were effective in conveying them to the young. In past centuries in the Western world and in the underdeveloped countries today, the school is asked to promote attitudes ("virtues") which the society needs more and more, but to which the everyday conditions of life are rarely conducive.

At the turn of the century, school psychology appeared and articulated the principles on which the schools had traditionally operated:

(1) The child's intellectual development is normally independent of his emotional development. School starts at an age when a child can function as an independent unit for several hours a day. The school takes him over for these hours and looks after his *intellectual* development. His emotional needs and development are left to the home, the family.

(2) Rewards and punishments that have proven effective in motivating children are used. If subtle rewards and punishments do not work, then a fuller dose will.

(3) Children don't like to work or to learn. The school must, therefore, "make" the child learn, and frequently check whether the portion of learning planned by experts has been taken in.

(4) Making the child do things he dislikes—sitting still and keeping his hands in a certain position, being quiet when he wants to talk, even standing in line and just waiting—all these were truly and honestly believed educationally beneficial to the development of character.

(5) It had been "established" by experiments with rats

110

and squirrels that human reactions were determined by habit. There were "laws of learning," including the "law of frequency" which held that the more often an act (behavior) had been performed, and the more often a specific response had been elicited, the greater was the probability that it had become a part of the child's expectable behavior.

(6) The other great power shaping the child was *imitation*. The child learned by imitating what he saw and heard, and he was most likely to imitate what he had observed most often.

The organization of learning was based on these views which supported the main reason for sending children to school: attitudes as well as skills needed in adulthood are best acquired in childhood.

Then came John Dewey's work. Childhood was seen by him not only as a preparatory phase, as a kind of dressing-room where human beings entered in an unkempt condition and which they left groomed and trimmed and thus properly equipped for later life. Childhood as a specific period of human life, with specific needs and values, had been discovered.

In addition to being able to take in attitudes and skills, children have potential abilities and talents which can be evoked and nourished in the "early formative" years but are much harder to elicit later. In other words, in childhood it is easier both to put things in and to awaken abilities and bring them out than it is to do later. With progressive education it became the school's task to promote the spontaneity, the freshness of youth—a very new function indeed!

Today it is easy to smile at the romantic exaggerations of progressive education, but the fact is that it changed not only the schools but the teachers of the young. Elementary-school and nursery-school teachers generally began their career with very different ideas from those with which they started their preparation for teaching. They changed in both what they wanted to accomplish and how to organize their classrooms.

To the functions of instilling into the child what he will need in later years and of protecting and nourishing what he brings with him, we today must add a third function. Most children, especially in the urban society of our times, need supervision and something to keep them busy outside their homes for long hours and long years. That this third point is sheer expediency may make some consider it wrong to ascribe to it the same dignity as that of the other two, but not recognizing this necessary "custodial" function interferes with the other things schools are supposed to do.

While educators and psychologists may differ about the most efficient way of learning, I see much agreement on the issue that *the school's primary function is to teach*. But there is no intrinsic value in longer hours spent in school. Indeed, the prospect of shorter hours is conducive to both better learning and better teaching. For the custodial function, other facilities are needed, clubs, youth centers, where youngsters are supervised and find worthwhile things to do.

Right now I see our teachers in public schools spending their time and effort on things which are not at all in the line of efficient teaching. I visit schools for various age groups fairly often and am often moved by the resourcefulness and dedication of individual teachers. But their number is in inverse proportion to the school's size. Now we also have a great variety of effective methods and ingenious teaching aids. The Armed Forces during the war years often accomplished teaching tasks in a fraction of the time deemed necessary before. But in our school system, neither outstanding teachers nor their methods come to our attention often enough because teachers are expected both to teach and to keep under control as many children for as long a time as they possibly can.

112

Too often today teachers as well as students "serve time." In the elementary grades, for example, teachers often use the first half-hour of the day—a time of great anticipation on the part of the child—to do their administrative work while supervising their class. The children do "busy work," things they could do at home or any time; those who are finished are expected to sit still or to read. In the average junior-high-school class, one must note how much time and effort the teacher is able to give to teaching those who want to learn as compared with the time that goes to subduing those who must sit in class and do not want to learn. A high-school diploma may mean that a student has learned certain things but it may merely testify to the fact that he sat still and kept out of trouble for thus and so many hours and years. In college some students may prefer to study certain subjects on their own and to report for a test; they are forced to attend classes and to sign their name to prove that they were bodily present for so many hours.

I do not dispute that at present children and adolescents (and society) are better off if they spend a number of hours in a place where they find something worthwhile to do than if they are always left unsupervised. But it is inefficient, inexpedient and undignified to confuse the function of promoting the best work, in any field of thought, skill or art, with the function of supervision, of custodial care.

Let me now briefly state the principles of psychoanalysis as they relate to development in the schoolchild and the adolescent (Although psychoanalysis has charted the very young child's development in far greater detail than it has that of the schoolchild or adolescent, our knowledge of older children is by no means scanty.):

(1) The child's intellectual and emotional development are closely interdependent. Attempts to foster the one without caring for the other are self-defeating. The young child's need for a fairly stable tie to a mothering person has

113

been greatly stressed in recent years, but the corresponding need of the school-age child for a stable tie to a superego figure has not found as much attention as it deserves. The schoolchild lives in a far broader social world than the preschooler and his needs, therefore, are not nearly so absolute. Yet a stable tie to somebody who knows what he does and how he fares, and whom he likes and/or respects, is vital to his social development. This need, to a certain extent, can be met in the family. Beyond that it must be met through membership in an informal or semiformal, stable, small group. Does the responsibility for providing a friendly guidance person belong to the school? Is the school as we know it today equipped to fulfill this function?

(2) Fairly stable ties to contemporaries are probably of equal importance. In our physically mobile society, the necessary ties to playmates are often broken to children's detriment.

(3) Seeing himself as a person who is worthwhile, competent, "good"—a positive self-image—is as indispensable to the child and adolescent as it is to anyone of us. Erikson has excellently stated the adolescent's need for ego identity, its sources, its vulnerable points. I want to stress the intensity with which even the young child observes himself, observes the reactions of others to him, the likeness and the difference between himself and others. He compares himself and his looks and behavior and possessions with others. This early self-image—in part realistic, in part grossly incorrect —develops in the adolescent into the sense of identity based largely on belonging to a group that enjoys acceptance and status. I think of ego identity as a bond to an ego ideal that either supports or interferes with whatever the child undertakes. The willingness of a six-year-old to listen to his teacher, to trust the child who sits next to him, to do his homework—all these and a thousand other daily requests are shaped by the image the child has of himself. On these

three vital emotional bonds—to a superego figure, to contemporaries, and to the self-image—intellectual development, the unfolding of talents, the acceptance of values are all predicated.

(4) During all development, activity replaces passivity of various kinds. The young child learns to manage his body, he learns to do things for himself, his understanding and his foresight grow. In the schoolchild these trends continue. It follows that the areas where the child makes choices should always be widening. Sound education must encourage physical and mental self-activity. Some schools do, but the trend in public schools is toward administrative units of such size that conformity to strict rules must take precedence over anything else.

Consider the network of petty rules imposed upon high-school students regarding attendance, use of library, trivialities like permission to go to the bathroom or locker. The suppressed but boiling rage is expressed in attacks upon teachers and in destructive acts upon school property. These outrages would not happen if there were not a general deep resentment among the majority of students and teachers who are cooped up in schools totally inadequate for their physical needs, let alone the intellectual and emotional needs of growing children.

(5) Most educators seem convinced that children do not like school work. It is interesting that diametrically opposed conclusions have been drawn from this conviction. The traditional school believes in the necessity of a complex system of forcing children to attend school, of assigning what has to be learned on a time basis and of checking regularly to see whether this has been done. Progressive educators, on the other hand, believe that learning should be postponed and the child's burden of academic work lightened. They also believe that children will gladly learn something if its usefulness for the child can be demon-

115

strated (e.g., being able to write or read a note, to count pennies and nickels for a purchase). Above all they believe in the great value of those children's interests that are spontaneous phenomena of natural growth, uncontaminated by social factors or pressures of any sort. While these notions are partly correct, they are far too narrow.

It has been my experience that our clearcut differentiation between "play" and "work" is not valid in the child's world, unless one takes these to mean "what *I want* to do" and "what *you want* me to do." The crux of the matter is that educators corrode and destroy the child's desire to learn and to work by the forest of their regulations ("Do this now—in this way—in this place—in this sequence") and by their basic fear that children will not learn what they must unless continually supervised, prodded and pressured.

My experience with children, in groups and individually, with teachers and student teachers, has been that most children can really like or "go for" most of the things that we adults want them to learn, provided the framework is right and the teacher interested in his teaching.

The child's desire to approach and to enter the adult's world is tremendous. It often hitches on silly things, but it is so powerful that it can be redirected and continue to be a strong incentive. The child wants to be able to do what an older or admired companion does, or what a respected counsellor or teacher seems to value highly. In short, social pressures and influences fashion the interests of children as well as of adults.

There are the "component drives" which seek gratifications, e.g., curiosity, the desire to explore, the wish to acquire and to have as much or more than one's neighbor, the drive to achieve mastery. Children start elementary school around the age of six, i.e., at the beginning of latency. This is the age when they have a grasp of reality and when compulsive traits come to the fore: the child likes to ac-

116

cumulate things, to measure what he has, to compare today's hoard with yesterday's, etc. He likes to repeat things,
to embellish and polish a performance. Indeed, if the
choice is up to him he often likes the very smoothness of
rote learning.

Tests have an important function: students want to know
where they stand. But again, tests can serve as a measure
against children or as a tool which works with them. If tests
are given at predetermined, regular intervals they will often not show the expected regular increase in knowledge
and skill. Learning occurs in spurts, not in regular steps.

Under simple (above all, primitive rural) conditions it was
the task of the school to stimulate, to bring the child into
touch with the tools of information, of learning. In a world
where information (newspapers, journals, books, TV,
radio, records) is over-abundant, the school's task shifts to
giving assistance in ordering the data which the learner has.
Today's children are not only the workers and bread-
winners of tomorrow, they are also the future participants
of fast increasing hours of leisure. For a constructive use of
leisure a variety of talents, interests, and versatile skills need
to be nourished in childhood and adolescence.

As I have said, school may be called upon to foster attitudes that society needs, but that conditions in everyday
life do not favor. In the early industrial era, the ability of
growing segments of the population to produce a specific
output over prolonged periods was needed. The school
promoted this ability, this attitude toward work while contemporary conditions did not. Today regularity, order,
cleanliness, conformity to rules may need reinforcement,
but they are not the school's main task. A very different
attitude is now needed. Many people are uninterested in
their work. The social conditions favor this attitude of unin-
volvement, which is conducive neither to good work nor to
mental health. School could counteract this aloofness, but

117

not by rigid timetables or external controls, which work against the investment of real interest. A school that leaves choices of many kinds to the student makes learning more efficient. I plead for such a school not only for its efficiency but because the experience of commitment to serious work is more significant than any learning content.

# Section III.
# Children's Play

You have found it a contradiction that living is to be playing, and that yet such emphasis is placed on serving. I think such contradictions are unavoidable and can not be properly dissolved, and this is not important either since they depend altogether on the subjective value given to certain words. In this case for instance, you have taken the word "service" much more seriously than the word "play," while I take both equally seriously. Playing, as the child does it and as Leo* means it, is perhaps best compared to the "playing" of music—this isn't anything serious either for wordly people and businessmen, but for the true musician it is the celebration of the absolutely holy. And just think how important the strict observation of the rules is even in every parlor game or card game. To submit to the rules, to take the game seriously, to play it with abandon, that is even in the superficial "play" of society the basic rule and conditio sine qua non. So I can not find any contradiction here.

Hermann Hesse,
Letter to Paul Schottky,
Middle of June, 1932
(quoted from Volker Michels, ed. *Materialien zu Hermann Hesses "Das Glasperlenspiel"*, vol. I. Frankfurt a/M.: Suhrkamp Verlag, copyright 1973; Suhrkamp Taschenbuch 80; p.56)

*Main character in Hesse's *Morgenlandfahrt*

# EDITOR'S COMMENTS

Psychoanalysis is a young branch of science. Its findings, theories, and claims were bound, by their particular nature, to challenge beliefs that were, and indeed still are, widely held and intensely cherished. The resulting public attitude was resistance, hostility, ridicule.

The same had happened to similar innovators: Copernicus, Marx, Darwin. The joke where a father tells his son, "Perhaps you are descended from a monkey, but not I," had a long life. However, Copernicus provoked the world more than four hundred years ago. Marxism and Darwinism are half a century older than psychoanalysis. The initial reaction to them is long forgotten. But the wounds that psychoanalysis suffered in its early struggles are still fresh.

So psychoanalytic scholars were driven into a defensive stance. They developed certain peculiarities of procedure and presentation that now appear as shortcomings. Lili Peller's writings on play are not free of such difficulties. Though they are overridden by the intrinsic values of her studies, and though readers will notice them anyway, it may be helpful to glance at some of them.

One is that theories are sometimes based on rather limited observations; this material is then made to support the weight of broad generalizations. Usually it supports them surprisingly well. Still, the method leaves a nagging feeling of being asked to believe something essentially on the

123

ground that psychoanalysis says it is so. Obversely, uncontroversial statements are sometimes buttressed with a reference to Freud, even though a generally accepted observation would still be valid without it.

The papers here assembled contain of course plenty of observation of children at play. They are derived to a very large extent from records of psychoanalytic sessions and from what went on in psychoanalytically oriented nursery schools. Still one may feel that the play and behavior of children here is seen through a one-way screen as it were, rather than in a less contrived give-and-take between a child and an adult observer in the family or in similar situations.

Depending on the audience for which she wrote, Peller used more or less technical psychoanalytic terms. It may be doubted whether their use always makes for greater precision for the reader, and they may sometimes tend to prejudge a problem.

A reproach that has frequently been leveled against psychoanalysis—and more often than not, too much has been made of it—is that it allegedly has been limited in its approach, and hence in its validity, by being tied up with the social locus from which it sprang, the middle class of early twentieth century Central Europe. Here again, Lili Peller is not entirely free of this shortcoming—perhaps nobody is? It is most important to note, though, that in her case this did not produce class bias. Her work was with children of all classes, and the outlook of the working class was hers as much as that of the middle and upper classes. This breadth of her understanding makes her papers on education and environment and on many other subjects—including, naturally, play—so especially valuable.

There are other unexamined assumptions, though. ". . . any activity which is pursued for the remuneration that society offers for it, is work" (p. 201). This is how work was seen in the big city, after it had become industrialized and commercialized, and before to "do it yourself" became the thing to do. Neither the pre-industrial peasant nor post-industrial man would conceive of work in this fashion. ". . . work must be carried to completion . . ." (p. 201)—this is the "Protestant work ethic"; though there were preciously few Protestants in either Prague or Vienna.

Once identified, these minor faults may be ignored. They matter little compared to the unusual positive qualities of Lili Peller's work: her genuine and empathic feeling for children, her unwavering championship of the child's rights and interests, her power of observation and reasoning, freedom from prejudice, her clarity and originality. Her major thoughts convey indispensable knowledge and information. Her minor remarks, scattered from a rich store of understanding, have that even rarer quality of stimulating thinking. A brief phrase may start the process of seeing things in a new light and arriving at new insights.

Her writings on play span a considerable stretch of time. She wrote variations on themes, presenting the same basic ideas in different formulations and contexts, adding new material and thought. We have therefore in this Section not tried to reprint any of these papers in their entirety, but have grouped them in three chapters corresponding to the main topics within the general area of play, as Lili Peller dealt with them:

1. Theories of Play.
2. Survey of Development and Types.
3. Play and the Theory of Learning.

We have in each of these chapters used parts of different papers and have indicated the source at the end of each such segment by using the abridged title, as follows:

*Theories*—"Die wichtigsten Theorien des Spieles" (1932).

*Education*—"Die Gruppenerziehung des Kleinkindes" (1933).

*Models*—"Models of Children's Play" (1952).

*Phases*—"Libidinal Phases, Ego Development, and Play" (1954). (This paper appears here in two segments; the references follow the segment in Chapter 2). Details on these four papers are found in the List of publications at the beginning of this book.

*Play and Learning*—unpublished manuscript.

We have eliminated most repetitions that could result from the use of several papers, but—on purpose—not all. Though we would not go as far as to subscribe to Lewis Carroll's facetious rule of evidence—what I say three times is true—we believe there is some good in the time-honored rhetoric of repetition. Readers may gain ease from facing an important thought more than once, especially when the author tells it with small but not insignificant modifications, as Lili Peller does.

Innumerable studies on certain aspects of children's play have been published. To list but a few recent ones: Susanna Millar, *The Psychology of Play* (1968); R.H. Herron and Brian Sutton-Smith, *Child's Play* (1971); M.W. Piers (ed.), *Play and Development* (1972) (particularly the papers by Lois B. Murphy and Erik H. Erikson pertain to our subject). These books also contain exhaustive bibliographies. Erikson's *Toys and Reasons* (1977) is this distinguished thinker's latest contribution to our field.

It may be of interest here that some of Peller's papers on play have been incorporated in books. Her 1955 paper "Libidinal Development as Reflected in Play" was both reprinted and translated. "Models of Children's Play" is included in the just mentioned book *Child's Play*, which collects in seven chapters papers of different writers to illustrate a variety of approaches to the study of the play of

126

children. In the chapter "The Psychoanalytic Tradition" we find the following paragraph relating to Peller's paper (p. 109): "In this chapter we include an article by Peller that is particularly insightful with regard to children's play, though in a fairly traditional psychoanalytic manner."

# 1.

## THEORIES OF PLAY

We are going to discuss briefly here several theories of play that have preceded the psychoanalytic view of the phenomenon. This review is based on Groos' standard work, *Die Spiele der Menschen*.[a]

1. THE THEORY OF SURPLUS ENERGY. —Going back to Schiller's *Briefe zur aesthetischen Erziehung des Menschengeschlechtes*, this theory was scientifically developed by Herbert Spencer. It sees play as "aimless expenditure of exuberant strength."[b] It explains it as life brimming over and stimulating itself to activity. We read that "as a result of the advanced development of man and the higher animals they have, first, more force than is needed in the struggle for existence; and, second, are able to allow some of their powers longer periods of rest while others are being exercised, and thus results the aimless activity which we call play, and which is agreeable to the individual producing it."[c]

This theory can not be simply discarded. It suggests itself especially when we consider youth, with its effervescent vigor that finds hardly any discharge but in play. Yet surplus energy can not serve as a general criterion of play. Even when energy is depleted, and indeed even in a state of exhaustion, there are a thousand occasions in the external world that stimulate the child to activity and play. We must conclude that surplus energy is but one of many possible conditions for play to arise and can not explain its origin as such.

128

2. THE RECREATION THEORY.—Its most scientific champion is Lazarus.[d] The basic idea is that "when we are tired of mental or physical labor and still do not wish to sleep or rest, we gladly welcome the active recreation afforded by play."[e] At first glance this seems completely to contradict Spencer's view. There play "wastes" surplus energy, here it serves to restore exhausted energy. But this is a contradiction in mere appearance: in many instances the recreation theory is a necessary supplement to the surplus theory. Take as example a scientist who after the day's strenuous mental work goes bowling in the evening, so that he discharges the rested and accumulated motor drives while letting the exerted mental energies rest and replenish themselves. The same activity appears from one angle as released of surplus energy, from the other as replacing expended force.[f]

An objection to both theories is based on the not infrequent observation that "a game once begun is apt to be carried on to the utmost limit of exhaustion."[g] Groos here adduces the phenomenon of automatic repetition to which he ascribed great significance in all animal life, and discusses the idea of "circular reaction" developed by Baldwin.[h] This refers to the phenomenon that reaction evokes anew the stimulus which had caused it. Example: A child hits his plate with a spoon. He may have produced sound unintentionally, but then he repeats his action, and its acoustic result now serves as stimulus for renewed action.[i]

Baldwin goes on to discuss the "almost irresistible urge to repetition." In view of the great importance of repetition compulsion in the psychoanalytic theory of instincts, I want to quote him extensively:

Life is as a rule preoccupied with the struggle for survival, we constantly see goals before us which we want to reach as soon as possible, and so we do not have the time to indulge that urge to repetition. Things are

129

quite different, though, when man steps out of the goal-oriented workaday life. Psychiatry offers pathological examples. Certain forms of mental illness manifest themselves in endless repetition of an exclamation or action. One woman mumbled constantly all day, "Oh Jesus, oh Jesus!" Another patient persistently spooned from an empty bowl.

The "automatic" or "continued" motions of the hypnotized belong in the same category. If the arms of a hypnotized person are rotated, he tends to continue the motion. He sometimes even goes on doing so, as a child might, when the order has been countermanded. Something similar can occur when great sorrow or great joy for a time throws us out of our goal-oriented life: here also the mechanical repetition of an exclamation or a purposeless action may result. The same phenomenon appears very clearly in the sexual intoxication of birds. Bell birds are reported to continue their mating call until they fall dead from the twig.[j]

Play likewise is such a stepping out from the workaday world. We should not be surprised that some play is continued to the point of utter exhaustion. This is particularly true of the play of children, as they can more completely than adults lose themselves in exclusive enjoyment of the present. "When the child hits upon the right combination," Baldwin says, "he never tires executing it. H. found unending pleasure in taking the eraser off a pencil and putting it on again, since each step acted as a new stimulus on the eye. This pattern is especially noticeable in the first attempts to talk."[k]

It is interesting to note that the inner kinship of such different impulses and actions as child's play, psychopathology, extreme emotional reactions of normal persons, is here comprehended in one far-reaching concept.

Karl Buehler has termed the phenomenon described by Baldwin the "functional pleasure" of the child.

We agree with the author when he says further: "This impulse toward repetition is doubtless the physiological reason for carrying on play to the utmost limit of strength."[1] However, this interpretation is not exhaustive: many psychological motivations are synergetic. It is only when these are clarified that the purely biological principle of repetition can be recognized.

So we come to the biological theories. Leaving aside the problems posed by Darwin's theories, we shall concern ourselves only with those views that refer to play as such.

3. THE PRACTICE THEORY. —Play is said to serve the practice and development of those abilities which the individual will need in its later life (struggle for survival). It is further said to be understood as "experimentation with the motor apparatus," and to make possible the "higher development of inherited capabilities" in a much higher degree than the fixed instinctual reaction can do that. The kitten is fascinated with running after a ball of wool because this is nature's clever way of preparing it for catching mice. Children of different cultures have different favorite games; in each case these copy such vital adult skills as fishing, hunting, or child-rearing. This theory supports the view that this is indeed a well-ordered universe in which every effort works in the right direction: even play helps to insure survival—if not now, at least later. Here we have play seen as relevant to the future of the race.

4. WUNDT'S THEORY. —The next theory on the other hand points to the phylogenetic past. Wundt lists three psychological criteria to explain play: its pleasurable effect, the unconscious or conscious reproduction of goal-directed actions, and the re-formation of the original goals into sham goals. Play mirrors "serious" actions of ancestors: combat games, hide-and-seek and pursuit games, collecting are mentioned as examples.

131

5. THEORIES OF HALL AND CARR. —G. Stanley Hall's theory of atavism (1908) and Carr's catharsis theory (1902) are already related to the viewpoint of psychoanalysis. Hall thinks that play brings out the hereditary endowment of mankind. Carr sees in play catharsis affecting asocial drives.

Summing up, we can say this: Each of the theories mentioned here contains elements of truth. It is not difficult to find numerous examples for each. None of them, however, can by itself do justice to the richness of the phenomenon known as play. Several of these theories taken together do not give satisfaction either, since they lack any inner relation to each other; in part they even contradict each other. Can we find a more satisfactory answer from the vantage point of psychoanalysis?

All theories discussed so far aim at explaining the "why" of play. All make a tacit assumption: that man, as a rule, has a rational reason for his actions. This assumption is considered so absolutely self-evident that it is never put into words. Man's performance is supposed always to have a reasonable, useful goal determined by the external world. This general and axiomatic assumption is believed to hold but for a few exceptions, and the task is to explain these. Man is conceived of as initially idle, becoming active and expending energies only when a real useful goal needs to be reached. It therefore causes astonishment to encounter instances where he stirs without need and expends energy uselessly. These "exceptions," this "deviant" behavior has to be explained. This is the origin of the play theories we discussed.

In substance the general attitude of 19th century science, which felt justified in proclaiming, in all areas, the primacy of the "useful" purpose over the purposeless instinctual. It was, e.g., absolutely "proven" for this frame of mind that human clothes had developed "for the purpose" of weather protection. The thought that they originally were just as much an expression of instinctual desire for ornamentation would undoubtedly have been branded "unscientific." The same turn of mind deems it paradoxical that a tired person may feel a need to play, "instead of" sleeping (cf. Lazarus). It did not fit into that orderly utilitarian view that psychological diversions could be more important to a person than regeneration in sleep.

The psychoanalytic view does not add a new theory to those we have discussed. It addresses itself to another aspect.

(*Theories*)

Freud derived his basic concepts mainly from the study of dreams, daydreams, neurotic symptoms, the phenomena of parapraxis, wit, and, last but not least, play. He deals repeatedly with the dynamics of play and also makes many incidental remarks about it. Waelder presented a psychoanalytic theory of play in 1932. To our knowledge, Waelder's presentation is the last systematic approach to play in psychoanalytic literature. Several excellent papers, among others Bally (1945), Erikson (1937, 1940), Hendrick (1943), dealing with one or another of its aspects have been published since, but there has been no attempt to fit the wealth of observational data into a larger conceptual framework. This may be due to a feeling that *play* is a descriptive term, more at home in academic than in dynamic psychology.

We believe that a study of the dynamics of play, of the motivations for play, of its changing form, style and range, offers increased insight into the interdependence of libidinal and ego development. The recent emphasis on direct observation of children may be expected to lead to a revival of interest in play.

In this paper we are not offering anything entirely new on play; nor are we attempting to revise the Freudian theory of play as presented so lucidly by Waelder. All we intend to do for the present is to apply some of the theoretical formulations laid down by Freud in *The Ego and the Id*. That is, we shall attempt to synchronize the psychoanalytic theory of play with our current psychoanalytic insight.

Waelder (1932) characterizes play as a method of "assimilating piecemeal an experience which was too large to be assimilated instantly at one swoop" (p. 218). An event becomes traumatic because there is "an onslaught of more events in a relatively brief interval of time than could be endured by the immature. . . . organism" (p. 217). The subsequent playful repetition enables the child to deal again with the painful situation, and to turn from passivity to activity. Waelder describes the various ways by which this can be achieved. The child may change the roles: in reality he was the suffering party or an anxious onlooker; in his play he turns aggressor. In another form of play the child changes the outcome of the situation, providing a "happy ending" to an episode which had an unpleasant outcome in real life. Finally, the very fact that an experience which was endured in reality is re-enacted in play constitutes a switch from passivity to activity.

The compulsion to repeat a traumatic event explains play activities carrying the greatest emotional intensity, the highest cathexis, yet it covers only a small portion of the many forms of daily play.

(*Phases*)


Play also helps the child to master a painful experience in other ways. In play he can become active in a situation in which, in reality, he was distressingly passive. A child who has been the anxious spectator of a painful scene may feel a similar need to re-enact what he has seen. Although he did not suffer himself, he was passive in that he witnessed the hurtful experience of someone else with whom he identified; hence the need to reverse the tables—to be active.

The very fact that in play the child can vary or terminate at will an experience which has caused him anxiety helps him to master that experience. This mastery produces pleasure. This expansion of the original concept of pleasure makes the theory of play an essential part of psychoanalytic theory as a whole and leads to a deeper understanding of human behavior. It does not, however, claim to explain all play activities.

The Freud-Waelder theory deals solely with this one function of play, in which the child who has had a traumatic experience attempts to come to terms with this experience. This play is of tremendous importance for the mental economy, but not all play is a repetition of painful experiences; and neither Freud, nor any other psychoanalyst, regards trauma as the only motivation for play.

A child plays because his play supports fantasies which give him pleasure, or imagery which compensates for keenly felt limitations, anxieties, and deprivations. An adult will play for exactly the same reason, but he also has other means of dealing with deficiencies or with a traumatic experience. He can, for instance, engage in endless repetitive talk about it.

Play permits us to return to an experience that has given us pleasure, or that appears pleasurable in retrospect. It also enables us to enjoy in anticipation something which may occur in the future. In his play, the child can turn back to his baby days or forward to adulthood. Play enables him to transcend the narrow confines of the Here and Now in order to overcome the destructive impact of shattering emotional experience.

Early play is the antecedent of, and the prerequisite for, conceptual thinking. Some salient features which make play the precursor of conceptual thought are as follows: the absence of any immediate or pressuring goal, the fact that

135

attention is not fixed upon such a goal but directed to the activity itself, the high libidinal investment in this activity, and interest in things in the environment mainly insofar as the child himself has first endowed them with specific roles, functions, and meanings. We must also point to the tremendous difference between play and conceptualization. Although imagination is the lifeblood of both, play is kept in motion by fantasies and their accompanying affects, but in conceptual thought there is a constant process by which the imagery is referred back to reality and/or to the conceptual structures of others.

The instinctive act (as the term is used in animal psychology) goes straight to its goal. The attractive power of this goal is so compelling that there is "no time, no place" for variations in the motor act, or indeed even for perfunctory perception. This is why experimenters can so easily fool an animal in oestro with a crude two-dimensional cardboard model, a dummy which resembles the sexual partner in one single aspect—its color, or scent, or its outline, etc.

Play on the other hand involves interactions with the environment which may be complex and varied, and which carry a high degree of libidinal investment, even though they do not necessarily "achieve" anything. For this last reason "playful" is often equated with "uninvolved" or "superficial" in everyday language, so that the distinction between true play and dilly-dallying is erased. True play is taken quite seriously and the player may invest intense emotion in his game. Sometimes learned activities are referred to as though they were the very opposite of instincts because the directness, rigidity, and blindness of instinct have been replaced by sequence, fluidity, and consciousness. But the real opposite of animal instincts appears to be play on the oedipal level and the later pursuits rooted in it.

(*Play and Learning*)

The psychoanalytic interpretation so far has stressed the emotional release gained through play. Children play in order to mitigate, to deny, or temporarily to solve a conflict. In play the child recaptures for a while the omnipotence he once believed he possessed. He repeats and gradually assimilates an experience that was traumatic or a narcissistic insult. Play may help him to overcome a specific fear. And, of course, play is a source of pleasure. In addition to these emotional values, we would like to discuss the benefits of play for the child's intellectual growth, benefits that are certainly not the cause of play, yet are inherent in it. Let us go to the very simplest quality of play: the playing child *repeats* an experience he has had, or a part of it. *Repeating it, he divests it of its uniqueness.* An event that has no precedent will overwhelm even the best equipped adult. Such events happen seldom to grown-ups. We can usually classify an occurrence in terms of past events or at least draw an analogy. The adult can in his thoughts go over the event that upset him or that he did not quite grasp. Reliving it in thought, he *reduces* it from a unique experience to one that can be classified with previous experiences.

The young child, however, meets "unprecedents" all the time. He has only a limited ability to recapture an image by repeating its verbal label or by repeating it in thought. Impressions that are unique are not amenable to laws. Play enables the child to reëxperience, to remold past impressions and events and their accompanying moods and emotions. *Playful repetition provides essential, possibly indispensable steps toward concept formation.* Freud defines thinking as test-acting (*Probehandeln*) carried out with a minimum of expenditure of energy. By pointing out the similarities between thought processes and direct action, by looking for their common denominator, we gain a better understanding. Can anything be gained by comparing formulas of *play* with the act of thinking? At first this seems a ridiculous comparison, almost blasphemous.

137

*Thinking* is a way of acting that respects the laws of reality. Play is largely wishful thinking, and as such ignores the laws of reality and poses as a "cheap" substitute for reasoning. Moreover, in play the expenditure of energy is big. Indeed, the overflow of useless energy has been considered the cause of play (Schiller-Spencer's theory of play).

Solving a problem through play thus appears the opposite of seeking a solution through reasoning. Yet the two share also certain features, above all the absence of direct and immediate consequences in the outer world. In thinking we pick out elements of reality and vary them; the same is done in play. Thinking is far quicker than direct action; steps taken in play can be instantaneous. Thinking requires imagination; so does play. Things that in reality are far apart in space or time can be brought into juxtaposition in the process of reasoning, but play also overcomes the obstacles of time and space with great facility. Play, as well as reasoning, is caused by an experience that was not concluded to our complete satisfaction. It was either too short, too sudden, unpleasant, or an insult to our ego, or we were not able to understand what was going on. Therefore, we are "at it," going over its various aspects in thought or play to be better equipped when it recurs or when we decide to seek it again.

Tentatively, we may say that a good deal of children's play is a crude kind of test action. In comparison to scientific thought, its tools are clumsy and inefficient. The adult in possession of the versatile symbolism of words can hardly estimate what it means for the young child to bring situations back by casting himself into different rôles, by play and pantomime. Play not only helps the child in his emotional adjustment; play activities are also the matrix of future realistic action and reasoning.

In conclusion, let us revert to the mechanism that seems to be at the root of most play: the turning from the passive to the active rôle. Being "passive" has several distinct meanings. It may, for instance, signify being physically inactive; it may also mean not knowing what to expect, being at the mercy of forces that the passive person cannot understand or predict, or being overwhelmed by a force or a person. Conversely, being in the active rôle may have any of the following meanings: being physically active, being informed and able to anticipate the next step, being superior in strength, leading.

The various types of passivity may befall a person separately or jointly and their traumatic effect varies accordingly. For instance, a tonsillectomy can be a shocking event if the child does not know what to expect—*e.g.*, that he will go to sleep, wake up with pains, be unable to swallow, and so on. If the child has been told about these things beforehand, he will still be physically inactive and a person much stronger than he will give the orders and inflict pain, yet the shock is likely to be far less severe. The child who has been taken by surprise, who has not had the chance to go over the event beforehand in thought, is more likely to play it out persistently afterwards in an effort at *adjustment and self-cure. Again, play seems to substitute for reasoning.* We can also put it in the short formula: play stands for pre-event anxiety, and anxiety for post-event play.

While the various formulas of play discussed here merge and overlap, certain groupings emerge. There are the play formulas that tell a story and in which several people interact. *Dramatic play*, as it is often called, may be instigated either by the child's wish to be grown-up—presto! And then it seems to say: "It's so hard to wait so long. At least make believe these things." Or possibly: "If I pretend it ardently, maybe it will come true." The rôles the child chooses are pre-stages of identification. Then there are play models based on the opposite formula: "I pretend to be the baby (or clumsy, and so on) in my play; then it's obvious that I am not

139

really clumsy (babyish)." Or: "If I make believe these things, they will not cling to me in real life." The child takes a rôle in order to accentuate the distance between himself and such behavior.

In either case, the child enjoys a gratification denied to him in reality or given in too small a measure. This kind of play helps the child to cope with the frustrations, the fears, the unfulfilled hopes, the disappointments, and the envy rooted in his situation in the family.

Manipulative play and play based on magic are basically different from the above. They are variations and ramifications of body skills and body controls, of oral and anal activities and of the one human relationship that precedes all others—*e.g.*, the infant's need for his mother. They are instigated by his efforts to derive gratifications from his own body or from his mother—not from his broader human environment. With the child's entrance into the Oedipal phase, these play patterns do not disappear, but they lose their prominence.

(*Models*)

In this study we consider play as instigated by the ego in its attempts to deal with blows or deprivations exerted by reality as well as with pressures originating in the id or the superego. According to A. Freud (1950) the ego reacts with anxiety, ". . . when it finds its existence or integrity threatened by dangers in the external or internal world. Such dangers can arise (a) from the strength of the instinctual demands themselves; (b) from instinctual demands which involve the individual in conflicts with the environment; (c) from instinctual demands which involve the ego in conflicts with the superego, as representative of environmental forces." Provided this anxiety is of low intensity, the ego may turn to play, e.g., to a fantasy which carries a tendency toward action and which is gratifying yet compatible with reality and superego requirements. Another prerequisite seems to be that the underlying conflict or its extent remain unconscious.

With Waelder we hold that the central function of play is gradual assimilation of anxiety, of a blow. But we also include anxiety arising from intersystemic conflicts. Play, then, alleviates anxiety. However, there are also play forms in which this function is marginal. Such play simply repeats or confirms a gratifying experience.

Before discussing specific types of play we shall deal with a few of its general features. In psychoanalytic literature the term "play" is at times used in a far broader sense than at others. We have adopted the broader meaning, our concept of play being approximately coextensive with the popular notion "play." Statements about play are sometimes couched in such terms as to exclude play activities of adults. Although adults have a smaller range of motivations for playing, they do play, and they seem to play more at the present time than ever before. Our survey is focused on children's play without excluding adult play.

All play brings wish fulfillment, pleasure, elation, a feeling of euphroia, well-being, a *Spielrausch*. Play, however, is not a direct manifestation of the pleasure principle. It is an attempt to compensate for anxieties and deficiencies, to obtain pleasure at a minimum risk of danger and/or irreversible consequences. Play is a step toward sublimation. The direct discharge of sexual or destructive drives is not play, but sexual and/or destructive elements enter into all play.

All play implies turning from a passive, receptive role to an active one. But this is not specific for play, it is rather a general principle of child development, as Kris (1951), quoting Freud, has reminded us recently.[1] Kris (1934) has coined a very expressive term to characterize creative or artistic activity: regression in the service of the ego. The

141

same might be said about play. Ego and id are on excellent terms in play. Play ceases to be play when the child loses his ability to stop *when he wants to do so*, when he becomes glued to one phase, to one episode. *Play then has become a phobic defense.* Frozen modes of behavior, obsessional rituals, phobic mechanisms obviously are not play, although they may have started as such. The adult watching play with benevolent interest quickly notices the transition.[2]

Small quantities of anxiety are mastered in play, but anxiety of high intensity disrupts play. A good example is provided by B. Bornstein (1935) in her analysis of a two-and-a-half-year-old child who had a phobia of lying down in bed. The little girl's ability to communicate by means of language was of course limited, and play was used to approach the phobic content, to give reassurance, etc. The analyst reports from the first meeting:

> Then in play I darkened the room with the window curtains and very quickly made it light again. I repeated this many times and had the child herself make the room light and dark, thus providing her with the twofold delight of a newly acquired ability to adjust the window curtains and a newly discovered knowledge that after the darkness comes the light. [At a later time] . . . . when I placed a little doll in the lying position she began to scream in fear and to tremble with excitement. In the next days her phobia became more extensive, so that no object in her presence could be placed in the lying position without arousing her anxiety and restlessness. [And again after a number of sessions:] . . . . She began to be somewhat more cheerful and active and allowed any object to be laid down in her presence, even though it still made her anxious. . . . Then in play the little girl tried to stretch herself out on the floor, but in so doing was seized by so

142

severe an anxiety attack that she relinquished this play for several days [p. 106].

As is well known, unconscious impulses can be acted out in play without reaching awareness. Further exploration in this direction could lead into interesting territory, but this would go beyond the scope of this paper.

We speak of play as long as the actions are initiated and terminated at will. In true play the fantasy is more highly cathected, more important to the player than the result of his motor action. (Games are excepted from this rule.) Play has a *cathartic* function: it serves as a safety valve for pent-up instinctual pressures. Here, as in other respects, play foreshadows the functions which the arts have in our psychic economy.

Play is indicative of the ego's resilience. In later life, the mature ego will act as a mediator between the demands of the id, the superego and reality. We have in mind an ego function closely related to Nunberg's "synthetic function" or Hartmann's "integrative function." The first successful mediations are achieved in play, and they are brought about by a mediator far weaker than the contending parties.

## NOTES

[1]We add that it seems to be a general biological law, a principle not only of ontogenetic but also of phylogenetic development. Plants are stationary and await the arrival of food, whereas animals can move and actively search for it. Cold-blooded animals depend on chance supplies of external heat, whereas warm-blooded ones actively maintain a steady body temperature. Animals submit to many environmental deprivations which man overcomes.

[2]"The indulgent attitude of [the grown-up] . . . . vanishes the

143

moment that [the child] ceases to make the transition from phantasy to reality readily, without any delay or hitch, or tries to shape his actual behaviour according to his phantasies—to put it more exactly, the moment his phantasy-activity ceases to be a game and becomes an automatism or an obsession" (A. Freud, 1936, p. 92).

## EDITOR'S NOTES

a) We have in the following substituted references to the English edition (Groos, Karl. *The Play of Man*. New York: D. Appleton & Co., 1901) for those to the German original used by Lili Peller, though we have in a few instances used our own translation.

b) *Op. cit.*, p. 362.

c) *Ibid.*

d) *Op. cit.*, p. 364 (the reference is to Lazarus, M. *Ueber die Reize des Spiels*. Berlin: Fred. Duemmler, 1883).

e) *Ibid.*

f) Groos, Karl. *The Play of Animals*. New York: D. Appleton & Co., 1898. p. 17.

g) Groos. *The Play of Man*, p. 366.

h) Mark Baldwin, Professor at Princeton University, wrote a number of books on problems of psychology and philosophy.

i) Here we have the germ of the concept of cybernetics, later developed by Norbert Wiener.

j) Adapted from *The Play of Man*, pp. 366f.

k) *Op. cit.*, p. 367.

l) *Ibid.*

# 2.

# SURVEY OF DEVELOPMENT AND TYPES

Herein we present a number of "models" or formulas of play activities, and illustrate them with examples culled from our experience and from literature. Undoubtedly this survey is incomplete. Even so, it may stimulate further observations and new interpretations of the material at hand.

*Choice Based on Love, Admiration.*—A child pretends to be some one whom he admires and loves and whom he would like to resemble. By and large, admiration and wishful anticipation of his own adult rôle determine the rôle he chooses. This is the type of children's play that adults find most amusing and that has been most frequently described, not only in psychological literature, but also in novels and poems. The child plays at being mother, father, or teacher; he pretends to be a king, a queen, or a fairy. At play he recaptures a fragment of his ancient belief in the omnipotence of wishes. He enjoys a power and prestige denied to him in reality.

When adults speak of "happy childhood," they probably have in mind the child who hobbles around in high-heeled shoes or who has draped around himself some piece of adult clothing and thus has jumped with great ease the gulf between wishing and being.

On closer investigation, however, the situation is not quite so carefree and happy. Admiration alone is seldom the basis for the child's choice; as a rule, there is an admixture of frustration, deprivation, or fear.

Michael, aged three years and eight months, has refused to go to nursery school, although all his friends are going there, and he thus remains without playmates in the park. Whenever a passer-by starts a conversation, asking his name, and so on, he answers, "My name is Michael Schoolboy," saying it with so much assurance that people are inclined to believe him.

There can be little doubt that Michael would like to go to school and be with his friends. But he cannot bring himself to leave his mother. In his playful change of name, the conflict is solved. He *is* a schoolboy. In fact, in almost every instance of such play one finds an element of fear or of envy accompanying the obvious admiration and love.

A *Rôle Assigned to an Inanimate Object.*—In a variation of the type of play discussed above, the child does not himself assume a rôle, but appoints a doll or a toy animal—or it may well be a pillow, a piece of wood—to the rôle of the child, the baby. To have some one depending on him indirectly changes the child's status. Or the child pretends to have an imaginary companion—a brother, a sister, or a dog.

Popsy made his appearance when Billy was about three and a half. We first became conscious of him when driving in the car. Billy always urged his father to pass other cars on the road and get to the "head of the line." But when a car passed us and sped ahead, Billy would chuckle, "My Popsy is driving that car. Doesn't he go fast?" Sometimes Popsy rode on the roof of our car. Sometimes he jumped from treetop to treetop beside the roadside as we went by.

Once when we commented on an attractive new

146

schoolhouse, Billy remarked, "My Popsy is a teacher in that school." That same night he got uncovered and called. As his mother tucked the blankets around him again, he whispered, "Popsy pulled those blankets off of me. Isn't Popsy a nuisance?"

The wishes, peculiarities, and possessions of this imaginary family member have to be respected. In a casual, apparently unintentional way this may give the child a chance to retaliate for some of the things he experiences. In a disturbed child, this mechanism is intensified and thus more obvious.

"David, aged two and a half, a very nervous child with a highly nervous mother, seemed quiet and comparatively happy in the first two days in the residential nursery. He was inseparable from a toy dog, Peter, whom he had brought from home. Peter slept with him, ate with him, was in his arms even when he was bathed and dressed, and David insisted that Peter should be taken care of as if he were another child in the nursery.

"When his mother visited him after two days, David had his first temper tantrum. He insistently demanded that she should kiss Peter on the mouth and hug him as if he were her baby. From then on and for quite a while he reacted with temper to any imaginary slight done to Peter. He would cry whenever another child would knock against the toy and would throw himself on the floor with despair whenever the dog inadvertently fell out of his arms. Peter is evidently a symbol for himself and has to be treated as he himself wants to be treated. His mother has to make up in affection to the dog for the wrong she had done to David by sending him away from home."[1]

147

The pleasure a child derives from his doll or Teddy bear stems largely from this source. The young child who is not under severe emotional pressure will play in this way intermittently, now feeding the Teddy with remarkable patience and carrying it with great care and a little later flinging it around carelessly. He assigns a rôle and forgets about it with equal ease. The significance of this type of play changes with the child's age. The five-year-old may play the maternal rôle all day long, but the two- or two-and-a-half-year-old, who is consistently gentle with his dolls, has in our experience been a person burdened by too many worries.

Barbe, aged three, lost her father in the war. Her grief-stricken mother has not been able to explain the father's absence to the child and consequently B. has a number of fears. For instance, she is terrified of the Santa Claus in the department store and does not even want to go near the store.

The consultant who sees mother and child presents Barbe one day with a chocolate Santa Claus, whom she takes with evident pleasure and no fear. Before leaving for home the mother wants to put the chocolate figure into a box, explaining that otherwise it might get broken, but Barbe objects. The mother proceeds to put it in anyway. Barbe is in tears. Her mother is highly annoyed with her unreasonable behavior. Barbe is alternately screaming and imploring her mother not to put Santa into the box.

At this point the consultant suggests making slits for air in the box and that solves the situation. Barbe calms down and permits her to put Santa Claus into the box. The child would rather dare her mother's anger than risk displeasing the chocolate figure.

*Choice Based on Fear.*—Whenever the child takes on the rôle of some one whom he fears, anxiety or frustration

148

determines his impersonation. Several of Freud's classical examples follow this line: a child plays at being the doctor, after the doctor has administered a painful treatment or performed a minor operation. Anna Freud reports the case of the child who conquers the fear of crossing the dark hall by pretending to be the ghost she dreads to encounter. By choosing the rôle of the doctor or the ghost, the child can switch from the passive to the active rôle and inflict upon another person—be it a child or a doll—what has previously been done to him. The change from a passive to an active rôle is the basic mechanism of many play activities both of children and of adults. It mitigates the traumatic effect of a recent experience and it leaves the player better equipped to undergo the passive rôle again, when necessary. This accounts for a great deal of the healing power of play.

*The Losing Party.*—In observing children at play, we see that while the dominant aggressive rôles are preferred, there is always some child willing to submit to the assault, to take the rôle of the sick child who has to swallow medicine and is sent to bed, or, in war play, to take the rôle of the hated enemy soldier who is invariably defeated. How can this be explained?

Several explanations suggest themselves. The very simple and non-psychological one is that a younger or less popular child fears that he will be excluded from the play altogether unless he takes such a rôle. Another explanation is that we have here early passive or masochistic tendencies. Finally the behavior can be explained by giving a broader meaning to the mechanism of "turning from the *passive* to the *active* experience." A child who himself chooses or consents to be the passive, the victimized party and knows that he can terminate this rôle whenever he pleases is not really passive. Even in the inactive rôle, he is self-steered and not a play ball.

*Incognito Indulgence.*—In contrast to the rôles described so far, which in the child's scale of values go in a direction "beyond and above" his present status, the child also chooses rôles that are distinctly "passed and below" him. For instance, he plays at being an animal or a baby. Freud states: "The wish which dominates childhood is the wish to be big and adult and do as the adults are doing." Why, then, should a child slip into a rôle that limits the powers he actually possesses?

Such a play rôle provides a convenient disguise for enjoying pleasures that are no longer compatible with the youngster's sense of his own dignity and grown-upness. This motivation can be understood if we consider how the young child is torn between two worlds. His superego takes its standards from his parents and teachers, whom he wants to please. Often, however, he cannot give up childish pleasures as quickly as he is expected to. Aware of the "subversive" elements in his own house, the superego of the early latency years is especially strict. Yet by announcing, "This is not me. It's a puppy dog," the child can permit himself to enjoy sniffing, crawling, getting dirty. By declaring, "I am a baby now," he can cuddle up, suck his fingers, insist on being carried around, talk gibberish. A child living under great pressure to be sensible and grown-up is more likely to select a rôle along this line. In one and the same play situation, a forbidden wish can be simultaneously expressed and disclaimed.

L., not quite five years old, insists for weeks and months daily on the following morning ritual: Her mother must greet her, "Good morning, Bambi." L. replies: "Good morning, Feline! You know, Feline, my mother died. Will you be my friend now?" To this her mother must answer: "Yes, Bambi. I'll always stay with you."

Often L. continues this rôle all day long. She has borrowed this scene from the Bambi film. There Bam-

150

bi's mother is shot and killed by the hunter and the lonely and distressed Bambi finds Feline in the forest and lives with her forever after. L. is a girl with many problems and her death wishes against her mother and the consequent fear that they will come true are particularly strong. About a year ago her baby brother was taken to the hospital where he died suddenly. Now L.'s mother is pregnant again and L. is terribly afraid and pleads with her not to go to the hospital.

In the past month the rôle of Bambi has provided L. with an excellent outlet for her own double-barreled wishes.

Bambi's mother was a deer, and people don't take it so seriously when a deer dies. After that sad event Bambi felt lost and lonely, but he got over the loss; so a human child would get over it, too, and find other friends, should his mother die. In the Bambi camouflage, loss and consolation can be lived through in phantasy without feelings of guilt.

It must be remembered that a child frequently assigns a rôle to an animal completely different from the one discussed here. A wolf, a horse, sometimes also a dog or a rooster may be symbols of great power and ferocity. In our examples, animals are a kind of "second rate" human beings. They feel and talk like human beings, yet they may indulge in actions that the child would consider beneath his dignity. After all, they are "only" animals and it is not upsetting when they lack the restraint expected in *homo sapiens*. On the other hand, it is permissible to do things to them that would be unthinkable with humans.

This type of play might be called "incognito indulgence." The child lends his motor apparatus to one part of his self and holds his superego in abeyance by declaring: "That's

151

not really me. You don't have to interfere." As in any make-believe, there is the implicit assurance, "All this is for a limited time only."

The prototype of this play mechanism is the dignitary, the Caliph Harun-al-Rashid or the Emperor Joseph II, who, shrouded in a cloak that provides convenient incognito, can visit all kinds of lowly places where he could not be seen if recognizable as himself.

An animal can enjoy feelings or show character traits that would be repulsive or cause feelings of guilt and shame in a human being. He can also be treated in a way that would be punishable if used toward a person. It works conveniently both ways, whether the animal is the subject or the object. The heroes of some of our most beloved children's stories are animals and thus can go through dangers and ordeals that would be outrageous in the human world.

Take Peter Rabbit. He really is a disobedient and greedy little boy who runs away from home. At the climax of the story, after stuffing himself with forbidden delicacies, Peter is chased by the old gardener who wants to kill him and put him into a mince pie. It would be outrageous in our day and age to tell such a story about a child. But story-teller and listener agree to call the hero a rabbit, and the plot can become more dramatic and much truer to the young child's hidden anxieties.

In more than one way this story follows the line of archaic childish reasoning: the impending punishment fits the crime. Peter is in a predicament because he ate forbidden things and now the gardener is going to eat him. It is tit for tat. As the story draws to its close, this horrible punishment is mitigated to one that is more likely to befall a naughty little boy: Peter is sent to bed without supper. But even this punishment still fits the crime. The characters in *The Wind in the Willows*, in Dr. Doolittle's books, and in many children's classics act in accordance with this "logic."

Seeing only the superficial, conscious aspect of a story,

educators have at times' objected to the unbiological thinking that is fostered as animals strut on their hind legs, talk, and are dressed like human beings. Yet more than 2,000 years ago when Aesop wanted to chide and deride human vices and weaknesses, he hit upon the same device; greed, vanity, and stupidity are somehow less offensive when encountered in animals. The implied accusation becomes less direct and loses its sting. After all, what can one expect from a fox, a peacock, or an ant?

The most recent and possibly the most popular addition to the long list of animal masks for human follies and foibles are Donald Duck, Mickey Mouse, and their consorts. In five minutes flat, the hero of an animated strip undergoes a series of atrocities that no exaggeration and no colorful details could make funny if they were happening to a human being.

*Clowning.*—Another mask that provides a convenient incognito is *clowning*. For instance, a child in a kindergarten has put on his cap the wrong way. He could correct it quickly and hope that none of his playmates noticed his blunder. (He would not be playing then.) Instead, he chooses another road: he repeats his mishap deliberately and in an exaggerated form, putting it, so to say, between quotation marks. Now he draws everybody's attention to his mistake, and he does not feel bad about it any more—just the opposite. After all, it is plain that he *chooses* to act this way.

The observation of a clowning child shows that there is more than one way of turning the tables, of switching from the passive to the active rôle. The clown does to himself what fate tried to do to him. That he gets plenty of attention may be called a secondary gain. The primary gain is that he need not admit—either to himself or to others—that he committed a blunder the first time. By deliberately repeating and paraphrasing it, he makes himself master of the situation.

153

A group of seven-to-nine-year-old campers stand on the platform near the train. Suddenly the locomotive releases steam with a loud hissing noise. H., who stands near it, almost jumps with fright. He notices that the others are looking at him, about to laugh. An embarrassed smile comes on his face and as the hissing recurs a few seconds later, he repeats and exaggerates his former movements. He throws his arms up, shrieks, and almost tumbles over. He repeats these antics with every blast of steam. Now he has the laughers on his side; he is the hero who parodies getting scared. He is not the victim of the situation, but the victor.

Clowning differs from the other models of play in that it requires an audience. It is as if the clown were saying to fate: "You thought you could lick me by showing me up as clumsy (or stupid, or ugly, or queer-looking). All right, I am not just a little clumsy (or ugly), I am very much so, but on my own choosing. You did not do it to me." Contrary to the other make-believe changes—"I am not envious or afraid. I myself am the giant, the king, the bogeyman"—this reversal cannot be enjoyed without the appreciative mirror of an audience.

Hiding one's own identity under the cloak of a clown, an animal, or a baby differs also in another aspect from the other paradigms of play discussed here. The others may be called *pre-stages of identification*. Being unable to achieve in reality a happy ending, an active rôle, or the strength of the aggressor, the child brings, at least in his play, things "into another order, more satisfying to himself." But in the incognito mechanism, the child adopts a way of acting not in order to incorporate it into his own person—as, for instance, in the identification with the aggressor—but in order to accentuate the distance, the veritable gulf between himself and such behavior. "*Facio quia absurdum*," seems to

154

be the principle of his actions. He rids himself of childish and ostracized impulses by acting them out drastically and copiously. He lends his motor apparatus to one part of his self while the other part—or his superego—pretends to be an uninvolved observer.

There are other instances in which we treat our own self as if it were another person and deal with another person as if it were our own self. There is, for instance, the mechanism that Anna Freud has called "altruistic secession," whereby we grant to and even encourage in another person an indulgence that our own conscience does not permit us.

Another example is the young child who tattles to his mother or teacher about the misdeed of a brother or a playmate. His denunciation of the other is not primarily malicious, as it might be in the case of older children or adults. Well enough does the young child know that he himself harbors similar "bad" desires. He uses his playmate to gain relief from his own guilty conscience.

In clowning, the child's superego disclaims what his bodily self does, while in tattling he clamors for the punishment of another person's misdeeds in order to atone for his own similar desires. In all these phenomena the gulf between superego and ego is temporarily wider than the distance between superego and another ego.

Thus far we have discussed *whose rôle* the child takes over and *why* he does so. Now we will follow another lead: to what extent do elements of the child's play copy a recent exciting or traumatic experience and to what extent are they *variations* of or *additions* to the past event. From the actor we turn to the plot.

*Deflected Vengeance.*—A child may suffer severe frustration without showing hostility against the person who disappoints or thwarts him. Instead, he vents his feelings on another person or on an object, often on his toys. Here the

155

hostility is *deflected*, as in the classical example of the play with the bobbin.

> "The child (about eighteen months old) used all his toys only to play 'gone' with them. He had a bobbin with a piece of cord fastened to it. He never thought of pulling it, for instance, along the floor, playing cart with it. Instead, he threw it with great dexterity into his crib which was covered so that the bobbin disappeared, saying his ominous 'O-O-O-O-' and then he pulled the cord so that the bobbin reappeared. . . . He greeted its appearance with a joyous 'da.'
> "Now the interpretation of this play was not difficult. It was connected with the great cultural achievement of the child, with his successful renunciation of instinctual gratification in permitting his mother to leave without remonstrating. Now he got even, so to say, by enacting the same disappearing and returning with the objects within reach. . . . The throwing away of an object, so that it was gone, could be the gratification of an impulse of vengeance against the mother for her leaving which in real life was suppressed. It could have the defiant meaning: 'Go away! I don't need you. I even send you away.' "[2]

Since it is impossible to avoid frustrations and disappointments in the child's daily life, this type of play can be observed in every nursery.

In a variation of this formula, only the *mood*, the general *feeling* tone, is taken from a recent traumatic experience, but the child's play actions do not copy the action to which he has been subjected.

Anna Freud has given an illustrative example of a six-year-old boy who had undergone dental treatment and came to his analytic hour in a very bad mood.

"The dentist had hurt him. He is angry and unfriendly and starts maltreating the things in my room. His first victim was an eraser. He wants me to give it to him as a present. I refuse and so he wants to cut it in half with a knife. Then he turns to a big roll of cord and wants this as a present, explaining to me how well he could use it as a leash for his animals. Again I refuse and so he gets a knife and at least cuts off a long piece for himself. But he does not use it. Instead, he cuts it all up into small pieces. Then he rejects the cord, turns to the pencils, and starts sharpening them indefatigably with a knife, breaking off all the points and sharpening them again and again. It would be wrong to say that he plays at being a 'dentist.' The image of the dentist does not enter his behavior. *His identification does not concern the person of his adversary, only his aggression.*"[3]

In our work with nursery schools, we frequently observed the following behavior: A little girl mercilessly spanks her dolls, puts them to bed for punishment, pushes them around, and so on. The teacher, naïvely assuming that the child's behavior mirrors the treatment she received at home, takes the first opportunity to talk to the mother. When the mother asserts that the child has never been spanked, and that the parents believe in lenient and progressive methods of education as sincerely as the teacher, the latter is nonplused.

The child's play in such a case reflects the feeling, not the treatment she experienced. The little girl felt her mother's impatience, anger, or hostility and uses "poetic license" in finding actions to express it in her doll play. She treats her dolls as her mother may at times *wish* to treat her.

*Anticipatory Retaliation.*—The actual situation may be even further removed from the impression we gain from the play in the doll corner. The mother is unaware of any

157

conflict or strain. Yet the child may be angry with her for one or the other reason. The child is the one who harbors hostile feelings against her mother and, therefore, expects her to retaliate. Indeed, with some children an unwarranted outburst of hostility against parent or teacher is a fairly reliable indication that they have done something forbidden. The underlying reasoning (conscious or unconscious) is, "I am justified in doing this to you as you plan to do it to me." The child's attitude may be called "anticipatory retaliation." (Credit for coining this seemingly self-contradicting term goes to *Time* magazine. It was used in 1948 in a discussion of our relations with Russia.) This mechanism was discussed by B. Bornstein, who calls it a "prophylactic aggressive attitude" and described several instances in which a child "takes over an aggression that he anticipates."[4]

Conversely, a little girl may be extremely gentle and kind with her dolls—not because her mother treats her this way, but because she would like her mother to be so kind and loving with her.

This indicates how careful we must be before drawing any inference about a mother's attitude. The child's play with her dolls may follow any one of these formulas: This is the way mother treats me, or this is how she *should* treat me or, this is the way she *feels* toward me, or, this is the way she will treat me once she finds out what I have done.

*Happy Ending.*—In other instances, the child's play mirrors and repeats a former experience except that the ending has been reversed from an unhappy to a happy one.

Shortly after Jonathan had moved from the city to a farm, he was playing with a visiting girl cousin in the yard when suddenly the lid of the dug-out on which the children were standing caved in and Eileen fell into the pile of manure it had covered. She struggled, yet sank

158

deeper into the oozy mass. Jonathan stood petrified, torn between the desire to run for help and his unwillingness to leave her. Fortunately, somebody soon happened to pass by and rescued the girl. Months later, his mother overheard him repeating the incident with his toys. His commentary ran: "The boy fell in splash! . . . But he is a big boy. He can get out all by himself."

Many of the ambitious daydreams of latency and later years follow the same formula.

*Magic (No Risk)*.—In another variation, the child repeats an everyday experience in order to gain the assurance that there will *always* be a happy ending, or, possibly, that it is within the child's power to bring about the happy ending.

"Hide and seek," the favorite game of most children between eighteen months and two years of age, is a case in point. The child "hides" in a nook or under the table and the mother has to look for him. He enjoys endless repetitions. At first sight this may seem a simpler version of the more skilled hide-and-seek play of older children. The real difference becomes obvious only after the adult, feeling that the act has been repeated in the same form often enough and is getting monotonous, tries to improve it by introducing variations. For instance, the mother begins to "seek" the child in places where she has not looked before and takes a longer time in finding him. But the youngster gets impatient and darts out from his hiding place, pointing at himself. "Look! Here I am!" Or the mother suggests that he hide in another corner, in a place where it will be more difficult to find him. This does not appeal to the child and he is apparently deaf to the remark that mother already *knows* the place where he had been hiding before. It does not matter to him, or it is more correct to state that this is exactly what he wants.

Thus the young child's hide-and-seek play follows a formula different from the game of older children. With them, it consists in pitting against each other skill and cunning in hiding and seeking, each player trying to outsmart the other. Each one hopes to win, but knows his risk of losing, and this suspense provides the spice of the game. The younger child's hide-and-seek game is but a pantomimic assurance: "Whenever mother is out of sight, I can reunite with her in a short time. *I* am the one who brings about our separation, and *I* can bring about our reunion. His hide-and-seek play resembles a square dance in which the couples part and weave their way in traditional figures through the dancing group to meet again.

"Goodbye, farewell, my dear old friend.
We'll meet again, you may depend.
We'll meet again ere long
In merry dance and song."

There is nothing new or unexpected in the stanzas and steps of a folk dance, yet the dancers enjoy the familiar sequence as the child relishes his well-worn pattern of play.

*Manipulation and Playful Repetition.*—In every type of play discussed thus far, some feature of reality is "canceled"—in fact, this cancelation seems to be the purpose of the play. From the actor's point of view, his version or his assigning of rôles improves reality. Now we come to forms of play that apparently have no intention of undoing events or of changing the status of players; their only purpose is to broaden and to vary contact with reality, as in manipulative play, or to prolong an experience, as in playful repetition. Everyday examples are throwing a ball, letting sand run through the fingers, opening and closing a faucet, and so on.

Do these activities belong to true *play?* Are they not either plain enjoyment or rational forms of learning, aiming directly at the goal of acquiring a skill or gaining information? For the time being, let us note that to exclude them is to ignore an important and at times revealing segment of the child's interests. Later we may discover additional reasons that favor their inclusion in a survey of play.

There is no plot in these activities. The child does not step into any rôle; there is no drama, no climax, as there is in play instigated by Oedipal tensions, and the child's actions do not seem to have a symbolic value. In a way, these activities are the direct precursors of later experimentation, of the physical, chemical, geographical explorations of the older child.

But they are forerunners only, and they are to a large extent evoked or accentuated by the child's emotional problems.

Martin, five years old, habitually visits his grandmother several times a week. One day he notices an egg-timer which had been within his reach all the time. For a long time he sits still and watches the thin trickle of fine sand run, turning the small hourglass over and over again. This simple manipulation and observation fascinates him and he repeats it on several visits. This is in contrast to his usual active and roving behavior. For the last couple of weeks Martin had heard many allusions about a baby brother or sister who will arrive after Christmas, and this is the month of July.

L., aged two years and three months, builds for height with extraordinary perseverance and skill. She has wooden cylinders, $3\frac{1}{2}$ inches long and with a base the size of a nickel, and she succeeds in putting four or five on top of one another before the structure collapses. It would be a skilful performance for a seven-year-old.

161

She has a blackboard which she uses but little for scribbling. Instead, she makes a wet spot on it—then blows on the wet spot and watches it disappear. This, too, she repeats many times, showing an unusual patience.

L. has been seen by a consultant because she has outbursts of rage, and attacks her mother, biting and scratching her. Her difficulties could be traced to a traumatic castration experience. Her only playmate and the only person she ever saw naked was a cousin, a year older, a very wild and aggressive boy. She also had very early and strict toilet training.

These are instances of seemingly purely manipulative play. The activity runs on and on in a rather monotonous way or possibly with a crescendo or diminuendo. Yet when the child's emotional problems become known, it appears that the manipulative activity carried out with innumerable repetitions was not chosen at random.

Of course, in a young child's day there is much playful manipulation that has no deeper emotional roots. It is characterized by less persistence, and the child does not become so oblivious of his surroundings, of other toys, of the ridicule of other people, or of parental prohibitions.

On the other hand, in children's so-called dramatic play with dolls, and so on, there are frequent interludes in which the ideational content runs low or gets confused and hazy and only the pleasure in some kind of manipulation or repetition keeps the children going.

Written records of children's family and household play have a tendency to gloss over its incoherences and sudden shifts. Adults are prone to read into the children's doings a progressive movement from one episode into the next. Yet the play of children under five usually resembles less a stage play and more a dream. There are duplications of persons

162

and episodes, sudden changes of locality—all of which just don't make sense, not even to the observer who knows the players well. It is amazing how children can apparently enjoy playing "together" for a long time, their ideas clicking for a while—then go far apart.

The child may modify his handling of a material, using it in many different ways and thus exploring it, or he may just repeat what he has already been doing. The doing as such seems to be pleasant enough to induce repetition. K. Bühler has termed this kind of activity with no goal "*Funktionslust.*" The mere functioning, the activity in itself, brings pleasure. This method of play belongs to the youngest age group. It includes the child's babbling monologues in which he pronounces sounds and syllables, listens and repeats and varies them; the long spells of playing with his fingers, his toes, or a rattle. If any imagery accompanies this play, he may have vague hallucinations of gratification and grandeur. There cannot be any plot, as there is no risk, no competition. In a sense, intending and carrying out coincide.

Manipulative play that is chosen with great persistence is related to the child's emotional tensions; it has symbolic value and merges into dramatic play. In later years, manipulative play—for instance, doodling—may return chiefly in stages of fatigue, or when a person is deeply preoccupied with an emotional or intellectual problem—in short, when part of his resources are drained off.

In academic child psychology, one often finds the statement that the younger the child, the shorter the span of attention. This is correct only when we try to force upon a young child materials and play methods that would be more suitable for older children. A child of eighteen months or two years when permitted to handle and explore mud, sand, or water will show remarkable perseverance and an even longer span of fully concentrated attention than older children with the same media and tools.

163

A play activity can belong to several models at the same time. For instance, Goethe's earliest childhood memory of how he threw all his doll dishes, one by one, out of the window and then let his mother's plates and cups follow because he enjoyed the cheerful clang of their breaking on the pavement outside, reads like an account of manipulative play. However, Freud's analysis shows that it was also an act of magic—namely, the symbolic eviction of a brother, who was about three years his junior. It was also an act of deflected vengeance. This shows that there is no rigid dividing line between various forms of play. (*Models*)

Each libidinal phase has focal anxieties and deprivations. There are frustrations and anxieties concerning the *body*. The awareness that our body is not at all times a perfect instrument to implement our wishes must come early, probably long before the end of our first year of life. The relationship to the *preoedipal mother*, the all-powerful mother as she is perceived, brings specific frustrations and fears. In the *oedipal period* the child is under the strain of instinctual drives which are incompatible with reality and even in compatible with one another. The oedipal tensions lead not only to the well-known inner conflicts, they also instigate and accelerate intellectual developments. Moreover, a wide variety of play activities assists the child in overcoming the blows and disappointments he suffers, and also in cementing his defenses against oedipal entanglements. In the *postoedipal* years, the dominant apprehensions concern *superego figures* and his own exacting conscience.

Each libidinal relationship causes anxieties or, to put it differently, each is harassed by deficiencies. Play is instigated in an effort to deny them, or to lessen them, or to work them through. Thus various types of play can be characterized by specific anxieties and corresponding fantasies. While these types of play have many similarities—

they use the same material, and, in part, have comparable "secondary play gains"[5]—they differ from one another in style, in social aspects, and in other respects. In order to gain a perspective on the various characteristics and meanings of groups of play, their differences and similarities, we have arranged them in the table given below. Needless to say, such a schematic presentation oversimplifies and even distorts developments which are slow and continuous.

With the appearance of chronologically later play groups, the earlier ones do not disappear. They persist or undergo modifications, reappearing in more complex and lengthier versions reflecting the child's progress of ego development. This is especially true of Group I. Fantasies of increased (or changed) body power and skill are incorporated in all play. Some play activities of Group III come to full blossoming only in early latency, e.g., after the appearance of Group IV. Of course, play forms of different types combine with one another and they also merge with other activities. Table I, presenting selected relevant features and typical examples, does not attempt to cover the vast field of play activities.

*Group I:* PLAY ORIGINATING IN THE RELATIONSHIP TO ONE'S OWN BODY

We preface the discussion of the characteristics of this group with a few play observations drawn from various sources, all of them antedating this study. A wider range of examples would be highly desirable but space does not permit it.

*Examples*

For two months, a three-year-old boy was frequently occupied with games of 'making coffee.' These sometimes bordered on compulsive behavior in the intensity of emotion he showed while playing with them, and his resistance at times to distraction. His favorite of many ways of 'making coffee' was by manipulating three ashtrays in imitation of a Silex machine, but he reduplicated this with many materials. He poured sand on his head and called it 'making coffee,' he pushed the dog into the piano and called it 'making coffee,' he slid down his father's back and the backs of chairs and called it 'making coffee.' There were many anal associations to the game and during this period he was specially interested in his own 'ga-ga' (faeces or anus) and those of animals, trolley cars, other people, etc. He sometimes called coffee 'ga-ga.' He talked about 'coffee go in at top, come out below.' Anal fantasies were the most constant association to these games, but they were not the whole story . . . [Hendrick, 1942, pp. 33-58].

Some children at this period (beginning of the second year) for a while disregard all toys and show little interest in their companions; they behave as if they were drunk with the idea of space and even speed; they crawl, walk, march and run, and revert from one method of locomotion to the other with the greatest pleasure. These children mostly use toys where they can include them in the continual game of moving. Chairs and pots are not used to sit on but are propelled about the room. Soft toys and animals on wheels are "taken for walks," balls are followed, and some children, after they have once gained an easy balance, show special pleasure in moving a toy along in each hand while they move themselves. Sometimes for an hour on end the whole population of the Junior Toddler room is on the move, circling around, crossing and recrossing like people on a skating rink . . . [A. Freud and D. Burlingham, 1944, pp. 15-16].

# SURVEY OF PLAY ACTIVITIES

| | CENTRAL THEME OF PLAY: OBJECT-RELATIONS: | DEFICIENCIES ANXIETY (denied): | COMPENSATING FANTASY: | FORMAL ELEMENTS, STYLE: | SOCIAL ASPECT: | PLAY MATERIAL: | SECONDARY PLAY GAINS: |
|---|---|---|---|---|---|---|---|
| Group I | Relation to Body ................. Anxieties concerning body | My body is no good I am often helpless | My body (its extensions, replicas, variations) is a perfect instrument for my wishes. Imagery of grandeur, of perfect ease | Hallucinations (pos. & neg.) rather than fantasies. Imagery increases pleasure, persistence | Solitary | Extensions & Variations of Body functions & Body parts. | Increased body skills & mastery. Initiation into active search for gratification. |
| Group II | Relation to Preoedipal Mother ................. Fear to lose love object | My Mother can— desert me; do as she pleases; | I can do to others what she did to me. I can go on (or quit) | Short fantasies. Endless, monotonous repetitions. Few variations. No risk, no climax, no real plot. Tit-for-tat | Solitary or with mother. Other children rank with pets, or things—not as co-players. Sporadic mirroring play | Maternal play with dolls, stuffed animals, with other children, and mother herself. Peek-a-boo. Earliest tools. | Rage, anxiety mitigated. Ability to bear delay, frustration. Initiation into lasting object relation. |
| Group III starts about 3 years | Oedipal Relations & Defenses against them. ................. Fear to lose love of love object | I cannot enjoy what grownups enjoy. | I am big; I can do as big people are doing. Family Romance | Spontaneity. Infinite variety of emotions, roles, plots, settings. Time is telescoped In later times: Drama, risk | Early co-play. Attempts to share fantasy. Fantasy always social Activity may be solitary or social | Dollplay: wide variety of events, of father, mother images: (pilot, nurse, magician, etc.) Creative play, Imaginative play. Use of emblems, props, insignia | Preparation for adult roles, adult skills. Co-play prepares co-work. Initiation into adventure, accomplishment. |
| Group IV starts about 6 years | Sibling Relations & Fear of superego and superego figures | I am all alone against threatening authority I cannot start all over again | Many of us are united. We observed rules conscientiously. I can live many lives. | Codified plot & roles. Importance of rules, program, rituals, formal elements. Reciprocity (Piaget) | Organized co-play Fantasy tacitly shared. | Team games Board games Organized games. Games with token armies. | Dissolving oedipal ties. Co-operation with brothers, with followers & leaders experienced as gratifying. |

The basic *topic* of these play-forms is the parts and the
functions of the body which the child paraphrases, varies,
or magnifies. The deficiency or anxiety which he experiences may be expressed as: "My body is no good, I'm helpless"; and the *compensating fantasy* may be: "My body, (its

167

extensions, replicas, variations) is a perfect instrument for my wishes, my orders." In this play the child obviously enjoys smooth easy performance and functioning as such. The accompanying fantasy does not tell a story as in the later groups of play. Rather there are vague images of grandeur or of perfect ease, and they account for the feeling of elation accompanying the play.

The toddler comes up frequently, or should we say incessantly, against the limitations of things he cannot do, either because he is not yet sufficiently skillful or strong, or because he risks punishment. Thus he begins to pretend, that is, to do things which are symbolic for a function of his body which he cannot yet enjoy or exercise, at least not to the desired extent. For instance, he does what he did before, but substitutes a socially accepted substance for the waste product of his body. He uses displacement. The most obvious example is play with sand, mud, and water. Another kind of earliest play deals with variations or extensions of his body, supporting a fantasy of great strength. A shovel is a more efficient scoop than the hollow hand. A wooden block is a better hammer than his fist. A ball skips and rolls without danger of a painful fall or bruised knee.

Implements used in play are at first experienced as substitutes for or improved versions of body parts rather than as tools (see preoedipal play). They become a part of the body ego—hence they retain a high narcissistic value in the adult's unconscious.

As we grow up, our body, our muscular apparatus becomes a far better executant of our wishes and orders, but it always remains far from the perfect instrument. Hence fantasies of greater skill or potency persist throughout our lives.

A brief reference to some of the patent *secondary play gains* may suffice: this play brings increased body skill and mastery. Play of any kind yields *functional pleasure*. This concept was introduced by K. Groos, while the term was coined by K. Buehler. Any observer of a child's play can confirm that it is an excellent descriptive term. In the play activities which paraphrase, vary or magnify parts or functions of the body or deal with their repercussions or counterparts in the outer world, functional pleasure is an even more conspicuous phenomenon than in later play forms.

Earliest play merges almost imperceptibly with non-play. This is one point on which observers of all schools of thought agree (see Groos, 1922; Piaget, 1932, 1952). The experiences of the preverbal period must needs remain subject to speculation. For this and also other reasons, earliest play forms may be considered a *prestage* of play. Jekels and Bergler (1940) speak of a prestage of the dream and we are following his model of thought. According to Jekels' thesis the earliest dreams are not guardians of sleep; to the contrary, their function is to remind the sleeper of life's enjoyments, to awaken him. Without this call he might remain immersed in sleep and never awaken. In a comparable way the earliest play may have the function of providing pleasure, pure and simple, not of achieving a compromise between the demands of drives and the dictates of reality, as does later play.

*Group II:* PLAY ROOTED IN THE CHILD'S RELATIONSHIP TO THE PREOEDIPAL MOTHER

*Examples*

a. Rose, 20 months, looked on with interest when several children had their noses wiped. Suddenly she picked up an old envelope, ran from one child to the other, and wiped their noses with it.

b. Paul, two years, loved to comb the other children's hair, disregarding the fact that they disliked it. He rushed from one child to another and maltreated their hair with a comb. There was only one child who did not mind, Larry, twenty months. Thus, whenever Paul had

169

made a child cry with his combing, he ran back and combed Larry, before he attacked his next victim. This game continued sometimes for several minutes.

c. Rose, twenty-one months, asked urgently "more, more," when she had finished her first helping. The nurse, who was feeding Christopher, sixteen months, next to Rose, left the table to fetch Rose's second helping. Rose immediately picked up the spoon and continued to feed Christopher.

d. Stella, eighteen months, was sitting next to Agnes, fifteen months. She heaped up a spoonful of food and put it into her own mouth, then she pushed an empty spoon into Agnes' mouth. This she repeated several times until she finally emptied the whole contents of Agnes' plate into her own [A. Freud and D. Burlingham, 1944, pp. 30-31].

Another example is the famous play with the bobbin quoted by Freud in *Beyond the Pleasure Principle*. The child who is often left alone begins to throw a bobbin out of sight and pull it back; he also makes his own image in a mirror disappear and reappear. In this category also belongs the peek-a-boo game played by infants all over the world. Many languages possess endearing terms for this play (e.g., "guck-guck" in German).

This group of play fantasies centers around the *preoedipal mother* figure who is the unfathomable source of comfort as well as of fear and terror. The central formula is: "I can do to you what mother did to me." The child makes his doll, or his teddy or a smaller child the recipient of maternal care.[6]

In hide-and-seek games he paraphrases her coming and leaving: "I can leave you as you left me." Running away and hiding behind a table or a curtain, he challenges his mother, playfully slipping out from her domination and protection.

Let us look at the *style* of this preoedipal play. There are countless repetitions with scarcely any variations. The underlying plot is extremely simple, it can be all told in one short sentence; maybe it is not even a real plot. The adult who plays with the child gets bored and tired long before the child has exhausted his desire for repetition.

Most preoedipal play appears monotonous to the observer because the underlying conflict is so simple, so monolithic. It is all based on one formula: Tit for Tat. There are only two actors, and all of the child's feelings are riveted on one person—his mother. He loves and fears her; he wants to have her all the time—to be like her, but also to replace her. The conflicts are not subtle, the player does not weave any risk or drama into his play acting. The mood of preoedipal play is often sober, serious, almost businesslike. All these characteristics are in direct contrast to the endless variety, the happiness, and the imaginative levity of later play on the oedipal level.

*Social aspects*: The child plays alone or with his mother and when other children are drawn into the play they serve as dummies rather than as co-players. The actively playing child often seems impervious to their mood and their reactions. (See example b, p. 169.)

The first animal play appears in the preoedipal phase. Roles of animals will remain convenient and well-liked vehicles, but their symbolic meaning will change completely according to the age level of the players. The toddler knows *one* relationship, i.e., that to his mother. Now the image of the preoedipal mother can be cast on an animal without deleting essential traits. Hence animals may arouse great tenderness, or fear, admiration, or hilarity. This may partly account for their popularity in toys, picture books, and nursery rhymes.

There is also preoedipal play without the dynamics of retaliation: the playful caressing of the child's body and the joking play with his hands or his face—naming the parts or enacting a little story, as in "this little pig ate roastbeef." The

171

child feels that his mother approves of his body, that his body is good and beautiful and that nothing is missing. Here our words may imply too much: we wish merely to convey the idea of the pleasure secured through this play and of the anxieties which are hushed.

We may make some speculative statements about the secondary play gains of preoedipal play. The child turns from the passive to the active role and by doing to others what the all-powerful mother has done to him, he can fathom his emotions of rage and anxiety. Rage is the most forceful, the climactic emotion of the preoedipal period (Brunswick, 1940). Incorporating the good and the bad mother may help the child remember the good mother in times of distress, and this in turn prepares the ground for an object relationship, e.g., for a tie lasting beyond the gratification of a need.

## Group III: PLAY INSTIGATED BY CONFLICTS ON THE OEDIPAL LEVEL

Play activities originating at the time of the oedipal situation and through the oedipal tensions show a far greater variety. The typical play of, let us say, four- and five-year-old children has a high visibility and has been extensively discussed in academic psychology. For instance, the children play house, furnishing a corner with some small pieces of furniture, doll dishes, small rugs, etc. Or, they put on some pieces of adult clothing or accessories and the insignia of a certain profession, and play doctor, cowboy, nurse, ship captain, etc. The trappings and the roles are taken from the outer world or from stories, but the problems the child tries to solve, the deficiencies for which he tries to compensate, are his very own.

The *anxiety* which this play undertakes to deny may be put into these words: "I am small, I am left out of the pleasures of the grownups," and the *compensatory* fantasy: "I am big, I can do what the adults are doing." Here we have the wish to which Freud gave central importance: to be big, to do as the big people do.[7]

The oedipal situation is, above all, the situation of the triangle (Freud, 1923; Brunswick, 1940). Relationships which were so simple in the preoedipal period now become entangled, aspirations soar and disappointments strike hard. The wide range of intense emotions is reflected in the vividness of play.

In many different settings, roles, and disguises the child pretends to possess privileges which in real life are reserved for adults; thus he derives satisfaction of his libidinal and/or destructive drives. On this level the playing child has the greatest leeway for his fantasies; his play activities are colorful and imaginative. His acute conflicts, his keen intelligence which is not easily led astray by conventions, impart to his play a vitality and a naïve urgency which become tempered in older children. The directness of the invented play situations, the intensity of emotions delighted observers long before the days of child psychology. It is not surprising that most of the play described in literature belongs in this group and that the term "play" is at times used as if it comprised only this group.

In one kind of oedipal play, the so-called dramatic play, the plot may be involved and tell a complete story. The play may have direction, successive stages, and later on drama and suspense. We observe a great deal of spontaneity and unforeseen developments. The average observer, that is, the observer with no special psychological interest, is charmed by the children's vitality, their facility of invention. Hence this type of play is so often remembered in autobiographies, or described in poems, and in the belles-lettres. The deeper reason why the adult is delighted to watch this role play is that the playing children have put themselves in

173

the place of the envied adults, have taken over their privileges and enjoy them without guilt feelings.

The mood pervading oedipal play is usually one of happiness, even of triumph, of a naïve invincibility. As Freud (1917, p. 367) puts it, ".... he who has been the undisputed darling of his mother retains throughout life that victorious feeling, that confidence in ultimate success, which not seldom brings actual success with it." The feeling of happy conquest which the mother's loving indulgence imparts to the favorite son is sought by every child in his oedipal play fantasies. Here every player becomes the hero whose wishes command fate.

In the oedipal phase the child also copes with intellectual problems which he cannot solve even if adults give him answers that are factually correct. This tension leads to developments outside the realm of play: the child's curiosity is greatly stimulated; he asks many questions and he learns a lot. But curiosity also leads into playful activities— riddles with surprise answers, tricky problems, and puzzles, and he begins to like witty rhymes, jokes, and puns.

*Social Aspects*: here several children share plot, plan, and play action; at least they make attempts at sharing them. They may form what Freud called a "closed system," or they may miss one another's intentions. In any case they attempt to communicate their ideas to one another and to co-operate, in marked contrast to preoedipal play.

They use props and emblems to support their fantasies. In preoedipal play the child used the simplest and crudest kind of tools, for instance, a stick, a spoon, a crumpled piece of paper, a mirror, but he did not arrange or invent any scenery, costumes or insignia. His fiat: "I *am* the mother," was enough; there was no need to support the illusion by dressing up to fit the role.

Oedipal play which is carried out with such great investment of affects, efforts and intelligence, leads to a wide range of secondary play gains. Let us first refer to the formulations of academic psychology which are very much to the point: through his play the child prepares for adult roles and functions, acquires skills which in his society will be useful to the future adult. (Play theories of Darwin and Groos.) But his play also yields an immediate gain: the tensions, the frustrations of the oedipal situation are alleviated, at least temporarily. As Greenacre (1948) puts it: "A generally expanding environment dilutes the genital urgency."

We have drawn the above examples from dramatic play. In other forms of play the kinship to the oedipal aspirations is less obvious. The child who takes tender care of a doll, pushes a toy engine, or erects a bridge, also gains privileges which in real life carry the sign: "Children Not Admitted." Tentatively we would say that all play in which the child does not merely dabble with materials but creates or constructs something is rooted in the strivings and the defenses aroused by the oedipal situation.

Creative achievements in the arts and sciences reached in later years are considered sublimations. It seems justified to consider childhood play, which is truly imaginative and shows glimpses of creative ability, as related to oedipal sublimations.

We cannot here enter into a discussion of play forms and fantasies based on defenses against the oedipal entanglements, e.g., the family romance and its offshoots. Some of these developments appear in day dreams spun out in children's literature. The family romance proclaims: "You are not my real parents." This may lead to the next stage: "In my search for them I must go far and wide," and this kindles interest in far-away countries and remote times. Or it may lead to the rebellious and self-assertive fantasy: "I don't need my parents; in fact, I don't need anyone. I can get along all by myself." In this context, Robinson Crusoe or Tarzan becomes the child's favorite story. The manifest content of these adventure stories describes the hero's survival as due to his valiant efforts, his courage, and inventiveness. On a deeper unconscious level he has rejected (or lost) his parents and his home to return to nature, that is, to the idealized image of the omnipresent, bountiful early mother. Twin stories are well liked by young children and they may represent another ramification of the family romance: an alter ego lessens the importance of parents, makes it easier to turn away from them (Burlingham, 1945).

*Group IV:* POSTOEDIPAL PLAY

Activities in this group include team games such as baseball, croquet, football, and also ten pins; dominoes, cards and board games. There are also less highly organized games like cops-and-robbers and hide-and-seek.

This type of play differs in some essential points from all previous groups, and the English language confirms our feeling of these differences by according to it a special name, i.e., "games."[8]

For the preschool child, members of his immediate family are the hub of his emotional world. At the age of five and six he seeks in various ways release from these attachments which have caused him so many painful disappointments. He turns to the fantasies of the family romance and also to organized games which offer him group attachments and mutual identifications with his playmates. Such feelings become the guiding stars of his play as the pretended adult role was the sun of his earlier play. The early make-believe castles were jerry-built and collapsed ever so often. The goals of latency play are more reality-adapted for two reasons: the older child has greater abilities and he aims at far more modest targets in his play fantasies.

It is customary to state that the child leaves the oedipal attachments for biological reasons and because of past frustrations. We would rather borrow a metaphor which Freud uses in another context: the tourist climbing the high steps on the pyramids of Gizeh is pushed from behind and pulled from the front by the escorting dragomans. The six-year-old who in our society enters school is also pushed and pulled. Biological reasons and repeated disappointments push him out from his early paradise, while beginning libidinal attachments to his playmates and to new father figures (teachers, older friends, etc.) pull him forward.

The games and sports played in teams are based on the fantasy of belonging to a group of brothers mutually and jealously guarding their prerogatives or of following a chosen leader. Needless to say that with this leitmotif fantasy other fantasies may coexist.

In the early postoedipal years there are also other pastimes. Anal sublimations appear on a higher level. Collections, with their competition and bartering, with cheating and prodigal donations, lead to cliques and countercliques, to deeds of love and envy. The world of his play interests engulfs the child with new hopes, new disappointments, and gratifications. Secret societies are formed, hobbies become important.

Here we shall discuss only the dynamics of *games*. The underlying anxieties are unconscious. If they reached awareness they would not instigate games. But if we, as analytic observers, put them into words, they may be phrased as: "I have to face authority, threatening dangerous authority, all by myself"; or: "I cannot go back and start all over again."

The formulas of the compensating fantasies run about this way: "I am not alone, there is a group of us and we are all united"; or: "We observed the rules to the letter." Strict rules are the backbone of games, and the players recognize them as absolute for the duration of the game. Their

177

meticulous observance gives independence from external superego figures. Or finally: "I can start all over again as many times as I want." To express it more forcefully: "I can live not one but many lives." The eventual end is pushed far away. The last formulas approximate more the fantasies of adults than those of adolescents.

The contrast with oedipal play is striking. There, the future was anticipated, transplanted right into the present, so to say, time was speeded up, telescoped. In games, time is treated differently. The clock is turned back, and the player returns to the beginning as many times as it pleases him. In reality one life course is allotted to each of us, one beginning and one end. The essential feature of games is that a new round can be started over and over again.

Another important aspect of organized games is that they foster identification with equals. In the oedipal phase the child identified with his father; now identifications with his peers come to the fore, and the family entanglements recede in importance. Homosexual strivings are channelized in team games.

A few comments on the *social aspects* of games: here the players definitely form a "closed system"; co-operation is well organized and must run smoothly or the game will be disrupted. In oedipal play, the players can miss one another for quite a while in their plans and in the meaning they give to roles and plots and yet go on playing happily "together." In games, the underlying fantasy is tacitly shared and carries but little emotional cathexis. This again is in sharp contrast to oedipal play with its affect-loaded fantasies.

A team in organized games of basketball, football, etc., represents a group of watchful and loyal brothers. Board games are one step removed from this arrangement: each player has at his command a group of faithful henchmen, a token army—the chessmen, checkers, domino bones or the handful of cards.

178

The plot is codified, and the roles, too, are frozen and conventional. Rules, ceremonies, rituals, are essential elements of all games. Formal elements are dominant.

Thus it may be, and often actually is, more important for a player to observe the rules than to attain victory. As long as both parties have observed the rules, they remain equals and friends. Winner and loser return to their initial equality; they shake hands. This custom does not indicate the winner's modesty or condescension; it is a ritual needed to re-establish the identification of all participants.

In contrast to oedipal play the players in games have little leeway for their actions, the plot follows a traditional pattern, it runs on tracks, unforeseen developments are limited to a narrow margin. The difference in the inner world of the child in the oedipal phase and the child in latency is reflected in their play activities. On the oedipal level play actions are confabulated on the spot, and thus they express so well the emotional tensions and conflicts of the child and provide relief. In contrast, "games" are not personal creations but traditional forms which are passed on from group to individual and from group to group. They lack the quality of spontaneity which seems one of the essentials of play. Yet another criterion is even more important: team and board games assist the player in dealing with his own personal conflicts. The young child gains a respite from his emotional entanglements through play fantasies because he invents them *ad hoc*—just to suit his immediate pressing emotional needs. The latency child in whom defenses have overlaid the oedipal strivings is helped by games precisely because their underlying fantasy is not spontaneous and not improvised, but impersonal and conventional.[9]

The backbone of games is competition. Rivalry and competition have appeared earlier in the child's life, in the oedipal phase, but there is a basic difference between this earlier competition and the later kind. Rivalry with father and/or siblings in the family is painful, but rivalry with playmates is by no means entirely unpleasant. Oversimplifying the issue, we might say: if competition at home could be eliminated, the competitor who wins the whole field for himself would be pleased. The opposite is true for the playfield: many of the things for which the playmates compete would lose their flavor if *others* were not competing for them. The see-saw of competition in games is rather pleasant, and even defeat is comparatively insignificant as long as it has been incurred according to the "rules." This is the salient point: the importance given to the *formal* elements of the game takes the sting and the shame out of defeat. This shift in focus impresses us as a protective device.[10]

The playing contestants strive for ascendancy during the game, but with each new round or new game they return to their initial fictional equality. The principle of "fair play" is an offshoot of the striving for equal status. Its furthest development is the *handicap*. A measured and timed *in*-equality is introduced in order to offset superior strength or skill of a participant or a team. The function of the handicap is to create an ideal equality of the players for the duration of the game, since in typical games victory would be without value unless attained on this basis of equality.

The libidinal goal of one period of life may become the content of a phobia shortly after (Freud, 1909). Kris (1938) points out that sometimes the object of anxiety of one period becomes the material for jokes and witticisms of the next. We add that a source of anxiety in one period of life often becomes the favorite play material of the slightly older child. The very young child wants to hear the *same* story told in the same way over and over (Freud, 1920). The unfamiliar causes displeasure, but shortly afterwards, in the early postoedipal years, new stories dealing with a wide range of adventures are well received. A similar reversal

180

can be observed in the way some games are played, e.g., hide-and-seek (Peller, 1952).

Banding together with equals, maintaining loyalty to the team, observing rules, and observing every one else's observance characterize many play activities of latency and adolescence. This mutual identification prepares the child for the loosening of his oedipal ties. Games are primarily the pastimes of boys, and one reason for this situation may be that the oedipal ties of the girl do not become so intensely taboo as those of the boys at the threshold of latency. Dissolving them is not as big and as urgent a task (Freud, 1931; Brunswick, 1940).

Let us glance briefly at other secondary play gains. Cooperation with peers, with a leader or followers, is a gratifying experience and is carried over from games into real life. The same applies to other socially approved attitudes (Piaget, 1932, 1952).[11]

The ego structures developed in latency are likely to lose their prominence and their rigidity in later years, but they remain part of our psychic equipment, and thus various types of codified games keep their attraction in later life. When the earlier groups of play reappear in later life they use very different material, they show great differences in the material they use and in their style, whereas activities of Group IV remain relatively unchanged from their first appearance.

We have pointed out a few of the characteristics of each group of play in the order in which they are presented in our table, that is, "horizontally." A "vertical" discussion of some points may be added.

The guilt feelings inherent in fantasies are handled differently in different periods of life. In the preoedipal and oedipal phases, the child neither hides nor displays his play fantasies; his attention is fully absorbed by his play. "The young child neither exhibits his play nor has he any inten-

181

tion of hiding it" (Freud, 1908). In contrast, the latency child feels ashamed of his daydreams and keeps them secret. To this we may add: besides his personal daydreams, the latency child has another type of fantasies. But these are group fantasies congealed into conventional forms long before his time, hence they carry but little affect. By and large they remain unconscious, but they are at the core of board games, team games, and the like.

Oedipal play reappears in later life, as enjoyment of the drama, novels, ballads, etc. The openness given to the fantasy counteracts guilt feelings and so does the emphasis put on aesthetic and formal elements. Moreover, the author, actors, and audience share in the creative effort, in performance and enjoyment. The listeners are by no means purely receptive, they provide the emotional resonance which is vital for the actor and the poet (Kris, 1952).

From one group of play activities to the other there is also a characteristic change in *intentionality*, preparation, and termination.

In the *first group* we gain the impression that the play activity is a chance event. We observe eruptions, shreds of activity which are chiefly short, but may be surprisingly long. They happen without any preludes.

Likewise, no behavior is observed heralding *preoedipal* play. The child plunges into his play and the observations reported, e.g., in *Infants Without Families*, convey this abrupt beginning and end. However, the skilled observer who knows the child, that is, his behavior in the immediate past, his mood on the day of observation, can with certain probability foretell the duration of a play form and the course it will take without outer disturbance. No such prediction was possible in the previous group.

*Oedipal play* has rudimentary or elaborate preparations. The co-players communicate to one another the theme of play or their plans, or the entire plot may be rehearsed

182

before it is mimed. The playing children take time out to dress up, to assemble scenery and implements, and to assign roles. Only after these preliminaries does play proper start. The play itself may have direction, successive parts, entanglements leading to a climax—in short it is structured and not a stretched-out, amorphous repetition, which is broken off by a chance distraction or by fatigue as is the case in preoedipal play.

In *games* the immediate preparations may not be more elaborate than in oedipal play, but there are remote antecedents. The plot, the roles, and the rules need to be told to the beginner only; the seasoned players are familiar with them. The props, the attire, the insignia, are not improvised immediately before the game starts; they are part of the child's social heritage. The time and location of the game may also be subject to long-term planning.

In conclusion, we return to a classical interpretation of a classical play memory. You are familiar with the play incident Goethe mentions from his earliest childhood—throwing all his mother's dishes out of the window—and with the interpretation given to it by Freud (1917): eviction of an unwelcome newborn brother. We wish to draw attention to one detail of the story. The child had started his mischief by throwing out his own newly acquired doll dishes. It was the applause of his audience which seduced him into doing something really forbidden, namely to break all the crockery he could reach on the kitchen shelves.[12] What would have been a rather insignificant, harmless play act assumed dramatic proportions on account of the acclaim of the audience—three middle-aged bachelor brothers seated at their window across the street: "My neighbors continued to signify their approval and I was delighted to have amused them" (Freud, 1917, p. 358).

About earliest memories, Freud (1917), pp. 358-359)

183

says: "It might rather be conjectured that what had remained in memory was the most significant element in that
whole period of life, equally so whether it had possessed
such an importance at the time or whether it had gained
subsequent importance *from the influence of later events.*"
The choice of this anecdote as the introduction to his life
history may not be unrelated to Goethe's vocation: the
writer and poet gives symbolical expression to impulses that
are socially not approved, to guilt-ridden conflicts. Actors,
audience and poet exculpate one another.

*(Phases)*

Some years ago I attempted a systematic survey of play.
Now I am trying once again, seeking greater simplicity with
a somewhat changed emphasis.*

The great change in a child's life is his entry into the
world of language. This metamorphosis establishes the
dominance of the "secondary" mental processes that are
not steered by affects, but by reality testing. The change
proceeds by small, hardly perceptible steps (as does the
transition from night to day); yet it generates revolutionary
changes.

Three broad groups of play emerge: pre-oedipal, oedipal, and postoedipal. Symbols abound in all play. But in the
first phase (Table, Groups I and II) symbols and the symbolized merge. The player interacts primarily with himself
or with a person whose otherness is not yet consistently
perceived. In the second phase (Group III), the oedipal
phase, his efforts to come to terms with himself and others,

*Lili Peller here refers to Phases. Her later study is a recapitulation.
We are including parts in this volume, both for their intrinsic value and
because we think it instructive to observe the changes in her presentation, due to her development as well as to the changed role of
psychoanalysis and the different mental climate in education. (Ed.)

including his investigations of reality, are honeycombed with symbolic expressions of his wishes and anxieties. He lives within a rudimentary framework of time, space, and causality. In the early postoedipal phase, these will be defensively accentuated and concretized, and thus postoedipal play (Group IV) is characterized by rules and conventions, rituals. The variety, spontaneity, and boldness of oedipal fantasies will be recaptured only much later—and then not in play, but in various art forms.

Here are thumbnail sketches of the types of play. There are two groups of preoedipal play: 1. the infant's play with his body parts, functions, and products, and with their replicas, extensions, and protosymbolic representations; 2. his play with the early image of mother. Imagery of grandeur, of perfect ease, seems to accompany his body play (Table, Group I), while "tit-for-tat" appears to be the basic fantasy of play with the mother (Group II). The one is relatively solitary; the other, social. Here I put them under one heading because of their strong interdependence, since the child's solitary play lacks zest and perseverance unless his mother plays with him and since it is predicated on her previous stimulation. For this reason early body play may be viewed as "self-mothering."

Self-observation enters even into the child's earliest play, as each action produces the stimulus for its own repetition. The ego is observer as well as actor. Although the child, or for that matter the adult, may appear to be "driven" in the play he enjoys, his actions remain play as long as there is some "elbow room"—as long as he maintains some minimal distance for self-observation and is able to step out of his play, to stop at any time.

At the oedipal level the child has acquired discursive language. His urgent wishes, which can not realistically be satisfied, compel him to seek symbolic gratifications. His play furnishes those pleasures which in reality are restricted

185

to adults and allows him to enjoy future privileges in the present. His play is colorful; there are unexpected spontaneous turns in it. Often it tells a story: there are successive stages, or even a plot. At this level one may also find play instigated by a traumatic event (cf. Freud-Waelder theory).

Children's overt behavior in the oedipal phase is largely shaped by the parents' attitudes towards the child's strivings. Indeed, this idea applies to all play activities. Adults tend to find it "charming" when a child playfully assumes an adult role, and this in turn not only encourages this kind of play but may also distort what the adult observer sees and reports. Therefore I want to stress that the child's play is not a slipshod or clumsy version of a stage play. Some parts are coherent, then come gaps, repetitions, incongruities. Parsimony and other basic requirements are simply not observed.

> The very perceptive director of a nursery school celebrated Purim with the children by permitting each child to come dressed up as he liked. In earlier years each child's role and costume had been planned beforehand to make sure that there would be no more than one queen Esther, one king, and one uncle Mordechai. With the latter arrangement, however, there were sometimes 3, sometimes 15 queens. No child seemed to mind that duplication: they even took pleasure in it.

A child's playful productions may be deeply moving, but they are not art.

With the passing of the oedipal phase, mental processes gain the ascendancy which are not steered by affects but are based in reality. We speak of the latency or postoedipal phase. The child is now consistently aware of the distance that separates his world from the world of adults. He be-

186

comes more attached to playmates who share his interests, his joys and his sorrows, and his play reflects this. Postoedipal play is primarily group play. The group may consist of several players—a team—or of one player who has a token group at his disposal. Its external appearance varies from marbles to cards to chessmen, but the symbolic significance of this group is always the same. It represents the hero's modest selfless helpers.

Our survey includes the play forms and hobbies of adults, which occupy an ever-growing place in their lives. Increased hours of leisure are, of course, a prerequisite for this phenomenon; but, in my opinion, they are by no means the cause. Adults in our highly industrialized society must adopt a broad spectrum of play forms in order to obtain what their impersonal and routine work can not give them. There is less and less opportunity to be spontaneous, inventive and daring in work, and thus less opportunity to invest libido. Today we turn to a wide variety of sports and collections for narcissistic gratification, for a sense of adventure and for a self-chosen team and competition. We turn to the enjoyment of, or amateur participation in, art and crafts, card games or board games.

In contrast to the child, the adult is often satisfied to be a spectator rather than an actor. Yet it is a misconception to consider a spectator as passive, as outside the game. He is passive if his inner participation is lukewarm, but it may well be passionate. In any case, the "passive" spectator— e.g., the audience in the theatre—is an integral part of any performance. Thus television studios have found that a "live" audience is essential to a good performance.

The materials, the setting, and some of the formal aspects of adult play may differ from those of children's play, but there is no essential difference. Indeed, if we were to omit consideration of adult play, we would blunt our ability to grasp the essence of children's play. The fantasies of adults

187

are fundamentally the same as those of children. Narcissistic gratification is found in sport, where the body performance is enjoyed and repeated with a persistence, and sometimes with a monotony, that those not addicted to that specific sport can often neither understand nor tolerate. Body extensions used for fishing, hunting, baseball or skiing are treated with "tender loving care," as are the objects of collections, whether many others share the collector's respect for their value or consider them bizarre trash. Derivatives of oedipal gratification are sought on the stage or screen, in books or pictures, in hobbies or travel, and post-oedipal gratifications are represented in games.

Some analysts hold the view that the adult plays in order to escape. This seems to me to be misleading for, in that case, one form of play would be as good as another. Actually, choices tend to be highly specific, and high libidinal investment is predicated on the choice. The adult, like the child, seeks in his play the fulfillment of fantasies that are meaningful to him now. However, adults face tasks and frustrations in their lives very different from those with which children deal, and they also have a wider variety of channels for expression open to them. The adult who has had a traumatic experience will not turn to play. He may, for instance talk incessantly about it, he may dream about it, or he may go into a psychotic episode, or he may sublimate or at least displace his anxiety in work.

In comparison with fifty or a hundred years ago, there is today a tremendous increase in adult play activities. Yet if we look to primitive societies the picture again differs. Perhaps in the distant past mankind put vastly more energy into activities akin to play than into work proper. It may be that this shift ultimately can be traced to the question: for whom does one work?

*(Play and Learning)*

188

# NOTES

[1]See *War and Children*, by Anna Freud and Dorothy T. Burlingham. New York: Medical War Books, 1943, pp. 133-34.

[2]Sigmund Freud in *Beyond the Pleasure Principle*.

[3] *The Ego and the Mechanisms of Defense*, by Anna Freud. New York: International Universities Press, 1946.

[4]See "Clinical Notes on Child Analysis," in *Psychoanalytic Study of the Child*, Vol. I. New York: International Universities Press, 1945.

[5]Our term "secondary play gain," analogous to Freud's "secondary gain" in neurosis, is helpful in the analysis of play and in integrating findings of other schools of thought with our findings.

[6]". . . . indeed the child plays the rôle of the mother not only toward itself but also toward other children, animals, and toys, and ultimately and above all toward the mother herself" (Brunswick, 1940, p. 298).

[7]". . . . that all their play is influenced by the desire which dominates this period of life, namely to be big and to do what the big people are doing" (Freud, 1920). See also a very similar statement in "The Relation of the Poet to Daydreaming" (1908).

[8]Incidentally, as far as we know, only the English language has this special term. (Nearest to it is the ancient Greek *agon*.) This is probably connected with certain sociological developments in the history of the Anglo-Saxon orbit. Many of the technical terms used in games, such as "fair play," "handicap," "umpire," have been borrowed by other nations.

[9]An analytic study of various board and card games, such old favorites as chess, checkers, dominoes, etc., and also of the team sports could provide important clues for our understanding of ego and superego developments in latency and maturity. Here we confine our discussion to a few general characteristics.

[10]In "The Passing of the Gentleman," W. N. Evans (1949) discusses the conception of chivalry and states that under certain

conditions "honorable defeat. . . . was preferable to inglorious victory. . . . The aim of the rivalry was not victory at any price, but the narcissistic satisfaction of proving one's own manhood" (p. 25).

[11]The first study of children's games—marble games as played by four- to thirteen-year-olds in certain parts of Switzerland—was presented by Piaget (1932). He not only records minute but significant details of the games and the exacting nature of the rules, but also gives to the reader an almost first-hand experience of how the children's verbal interpretations of these rules are reasonable and coherent for a long period, then show inconsistencies and irrational elements which completely escape the young players' attention.

Piaget divides childhood play into three stages, successively characterized by the use of *practice, symbol* and *rule*. In their content these three stages of play correspond approximately to my group 1, 3, 4 whereas my group 2, i.e., play under the dominance of the relationship to the preoedipal mother, falls between Piaget's group 1 and 2.

Thus when it is a straight tit-for-tat, for instance: the child who just was fed, picks up the spoon to feed another child, it would come under the heading of play which is "sensorimotor practice" because the child's action is "only a reproduction of itself," but if the child takes a piece of paper and pretends to eat it (Piaget, 1952, p. 96) he uses "an inadequate object" to present an absent object—hence there is the beginning of make-believe and thus "symbolic play."

These remarks merely point to superficial similarities and differences between Piaget's grouping of play activities and a psychoanalytically oriented survey. Piaget's conception of play, his choice of criteria, differs basically from ours and only their exhaustive presentation can do justice to his consistent, imaginative and highly perceptive studies.

[12]Freud cites four other clinical examples of children throwing dishes and other household effects out of the window and in each instance the child acts out his own impulse and is not egged on or seduced by adults.

# REFERENCES

Bally, G. (1945), *Vom Ursprung and von den Grenzen der Freiheit*, Basel: Schwabe.

Bornstein, B. (1935), Phobia in a Two-and-a-half-Year-Old Child. *Psa. Quart.*, IV.

Brunswick, R. M. (1940), The Preoedipal Phase of the Libido Development. *Psa. Quart.*, IX.

Burlingham, D. T. (1945), The Fantasy of Having a Twin. *This Annual*, I.

—— (1946), Twins. *This Annual*, II.

Buytendijk, F. J. (1933), *Wesen und Sinn des Spieles*. Berlin: Wolff.

Erikson, E. H. (1937), Configurations in Play. *Psa. Quart.*, VI.

—— (1940), Studies in the Interpretation of Play: Clinical Observation of Play Disruption in Young Children. *Genet. Psychol. Monogr.*, XXII.

Evans, W. N. (1949), The Passing of the Gentleman. *Psa. Quart.*, XVIII.

Freud, A. (1936), *The Ego and the Mechanisms of Defense*, New York: International Universities Press, 1946.

—— 1950, The Significance of the Evolution of Psychoanalytic Child Psychology. *Congrès International de Psychiatrie, Paris 1950*, V.

—— and Burlingham, D. T. (1944), *Infants Without Families*, New York: International Universities Press.

Freud, S. (1908), The Relation of the Poet to Daydreaming. *Collected Papers*, IV. London: Hogarth Press.

—— (1909), Analysis of a Phobia in a Five-Year-Old Boy. *Collected Papers*, III. London: Hogarth Press.

—— (1917), A Childhood Memory from *Dichtung und Wahrheit*. *Collected Papers*, IV. London: Hogarth Press.

—— (1920), *Beyond the Pleasure Principle*. London: Hogarth Press, 1922.

—— (1921), *Group Psychology and the Analysis of the Ego*. London: Hogarth Press, 1922.

—— (1923), *The Ego and the Id*. London: Hogarth Press, 1927.

—— (1931), Female Sexuality. *Collected Papers*, V. London: Hogarth Press, 1950.

Greenacre, P. (1948), Anatomical Structure and Superego Development. *Am. J. Orthopsychiat.*, XVIII.

Greenson, R. R. (1947), On Gambling, *Am. Imago*, IV.

Groos, K. (1896), *Die Spiele der Tiere*. Jena: Gustav Fischer, 1930.

—— (1922), *Das Spiel*, Jena: Gustav Fischer.

Hartmann, H. (1948), Comments on the Psychoanalytic Theory of Instinctual Drives. *Psa. Quart.*, XVII.

—— (1952), The Mutual Influences in the Development of Ego and Id. *This Annual*, VII.

—— Kris, E., and Loewenstein, R. M. (1946), Comments on the Formation of Psychic Structure. *This Annual*, II.

Hendrick, I. (1942), Instinct and the Ego During Infancy. *Psa. Quart.*, XI.

Huizinga, J. (1938), *Homo Ludens*. Basel: Pantheon.

Jacobson, E. (1946), The Child's Laughter. *This Annual*, II.

Jekels, L. and Bergler, E. (1940), Instinct Dualism in Dreams. In: Ludwig Jekels, *Selected Papers*, New York: International Universities Press, 1953.

Jones, E. (1930), The Problem of P. Morphy: A Contribution to the Psychology in Chess. *Essays in Applied Psycho-Analysis*. London: Hogarth Press, 1951.

Kris, E. (1934), Psychology of Caricature. In: *Psychoanalytic Explorations in Art*. New York: International Universities Press, 1952.

—— (1951), Some Comments and Observations on Early Autoerotic Activities. *This Annual*, VI.

—— (1952), *Psychoanalytic Explorations in Art*. New York: International Universities Press.

Lantos, B. (1952), Metapsychological Considerations on the Concept of Work. Int. J. *Psa.*, XXXIII.

Loewenfeld, M. (1935), *Play in Childhood*. London, Gollancz.

Nunberg, H. (1931), The Synthetic Function of the Ego. *Int. J. Psa.*, XII.

Peller, L. E. (1952), Models of Children's Play. *Ment. Hyg.*, XXXVI.

Pfeiffer, S. (1919), Aeusserungen infantil-neurotischer Triebe im Spiele. *Imago*, V.

Piaget, J. (1932), *The Moral Judgment of the Child*. New York: Harcourt.

—— (1952), *Play, Dreams and Imitation in Childhood*. New York: Norton.

Reich, A. (1949), Structure of the Grotesque-Comic Sublimation. *Bull, Menniger Clin.*, XIII.

Waelder, R. (1932), The Psychoanalytic Theory of Play. *Psa. Quart.*, II, 1933.

# 3.

# PLAY AND THE THEORY OF LEARNING

It is my belief that the child's essential learning takes place in play and not in a situation of environmental pressure. Learning theory takes the opposite view. The experiments designed to evoke learning work with rewards and punishments—i.e., with environmental pressure.

As I have pointed out several times, psychoanalysis takes the position that the mental apparatus has as its primary goal the avoidance of displeasure and the attainment of pleasure. There is an early, quick but unreliable way to pursue this goal, and there is a later way which is less hasty and more reliable in its outcome. We speak of the two principles of mental functioning: the pleasure principle and the reality principle. The latter term is misleading: not reality is the focus of the reality principle, but pleasure; however, reality is not ignored, as it is in the earlier phase.

We have suggested in our survey of play that the infant derives intense narcissistic gratification from all that his body can do or produce, and from the things he feels to be similar to these. Through his early repetitive play the infant gradually comes to love those things that he manipulates, and his pleasure induces him to repeat and vary his action. His perceptual and motor skill and his knowledge grow in range, precision, and perseverance. He learns because he enjoys his play.

Play may be divorced from the fulfillment of physiologi-

194

cal needs, but the healthy infant is busy playing all day long. He thrives and develops through play. The self-image which he develops in his early body play and the skills he learns will later enable him to do useful things. I believe that little that is really new is learned in a situation of need, and that in such situations the child—or, for that matter, the animal—simply applies what he has already learned in play ("animal" here refers to higher animals—for the lower species, both learning and play are either absent or vestigial).

Learning theory has in recent decades been responsible for a stupendous amount of experimentation at American universities. However, the question whether learning takes place in play or in a situation of physiological need (receiving a food award, avoiding the pain of an electric shock) does not seem to have even arisen and thus has not been the subject of experimentation. Yet, since 1929 a number of observations which support my view have been on record. For instance, Hilgard reports in his *Theories of Learning* an experiment with rats in a maze. There were two groups of rats. Group A was permitted to explore the maze for ten days without any reward. On the eleventh day a reward of food was given to Group A, and to Group B who had not yet experienced the maze. On the twelfth day Group A surpassed Group B in their ability to negotiate the maze.

This seems to me clearcut evidence that learning took place during the time when the rats were engaged in playful exploration of the maze. Yet the experimentor, and other learning theorists, explain the results differently: They refer to the learning that took place without reward as "latent learning," the implication being that "latent" learning is not yet real learning, and that the reward transformed latent into manifest learning. The introduction of this concept of latent learning obviates the need to make two major theoretical changes in the edifice of Learning Theory that would otherwise be unavoidable: 1. the notion that there is no need to deal with behavior that is not visible, and 2. the principle that all learning is adaptive and caused by environmental pressure.

A very skillful student of animal behavior, Schiller, provides even more telling proof that learning takes place in play.* He reproduced Koehler's famous stick-using experiments with chimpanzees and obtained very different results. He states that Koehler's observation

> points out that the joining [of two sticks] was made in play, but then was immediately utilized for work. My chimpanzees learned it rapidly after a few trials, but they played a lot with the double stick before incorporating it into the problem solution.

He continues:

> The same animals who performed the stick-connecting in play were not all able to solve a pulling-in problem by connecting the same sticks. . . . The problem of joining sticks was never solved . . . by animals who had not performed the connection in play. They were more retarded in utilizing it for work than the ready players. It is obvious, then, that presence of the play-performance is a prerequisite for the solution of the stick-joining problem. The pattern must be readily available before it can be utilized, and it is not the pressure of a need that makes it emerge, but on the contrary, such a pressure represses it, if it is not highly available.

*Cf. Schiller, P. H. "Innate Constituents of Complex Responses in Primates," Psychological Review, 59, 177-191, 1952. This author should not be confused with Friedrich von Schiller, the famous 18th century German playwright, poet, and philosopher, whom we mentioned as the originator of the "Schiller-Spencer theory" of play. (Ed.)

Schiller's description leaves no doubt that the animals which he observed learned the new behavior in play, improved it in play, and often preferred playing to the "useful" application of the skill they had acquired. He also quotes this observation by Birch (1945):

> Chimpanzees 5 to 6 years of age were quite clumsy in their first attempt to use sticks as implements, but the same animals, after having had access to sticks to play with for three days, showed remarkable improvement in problem solutions.

It is interesting to note that Schiller, despite his own findings, refers to the "purposeless motor patterns" of the chimpanzees and to their "learning without any specific motivation." His description leaves no doubt that the chimpanzees derived pleasure from their play, but he obviously did not see this as either motivation or purpose. Such narrow definition of terms blocks the path to better understanding of human behavior.

*(Play and Learning)*

As far as educational literature has been influenced by psychoanalysis, it has recently on occasion equated the play of children with daydreaming of adolescents and adults. That the two phenomena are developmentally identical is indeed the decisive point for the analytical psychologist; but the practitioner (and education is a practical field) can not take this viewpoint.

Freud has in another context compared the daydream to a protected wilderness area. Both are reservations set aside to enable original conditions to survive. Children's play is not such a reservation. Indeed, it is largely the opposite: the child keeps trying again and again to work through the stimuli that accost it from the outside.

197

The adult who observes the playing child fondly admires his inexhaustible imagination—i.e., his ability to create distance between himself and the reality that hems us in. The admiration is based on the thought, this child is still so small, and already he has so much imagination. But the distance from reality is a given for the child, has been with him from his origin. If any "achievement" is to be seen in the child's play, it is rather in the very opposite: in his ability to approach reality through play, to master in due course all the new things that forever claim his attention, the demands of reality.

Seen thus, child's play is as purposeful a device as the dream. The dream masters excitations that approach us from within, as experiences of the day have stirred up the deepest layers. Play masters excitations which as a rule are coming directly from the external world; it is rare that they already raise any claims from inside us (we are leaving the layering of that "inside us"—i.e., of the ego—outside of consideration).

The function of play is at least as vital as that of the dream. Let us continue this teleological consideration. The dream gives us but a primary transformation of our wishes and impulses. The resulting absurdities are unimportant since sleep inhibits our motor action and they therefore can not affect reality. It can likewise be said of play that what absurdities it contains remains innocuous (or almost so?), as the child lacks the physical and mental powers to translate its fantasies consistently into reality.

Child's play, however, is not to be considered mere fantasies which the child acts out instead of merely imagining them. It is rather a synthesis of fantasies and suggestions from the external world. "Suggestions" sounds harmless, but the word must cover all the demands and frustrations which the external world inflicts on the child. Play is an important help to the child in overcoming these hardships.

198

It is the approach to reality that fits the child. At least a great part of play has this function.

We damage the child if we impair his play activity, but also if we overly foster play that is removed from reality. If so many educators glorify play removed from reality, this is less a matter of pedagogy than of the adults' psychology. The adult uses every opportunity to escape oppressive reality.

In play the child learns to tolerate reality. But he will only recognize and draw into his play such reality as is pleasurable, alluring, and interesting. If it isn't, he will withdraw as much as possible into himself even in his play.

If education wants to help the child to control his instinctual impulses, it must give him the chance to engage in activities that for him are pleasurable, and that at the same time demand the commitment of his entire intelligence. Only if both these conditions are fulfilled will it be possible to contain the aggression, the domineering drive of the child and to lead toward sublimations.

Education can fall into two errors:

Activities are permitted without regard for the child's wishes. This mistake is mostly found in school. The performances it demands of him do not flow from his original tendencies. Seen from the aspect of the child's inner development, they are rather arbitrary.

Or, the activities put at the child's disposal are pleasurable enough, but they allow his energy to fizzle out in the area of the playful instead of utilizing them to overcome difficulties and thus to elicit and stress them. This is the mistake committed in the usual occupations in nurseries schools.

The child comes to nursery school to play. At six he gets to school and has suddenly to produce performances which are precisely normed as to content and timing. Neither offers much of an opportunity for sublimation. We consider it the superiority of the Montessori method that it opens up to the small child opportunities for activity which were so far (in our cultural environment) out of his reach.

The teacher whom we tell of a special method of education and instruction will be ready with the question, but how will the child be able to acquire the knowledge and skill demanded of him on his respective age level? The psychoanalyist will raise the opposite question, how does this method help the child to control his instinctual impulses?

(*Education*)

Play activities can be regarded as primary processes that are not merely carried out in thought but are in addition acted out. There is an admixture of secondary processes; it increases substantially as the child gets older. Reality testing is never as rudimentary in play as it is in dreams (contrary to the more customary viewpoint, I consider the thought "this is only a dream" to be a kind of reality testing.)

As a definition of play this is obviously too broad. Psychotic and neurotic behavior on the one hand, and artistic and scientific pursuits on the other, are not play—though the latter are rooted in it and often merge with it. Compulsive, self-injurious, or highly formalized (stereotyped) behavior falls outside the area we have delimited as play.

I consider play the matrix of all our later interactions with out environment. Skills and objects are used for symbolic gratification before they are used rationally for the gratification of physiological needs. We might express it even more strongly: Through play the child learns to use things in a sober way. As the child plays, his awareness, knowledge, and skill grow. Most of all, the range of the pleasures he can experience grows.

An adaptive act reaches its goal and is completed, whereas play actions can be repeated—indeed, they ask for repeti-

200

tion and variation. The playing child responds continually to self-initiated stimuli. Higher animals also play. But maternal care covers only a part of their physiological needs (food, warmth, protection from enemies) and that for a limited time only. Adaptive, realistic actions therefore compete with play and often take precedence over it. The human child, however, puts from the beginning of life all his zest into play pursuing it with greater abandon and persistence than any other primate.

The early play forms precede the acquisition of language. Many statements in the literature about play are quite correct—except that they leave out the early play forms. Huizinga saw play as the most characteristic function of man and developed the thesis that all our cultural achievements—science, art, religion, philosophy, law— originate in play. He gave this definition:

> . . . a free activity standing quite consciously outside "ordinary" life as being "not serious," but at the same time absorbing the player intensely and utterly. It is an activity connected with no material interest, and no profit can be gained by it. It proceeds within its own proper boundaries of time and space, according to fixed rules and in an orderly manner.

While excellent in the way in which it points to the salient features of play, this definition is too narrow. We may try for a sociological definition—a far simpler undertaking than the psychological one.

Sociologically speaking, any activity which is pursued for the remuneration that society offers for it is work, while play needs no such recognition. From this follows another distinction: While work must be carried to completion, play can be stopped any time we like. The same activity, however, may be either work or play—e.g., we can collect

201

stamps or play bridge as a hobby or as a way of making a living.

Ego interests, instinctual drives, and super-ego demands arrive at a modus vivendi in play. The immediate results of play are inconsequential; unlike work, they have little impact on the player's physical environment. Such useful and not ephemeral changes that do occur are unintended side effects. Play, however, changes the player. It alters his emotional balance, mood, skills, understanding, self-image, and the range of his imagination. It is because play changes the player that it is the matrix of all other human achievements.

(*Play and Learning*)

# Section IV.

## Language—From Children's Books to Language Theory

# Editor's Comments

This section of our selection represents the development of Lili Peller's interest in language and literature. I remember the exquisite collection of old children's books she started back in Vienna, and how she got us intrigued in recognizing the value of style and of illustrations in books for children. Then—as in everything else—her interest moved from the joy of seeing children respond to books to fascination with their intrapsychic response to reading (see her papers of 1958 and 1959, numbers 2 and 3 in this Section), and finally to the development of language. She eventually joined the Study Group in Language Theory and Psychoanalysis at the New York Psychoanalytic Institute. Dr. Victor H. Rosen, the chairman of the Group, spoke of this at the Memorial Meeting for Lili Peller in 1966:

> I knew Lili Peller well for only a little more than two years before she died. Before then, I knew her from her writings, as a casual acquaintance, and as an intent thoughtful listener who attended many of the same psychoanalytic meetings that I did. One day, having heard of the Study Group, she asked me if she could join as an "observer." With her characteristic humility she seemed to be saying, "I will just listen and not bother any one with my own ideas." I told her that her presence in the group as a fully participant member

would place us in her debt. Lili had just published one of her best papers on "Language and Its Pre-Stages,"* and I knew that she had more to teach us than she had to learn from us. In this paper she developed the stimulating and, I thought, quite novel hypothesis that human instinctual structure has more to do with the phylogenesis of language than man's complex ego equipment (although she would say that both were necessary).

This idea is, of course, closely akin to what has since become known as the Chomskian Revolution in linguistics.

*The Uses of Enchantment* by Bruno Bettelheim, a man whose thinking had been shaped by the same milieu as Lili Peller's, was written more than twenty years after her articles on the emotional meaning of stories for children. His book focuses on folk fairy tales and their special quality to help children in the oedipal phase to come to grips with problems of their role in the family, and as a "by-product" to strengthen the relationship to the story teller—mostly the mother. For severely disturbed children fairy tales had been, in Bettelheim's experience, especially helpful.

Lili Peller looks at children's literature more as it affects and entrances children after they have learned to read, and pre-adolescents. Both authors seem to bring to the discussion a good deal of their personal experience. Bettelheim writes in his introduction how much he thanks his mother for having introduced him to "the enchantment" as a listener; Lili Peller, the independent child and student, found this satisfaction in her own activity.

Her move from the more concrete thinking and writing, as in the papers of 1958 and 1959, to a more abstract level,

*A part of this paper is contained in Section II of this book, and a smaller part opens this Section.

as we find it here and in "Freud's Contribution to Language Theory," was probably a sign of two developments in her life: less input from daily contact with children and their teachers, and the high level of maturity which helped her deal with complex thoughts and formulations. Here is an example of Peller's ability to formulate, from a paper included later in this Section.

That a child envies the grownups has always been known, but Freud pointed to the direct gross male (or female) aspirations which go with the wish to be big. These fantastic aspirations make the child's happy illusions and his downfall so intense and potentially traumatic.

# 1.

# FROM "LANGUAGE AND ITS PRE-STAGES"

Language is a powerful tool influencing the child's life. The development of language and hence of language skills promotes or retards all segments of the child's cognitive development. It is well known that children from lower socioeconomic strata score on intelligence tests as a group significantly lower than children from privileged homes. This used to be ascribed to factors inherent in the respective genetic makeup of the groups. The lower economic strata were considered to be on the whole less endowed intellectually. Today this difference is related primarily or fully to the differential cultural levels of the children's homes.

Could instruction influence and improve the intelligence of children from underprivileged homes? The answer is that the child's vocabulary (the range of understood words) can be increased by direct instruction and a greater vocabulary gives a higher rating on an intelligence test. Indeed, even the presence or absence of a TV in the home seems to influence children's test performance. Yet after participating and watching the nursery school field for over forty years, I have learned to watch carefully the effects of any direct teaching and any specific exercise introduced in the nursery school. But nursery schools are or could be well fitted for another significant contribution; they could offer opportunities for *observing language development*. This could be done without major changes or investments. It is impos-

208

sible to study the specific features of the child's language in a laboratory as we study and test narrowly defined skills or specific information. Prolonged language studies can only rarely be carried out in family homes. They presuppose an environment where activities are organized, yet flexible, a setting encouraging outgoing, spontaneous behavior. In nursery school we could study the changing pattern, the changing functions of language, the influence of play-mates, of important emotional events in the child's life, the interdependence of language with other segments of early development. My hunch is that the next significant advances in our understanding of children's development will come in the field of language.

# 2.

## DAYDREAMS AND CHILDREN'S FAVORITE BOOKS

## PSYCHOANALYTIC COMMENTS

When well-known authors write for children they seldom take pride in it. In former centuries they often chose a pseudonym, while more recently they apparently consider it necessary to explain it—albeit apologize for it. (A closer examination of the field necessitates a revision: since about the 1930's the writing of a children's book has for many writers become a token of "having arrived," of being a successful author.) Ironically enough, there are quite a few authors whose other writings have sunk into oblivion—yet the children's story they wrote has kept its freshness and is still in print. Their name would be forgotten if it were not for the juvenile they wrote. A writer may tell us how he tossed off a children's book in a few leisurely hours. While this is not likely to increase the general public's respect for juveniles, it makes us more curious about the vitality of the daydream behind the story.

In recent decades the esteem for writers of children's books has greatly risen, in line with the general tendency to relish a much wider range of productions in all fields of art (for instance, primitive, exotic, psychotic, and frankly amateurish art). In keeping with this trend, a publisher sometimes even brings out a story written and illustrated by a child. Such a book may be very appealing because its author is so genuine, so earnest, so involved in his own writing—but as a story it usually falls flat.

210

Six-year-olds Absorbed in Reading a Story Together

—Photo by Fritz Winter

But a child can spin a daydream with such emotional intensity that he will remember it in later years; indeed, he may live his life under its spell. This is especially true when at a time of inner turmoil, he encounters his own, his private daydream woven into a story. Sometimes we discover only in analysis the strong grip that an early story has had on a person's life. Usually it is one scene of the story or one story character which is vested with emotional significance.

"The poet arouses in us emotions of which we hardly believed ourselves capable" (Freud, 1908). If the adult reader cherishes this ability of the poet, the child with his unlimited eagerness to savor life is wide open to the magic of the storyteller.

A fear or anxiety which remains covered up in everyday life may become broadly visible through the child's reaction to a story. But while a tale may frighten a child, it may give relief too. He discovers that he is not the only one in the world who harbors fears or hatred or spite, emotions that are socially unacceptable. Thus the recent well-meant endeavors to purge stories of all cruelties, of all mean feelings and of vengeance may actually increase a child's guilt feelings and the burden he carries unaided.

"The poet enables us to enjoy our own daydreams without shame or guilt" (Freud, 1908). The story gives greater emotional courage to the child's own daydream. On the intellectual level he acquires new dimensions, new concepts and images for his reveries. Before he encountered the story, his own daydream may have been unconscious or conscious or have lost access to consciousness (becoming repressed), and now regains it or comes close to consciousness. The child identifies primarily with the hero. Yet things are not always so simple and transparent: the listener may also identify with the antagonist—a point mentioned by Buxbaum (1941).

212

Earlier studies emphasized the direct gratification a story can offer: there are the scoptophilic and oral aspects, the taking in through eyes and ears. The excitement accompanying a thrilling story (producing red cheeks, glassy eyes, tenseness or restlessness) seems comparable to masturbation and sometimes merges into it. Yet the support of defense functions through reading appears far more prominent.

On a deep level, the child's desire for stories is related to the desire to see what the adults are doing. In the "Children's Hour" the child travels beyond the walls of the nursery, seeing and listening to what goes on in the adult's world. For this excursion, however, he has his parents' sanction; the storytelling adult has taken his hand and leads him there. It is not an illicit transgression. The "Children's Hour" occurs at dusk and if it was successful, i.e., bringing excitement and relieving it, the story hour detracts from the anxiety-filled wish to peek when the "Parents' Hour" comes later at night.

A story heard today may be retold tomorrow with great though unconscious distortions. The reverse is also true: apparently insignificant details stay amazingly fresh in the memory after decades. The retelling of a story almost resembles a projective test. Obviously, the tale is either faithfully preserved or changed and garbled up, according to a person's daydreams.

I am venturing another suggestion: children are presented with stories at a very early age and the experience of gaining pleasure from something that is past, that is gone, may lead to an increased cathexis of his own memories. If my view if correct, fantasy here enhances contact with reality.

"The young child lives at first entirely in the present." This is well known and can be translated into psychoanalytic terms: at first only the concrete Here and Now is

213

cathected. Memory traces are hazy and fragmented, unless there is a reason for cathecting them. After having savored gratification from a narrative, from a pleasing account, there will be an added incentive for a young child to extend interest to his own private store of images, to his memories.

Dream, daydream, story—they are related, yet distinctly different; indeed, so different that we lack a term encompassing them all and thereby pointing to their common denominator. A story, even a highly fantastic one, follows mostly the secondary process.[1] Yet while seemingly all absorbed by the story, the listener may spin his own daydream. The story supplies the key word or the allusion which triggers off his own fantasy.

I am going to discuss a number of typical childhood fantasies and some of the stories built on them. Let us start with a plot intended for the very young.

### The Fantasy of Loss and Return

A child loses his mother and, after dangerous adventures, is reunited with her. Any number of stories use this plot. Because it appeals to the youngest listener, the child in the story is often an animal child. This has the advantage that more gruesome adventures can be included. With an animal as the central figure, the storyteller can introduce the cannibalistic fears and fantasies of young children and thus increase the drama (see, e.g., *The Story about Ping, the Duckling; Peter Rabbit; Curious George, the Monkey*). It is the child who acts out, who runs away, but his leaving is often preceded by some fault or negligence of his mother (or protector) mentioned very casually, and hardly noticed by the reader—the story really gains momentum with the child's escapade.

Let us look at the best known story for very young children, *The Tale of Peter Rabbit*. His mother warns him not to

214

go *near* Mr. McGregor's garden. She has hardly left on her shopping trip when Peter runs right into that forbidden territory. He finds it absolutely full of delicacies, young radishes and tender salad leaves, but Peter's happiness in stuffing himself is very short-lived. He is chased and almost caught and killed. Is it all Peter's fault? It looks this way, yet it never would have happened if his mother had not considered a shopping trip more important than looking after her children.

And so it goes also in the other stories. *Curious George* would not have ended up in jail had his protector not left him alone on their very first day in the big city where George was surrounded by gadgets tempting him to manipulate them. It is the mother who, by turning her attention temporarily to other matters, loosens the bond between herself and the child (A. Freud, 1953). Even in this simplest type of story there is a conscious plot and another one which reaches consciousness for a brief moment, then sinks back to the preconscious or unconscious. Yet this part contributes to the story's emotional appeal as well as to the motivation and the plausibility of the story hero's conduct. In all art, essential parts remain on the unconscious or preconscious level, and the nursery tale is no exception.

In these stories for very young readers, animals feel, behave, and talk like human beings. But these fantastic elements are not essential; the very same daydream may also be expressed in a cogently realistic story; see e.g., *Oley, the Sea Monster*. Oley is a baby seal that gets picked up and carried away by a sailor while his mother dives for some food. An exciting adventure story follows, with funny and with deeply moving events—but nothing that could not have happened in reality. The book even carries a map showing the route through the Great Lakes, the St. Lawrence and around Nova Scotia by which Oley swam back to his mother.

Tales of *fantasy* and realistic, "true" stories are considered to be basically different, yet we find that every childhood fantasy can become the backbone for either type of story.

*The Fantasy of the Reversal of Roles*

The young son (the small one, the simpleton), the shy one who always is left out of things, proves to be stronger than all his older brothers when a great danger arises. Thus he not only slays the dragon and wins the princess, he also rescues his friends or his father's kingdom—in short, he becomes the beloved and admired benefactor. This is the core of many fairy tales, in which it is often the third, the youngest son whom nobody has taken seriously, and who wins after his older brothers have failed.[2] This is the plot of *Hop o'My Thumb*, of John Ruskin's famous *The King of the Golden River*, and also of the Biblical legend of Joseph and his brothers. The contrast of who seems to be strong and powerful and who is small and helpless, and the sudden unexpected reversal of roles provide the spice of these stories. Again there are completely realistic stories with the same plot, for instance the French story *Moustachio*. Moustachio is the smallest dog in his village, indeed, ridiculously small. Yet on the day of the great hunt, he is the one who finds and holds the vicious wild boar at bay until his master comes and fires the deadly shot. The storyteller's skill, his use of relevant details, makes the improbable victory plausible. Touches of humor are used for the same purpose. Maybe the bigger dogs could not penetrate the thicket surrounding the boar's cave, while agile, small Moustachio could slip in? Maybe he was pursuing a field mouse and got near the boar's stronghold merely by accident? The fact remains that once there he fiercely stood his ground, and thus from being the butt of ridicule he rises to fame.

216

## Heroic Tale—Oedipal-Level Stories

In these tales the hero obtains the goals of oedipal wishes in a form which is acceptable to the ego of the latency child. What we know of other latency fantasies also applies here: their ingredients are akin to those which in stories, dramas, operas, and ballads appeal to an adult audience. The essentials of these fantasies have been presented by Freud (1908, 1909b), and its juvenile version was studied by Friedlaender (1942), whose work remains to be of basic importance.

The hero or the heroine lives with one parent or some relatives. Thus at the outset of the story the parents, or at least the parent of the same sex, have been eliminated without the hero's guilt. The grownups in the story accept the child hero as one of them, not as a child. The story depicts the hero's struggle against adverse circumstances and against the villain or villains. But being fearless, resourceful, and a paradigma of many virtues, his eventual triumph is assured.

Friedlaender mentions the following favorite books which use this fantasy: *David Copperfield, Jane Eyre, Treasure Island, Emil and the Detectives*; Anna Freud (1936) has already pointed to *Little Lord Fauntleroy*, and to various fairy tales. Friedlaender attributes the overwhelming popularity of *Jane Eyre* to the fact that in this story the oedipal wish attains a "relatively undisguised" fulfillment. Here I do not follow her. It is the very art of storytelling that the fulfillment of the primal wish is achieved and at the same time skillfully veiled. Occasionally, it even remains barred from consciousness. There is only one other alternative left to the artist: a hero (or heroine) who attains undisguised gratification goes to his own destruction—like Oedipus. But Jane, after long and tragic trials and tribulations, eventually marries her man, and they live fairly happily ever after. Throughout the story, Jane is a very proper girl. I do not agree that in her story the oedipal fantasies "break through

217

in almost bare-faced fashion." Yet Friedlaender is right in one point: the gratification in Jane Eyre seems more direct than, for instance, in *Treasure Island* or *David Copperfield*.

A remark of Freud helps us to understand Jane Eyre's seemingly more overt wish fulfillment. In his story the poet may incorporate the boy's version of the oedipal wish—centering on gratification of aggression and ambition—or the poet may build the story on the feminine counterpart and focus on direct libidinal gratification: a prince charming who leads the heroine home. But it is a difference of focus only—both versions contain or allude to both gratifications, the erotic and the ambitious one.

*The Little Mermaid* also belongs to this group, and from this old favorite we get another glimpse of how a poet uses his materials: the little mermaid's older sisters too have taken good looks at "the upper world," each one enjoying this privilege on her fifteenth birthday, but none fell hopelessly in love with a human as she does with the prince. The fairy tale does not give the reason for this infatuation at first sight—otherwise it would not be a fairy tale but a case history. But at the beginning, when we hear of the sisters' early childhood, there is an incidental comment about the flower beds which they owned and tended and how each one decorated her plot with shells and many strange objects, while the youngest had only one figure on hers—the statue of a little *boy*, a statue of white marble which had come down from a sunken ship. By chance or choice the image of a human was imprinted upon her in her sensitive childhood years. This part of the plot is crucial in understanding the heroine's later behavior, yet it quickly slips from the reader's awareness. The poet moves us, then provides other details superseding the one through which he drew us into the story and evoked our unconscious understanding.[3]

218

While many stories employ the same basic fantasy and thus have similarities, we also find that every single story deviates from this fantasy and has unique features—if it were otherwise, we would not be dealing with works of art.

## The Bad Boy Story

The two foregoing fantasies—Reversal of Roles and Hero Story—are variations of the same daydream. There exists a third variation: the Bad Boy Story. The hero, as you remember, is all virtue. The only point where he deviates from a schoolmaster's ideal is his fearlessness, indeed his defiance of persons in authority.

Now the main figure in the Bad Boy Story is the hero's antipode: he lacks all the hero's virtues and he makes a big display of his badness. But in one point he does resemble the virtuous hero: he, too, is impervious to the general awe accorded by everybody else to the story's father images. Actually, not many stories exist in which this fantasy provides the main plot. There is the anonymous *Bad Boy's Diary*, and Crompton's *Just William*. In German we find the famous *Lausbuben Stories* (L. Thoma) and the pranks of *Max and Moritz* (W. Busch).

My impression is that these tales are not really children's high-ranking favorites. They are cordially received by "staid and sober men" whom they support in reminiscing about (and aggrandizing) their own boyish daredevil adventures. This kind of nostalgic reveries might be called daydreams in reverse, i.e., daydreams projected into a mythical past instead of into a rosy future.

While accounts of carefree badness seldom provide the core of a story, they are often woven in as a side line (the most famous example is *Tom Sawyer*).

## The Fantasy of Having a Twin

This fantasy has been dealt with so lucidly by Dorothy Burlingham (1945, 1952) that I will quote only briefly from

219

her findings and supplement them. She considers it "a conscious fantasy, built up in the latency period as the result of disappointment by the parents." The child searches "for a partner who will give him all the attention, love and companionship he desires and who will provide an escape from loneliness." To this we may add that this fantasy of a companion whose devotion never falters also gives relief from sibling competition and rivalry. Moreover, it not only compensates for the disappointment inflicted by the parents, it may also serve as a defense against oedipal seduction through parents who tend toward too much physical intimacy with the child. Like many latency fantasies, this one may present a shortcut to grownupness. Burlingham also mentions the fantasy's narcissistic gratifications: "Self-love appears under the mask of object love."

As a variation of the twin fantasy she denotes the fantasy of an animal companion, an "understanding, dumb, always loving creature." In this group belong the many fantasies of a boy-dog or boy-pony friendship, which have been woven into perceptive stories, sometimes combining autobiographical elements (Steinbeck, *The Red Pony*). There are many beloved and famous horse stories for boys and girls. In the girl's fantasy, the horse, according to Friedlaender, stands for the lost penis. In my opinion, the colt, the kitten, or the puppy in the boy's story substitute for a baby, and this meaning may also shine through in an autobiography. Thus, both sexes derive gratification by making the pony or the dog the symbol of what they cannot have in reality. The boy's wish for a baby is more dangerous than the girl's for a penis and must be removed further from consciousness.

In some stories twins are given dissimilar characters so that "they are as two halves of one person," and "talk and behave as complements to each other" (Mark Twain's *The Prince and the Pauper*).

Burlingham discusses "absolute identity in appearance,"

and this feature of twin fantasies is subject to exceptions in the way all typical features of fantasies are. The example which comes to mind first is the picture story of *Max and Moritz*, a real childhood classic. A wisp of Max's hair stands up, while that of Moritz streaks all down; their clothing is different. Otherwise, in all their famous-infamous pranks, not one difference between them pops up—their unity in defying authority and planning mischief is perfect.

Another story built on the fantasy of invincibility achieved through doubling or multiplying the hero is told in the old folk tale of *The Five Chinese Brothers*. One of the five brothers, who lived with their mother, was unjustly accused of a crime and sentenced to die. Now all of the brothers looked exactly alike, but each one possessed a unique magical gift—the neck of one brother consisted of iron, the legs of another could stretch indefinitely, etc. The condemned brother accepts his death sentence, asking only permission to go home first to bid good-bye to his mother. Knowing that the judge has ordered him to be beheaded, the brother, whose neck cannot be cut, goes instead. Well, the executioner does not succeed in chopping the man's head off and so the judge orders death by drowning. But again the brother is allowed to go home to take leave from his mother. Next morning, the third brother steps in for the condemned one, and as he is thrown into the deep ocean, his legs stretch and stretch until they reach ground. And so the brothers replace and save one another until the watching crowd gets tired and the judge gives up and declares the boy's innocence.

## The Stories for "Have Nots"

This group may not seem to be a counterpart to the others mentioned so far, but rather a catchall term for a number of types, namely, for all stories which owe their special appeal less to the tale they spin or to the story characters they bring to life than to the *milieu* they describe. This discrepancy disappears when we extend the meaning of the term "daydream" to indicate not only a narrative, a sequence of events, but also a static *tableau*, the vision of a blissful scene, which includes the daydreamer in his enjoyment of a coveted environment. The readers of these tales are recruited from the ranks of those who pine for an ambiance not attainable to them in reality. Here we think of the story describing ways and joys of *teenagers* for those who are still too timid or too young for them; there are the stories of *school life*, i.e., life in a British public school for those who are too young, or, more often, who do not quite belong to the socioeconomic strata who can afford such a school (Orwell, 1939). There are *nature, mystery, adventure, big game* and *Wildwest* stories for those who are barred from these experiences in reality. One generation ago, youthful readers loved historical novels which took them into a romanticized past. Today, stories of space travel have partly replaced them.

Of course, all these stories have also a hero; he has satellites and adversaries; there is a plot, and the story may represent hack-writing or may be well done—in either event a greal deal of the attraction is due to the coveted milieu into which the readers are transposed. This is their bait; and this formula is by no means restricted to juveniles but accounts for the popularity of many books, movies, and plays for all ages.

Books may give pleasure through more than one fantasy. Biographies enable the reader to identify with a father image. You have to be famous to rate a biography, and achieving fame can be translated into psychoanalytic concepts as achieving a flamboyant oedipal victory. But a well-written biography does more than this: by reporting personal anecdotes, by letting the reader in on trivial day-by-day incidents, it fosters in him the illusion of hobnobbing

222

with the great and the mighty. This is our reason for mentioning biographies here among the "Have Not" stories. (Receiving factual information may of course be also highly pleasurable, but is outside our topic.)

I suspect that the countless "How-To-Do-It" books, pamphlets and magazines describing hobbies and skills of amateurs are cherished not only by the "doers," to whom they deliver technical information, but also (or mainly?) by the "idlers," for whom they substitute for the doing. Not only an imaginative tale, also a sober step-by-step account can incite and feed daydreams.

I have presented typical daydreams paraphrasing the important emotional constellations of childhood. There is the relationship of the little child to the protective and despotic preoedipal mother. The young child cannot fight her, nor oppose her—the drama is restricted to the possibility of escape and return or rescue. The Loss-and-Return fantasy is really an elaboration of the infant's earliest play activity, the peek-a-boo game. There the plot also consists of separation and reunion.

Several types of daydreams mirror the oedipal tension. The Reversal-of-Roles fantasy deals with the relationship to older siblings and to the early father, experienced as fearfully big and strong. The Hero and Heroine fantasies refer more directly to the oedipal constellation. The Bad-Boy stories glorify open defiance of all father images. Actually both the Hero and the Bad-Boy stories tell of oedipal victory, but the bad boy's triumph is quickly attained and short-lived, while the hero attains his goal the slow and arduous way. There are the fantasies of having a twin, an alter ego, or a most faithful companion; and finally the last-mentioned omnibus group which "sells" admission to the coveted but unattainable milieu. Thus daydreams born and fomented by all basic childhood constellations seem

223

covered—but the best group of stories for the young child is still to be discussed.

## The Early Tale

I am speaking of such universal favorites as the *Christopher Robin* stories, *The Story of Dr. Dolittle*, the *Mary Poppins* books, and Grahame's *The Wind in the Willows*. In some respect, the books of *Babar, the Elephant* also belong here.

In all groups discussed so far we find books which are little masterpieces and others where the writer has learned the formula and uses it glibly. But in this last group I know of no such hack-writing. These are tales which cannot easily be imitated. If not handled by a literary master, the plot would fall apart, and there would not be left a story worth the telling.

In *Winnie—the Pooh*, for instance, there is a group of toy animals who for all intents and purposes are alive, although they are at the same time plain stuffed animals. Each one lives in his own house—but all are within easy walking distance from each other. They share adventures and expeditions and all kinds of pleasures and hardships. Winnie—the Pooh is not their leader, but ranks first in seniority, he is *primus inter pares*. And he is a conceited, greedy, but lovable toy bear. The real leader, the figure who turns up in emergencies, is Christopher Robin, the five-year-old to whom they all belong. Only a few lines of each chapter deal with C.R. in person, but when he is badly needed he is right at hand. The personality of each toy animal emerges clearly and so do the positive, the likeable as well as the weaker qualities of its character.

Now let us take a quick glance at *Dr. Doolittle*. He is an elderly, smallish, shy doctor. The drawings show him pot-bellied, bald, a rather ridiculous figure. His outstanding qualities are his simplicity and kindness. No part of the globe is too distant to travel to when he learns about sick animals in need of his magical cure. His home is in the English country side; originally his sister kept house for him, but she became disgusted and left when the doctor refused to give up the crocodile who ate up the linoleum. As the tale begins, the good doctor lives all alone with his faithful animals, a parrot, a dog, a baby pig, an owl, a duck, and a monkey. These, his household companions, are introduced by name and drawn as individual characters. Besides them are nameless throngs of animals who move in and out of the story.

The central figure of another classic series is *Mary Poppins*, the governess whom the eastwind blows into the home of four children at number Seventeen Cherry Tree Lane. The pictures show her rather unkindly as an old-fashioned, bony spinster with quite shabby yet frilly clothing and accessories. She is at times harsh, moody, often snappy in her commands and answers—but she works magic and enjoys a terrific reputation with various mysterious personages. Her children have wonderful adventures and thus are willing to put up with her occasional bad days.

And, finally, *The Wind in the Willows* (*The Wind in the Reeds*, as it was originally called) tells the story of four devoted friends, Toad, Rat, Mole and Badger. Each one has his own house and each house is quite different from the others. Rat lives at the bank of the busy river, Toad is rich and keeps residence in a splendid mansion, Badger's ancient and many-chambered home is in the Wild Woods, and Mole has very modest ("compact," his friends call it) quarters underground. Among the friends there is continuous visiting, passing by and dropping in, and staying for hours and days and sumptuous meals. These casual visits alternate with adventures undertaken jointly by two or three of them. The Almighty Protector of this chummy group appears only once. He is the Piper-at-the-Gates-of-Dawn, whose presence is felt long before he is seen, whose sweet chant is heard before he appears as a faun-shaped figure. Yet his animals know that in distress he will be at their side.

The togetherness of these friends, their deep loyalty, fills the book and shows in their cozy visits as well as in their wild and glorious adventures. Their enemies are nameless and faceless flocks of animals. A few incidentally introduced humans stay at the fringe of the narrative and their feelings remain hazy and are not really woven into the story. They appear and disappear as their function in the story requires, not growing into story characters.

Here are four obviously very diverse tales. They differ not only in plot, in characters, in style, they also appeal to different age groups and are far apart in their literary levels. What, then, do they have in common? In each story we find a Group of loyal friends and we find a Protector who can work magic (at least in the eyes of his entourage; whatever five-year-old Christopher plans or figures out appears as magic to his toy animals). Every member of this group has unique gifts and skills and foibles. In the animal stories there is usually *one* of a kind, one of a species, and animals who in reality could never live together, like a badger and a toad, or a pig and a parrot, are intimates. No member of the circle is defined as either young or old, as male or female.[4] The magician-protector's sex is given, but he (or she) is of an age or appearance where genital maleness or femaleness is of little consequence. (To recapture their similarities as well as their crass differences let them pass quickly before our mental eye: the pathetic little doctor with his top hat; Mary Poppins with her shabby, old-fashioned bag; Christopher Robin who is still more a baby than a regular boy; the frail but very rich Old Lady, who equips Babar and later his royal residence, Celesteville; and the early Piper, the Faun whose form, barely perceived, dissolves, and melts into the foliage.)

The magician-protector stays offstage or near the wings

and the friends' actions and their feelings really carry the story. The character of each one of them is etched distinctly, although age and sex are left vague. In these tales *the two great dichotomies, male-female, old-young*, which pervade and shape our life and bring so much pressure upon the ego of the young child, are mostly nonexistent. These stories seem to say: "See what good times and how much adventure you can have if you just forget and ignore those things."

The friends in these stories are devoted to one another, yet their love is conflict-free. There is no jealousy. Let us see what else is absent. Family relations of all kinds are nonexistent or they are at the very fringe of the story, and the feelings of these incidental relatives for one another are luke-warm in comparison with the ardent loyalty and the intimacy welding the friends together. The exception here is a parent's love for its small, helpless baby. Kanga loves Roe, Otter loves Little Portly.

In all the chapters of contended home life or risky adventures nothing happens that would suggest a comparison between what Tom does and what Dick does, or between their appearance. And perhaps as a further assurance against the pressure of comparison, of jealousy and competition, most of them belong to different species. Who will compare a monkey with an owl or a mole with a toad? The members of the closely knit circle are not measured against one another. And more than this: their earlier self is not compared with their later self. They are the same people at the end of the story as they were when we first met them. This, too, is in sharp contrast to the hero of the oedipal tale, who at the close of the story is not only in different circumstances, but is changed, an "improved" person. The good and the sly and bad people he met, the events he went through, joy and sorrow, love and loneliness—have molded him. The endearing characters of Lofting's, of Milne's and of Grahame's tale remain throughout the story what they

227

were at the very beginning. Each one is as boastful or greedy, or as kind or gullible as we found him when he first entered. This is not because these stories, by and large, appeal to younger children who are but little aware of the passage of time. After all, heroes intended for a very young age group (e.g., Pinocchio or Bambi) grow up and change, and this recasting of their inner self becomes an essential part of the story. But the heroes of the Early Tale are static characters.[5]

The reader of the oedipal story identifies with the hero and with his success, and by doing so he vicariously shares the hero's pressures. The charm of the Early Tale may be due to their complete absence.

Frequently the characters of these stories wear animal masks.[6] These are mask of animals rather than real animals. Not only do they talk and wear clothes, but besides giving them a few convincing and specific animal features, there is no attempt to present a biologically correct picture of their animal life. Why, then, are these animal masks employed by the writer? A human character who in a story is not defined according to his approximate age remains so vague, so insipid, that he does not win our interest, and a human being whose sex remains undefined arouses anxiety. In the Early Tale the animals are depicted with just enough authentic detail to screen the absence of those features which are usually indispensable for creating a plausible character, i.e., the missing age and sex. *The animal mask supports the mechanism of denial.* The paucity of concrete features gives them a heraldic quality.

In the preoedipal phase the child is almost unaware that there are men and women. The difference he perceives is between him and the adults, the persons who can fulfill his wishes or deny them all. The world is divided into children and grownups. In the oedipal phase he is aware of sexual differences but likely to forget that other division which formerly loomed so large, he is cocky enough to consider himself the equal of his parents. I know that I am over-simplifying—yet basically this is correct: from being innocent of one of the great dichotomies (male-female) the child turns to ignore the other one (child-adult). Time and again, however, this dichotomy is sharply brought to his attention. He is only a child and thus can neither be his mother's partner nor his father's successful competitor. In his happy moments he succeeds in denying that he is small and unequipped for being a lover, but painful experiences bring him brusquely back to reality. That a child envies the grownups has always been known, but Freud pointed to the direct and gross male (or female) aspirations which go with the wish to be big. These fantastic aspirations make the child's happy illusions and his downfalls so intense and potentially traumatic.

At this point I thought I had discovered a new way of looking at the oedipal constellation. But then I happened to scan the last pages of Little Hans's case history and came across the daydreams he produced at the end of his analysis (Freud, 1909b). Hans has two "happiness fantasies" ("*Glücksfantasien*"), which testify to his newly-won ability to cope with the pressures in his life. The plumber comes in one fantasy to screw off his buttocks and his penis and to give him larger ones instead; in the other, Hans has many children and takes them to the toilet, wipes their behind, their "podl," in short, does everything a mother does with her little children.

With these fantasies Hans has regained his former cheerfulness. They provide the gratifications from which reality excludes him because he is only a little boy. With the first fantasy he denies the gulf separating the boy from the grown man, while the second cancels the difference between male and female. The Early Tale employs the oppo-

229

site technique: the confining and often painful dichotomies are blissfully absent or irrelevant for the story characters.

The Early Tale builds on the defense mechanisms of denial. A quick glance at another story character may clarify what is being done here. *Peter Pan* is a little boy who refuses to grow up—that is, he is well aware of the difference between old and young, but says NO to something he does not like, he *negates* the need to grow up. The Early Tale goes one step further: there nobody heard of such a thing as growing up. The animal friends are a delightful mixture of childishness and grownupness.[7]

At the core of every successful story there is a universal daydream. The tale begins, the curtain rises, the reader identifies with the hero, and enjoys experiences inaccessible to him in reality. The intensity and the grip of emotions he finds in the story would at times be painful in real life.

The pleasure yielded by a daydream is intense, yet definitely restricted. The storyteller makes the daydream articulate, hence communicable, and he makes it ego-syntonic, thereby changing and multiplying the enjoyment. The hack-writer takes the daydream and uses it pretty much "as is." The poet paraphrases and veils it, and he even destroys some of its easy and glib gratification.

Earlier studies had assumed that the story in which we meet our own daydream makes it fully conscious by lending words to it. I believe that essential parts of a story, of its plot, of the story characters' motivations and conflicts remain unconscious or preconscious and *for this very reason* arouse our emotions, our sympathy most effectually. Here a good children's story shares the dynamics of all art.

Many nursery tales employ magical features, i.e., denial in fantasy. Miracles happen with complete ease and make the story possible. The well-known traditional fairy tales are very old and come to us from a time when adults, too, believed in magic. In a preliterate world the laws of reality have less validity, they are less stringent for the reasoning of anyone, child or adult.

The storyteller, like the poet, must believe in the tale he spins. If he makes a conscious effort to write "for little children," his story is likely to sound concocted or it becomes pedantic. This may explain why the majority of fairy tales written today are so trite and syrupy. But recent decades have given us one type of story where fantastic happenings are closely interwoven with highly realistic and prosaic details which in a way deny the first denial. The reader is shuttled between the two, and this double denial may account for the story's ability to hold his interest.

The sincere modern fairy tale is at home in both the world of magic and denial in fantasy *and* in the well-observed world of sober, everyday reality.

We have discussed daydreams, paraphrasing important human relationships and aspirations, and we also took a close look at one type of contemporary fairy tales. Because these stories usually appeal to young children and because they remind us of a simple, carefree age, we called them "Early Tales." In these stories, problems of genital sexuality and the slow encroachments of death are eliminated. Yet thanks to the poet's art, the sutures where these powerful realities were cut out from the fabric of human life are invisible.

## NOTES

[1]To equate fantasies produced in analysis, in traditional epics, and in dreams, as Róheim (1940) does, seems to me incorrect.

[2]Why is it usually the *third* son who wins? We may think of the symbolic significance of the number three (Abraham, 1923). However, reasons of plot construction offer another explanation.

Were the story to speak of one older and one younger brother, the contest between them would resemble too closely the father-son contest, and thus conjure up the oedipal struggle; on the other hand, the account of deeds of a larger number of brothers might be too lengthy, too repetitious—three is the smallest crowd. Finally, the story of the youngest son who succeeds where his older brothers lost out may be a faint memory of archaic conditions where elder sons were murdered or exiled while the youngest, born when the father's strength was declining, stood a better chance of becoming his heir.

³Discussing the simple tales of *Peter Rabbit* and *Moustachio*, I have pointed to this technique. The story brings an almost hidden or insignificant experience of the hero which seems unrelated to the events yet illumines, indeed accounts for his later feelings and actions. This belongs to the general principle of "aesthetic ambiguity." To quote Kris and Kaplan (1948): ". . . It is not to be supposed that the multiple meanings of which we have been speaking are clearly and distinctly present to the mind of either artist or audience. For the most part they remain 'preconscious'—i.e., though not conscious they can become so with comparatively little effort if the interpretation becomes problematic at that point. It is because they are in the 'back of the mind' in this sense that they contribute so much to poetic effectiveness." The authors refer here to poetic language. Nursery tales are narratives and we think of them as the child's equivalent of the novel or short story. Actually they are closer to drama and poetry. Their language is poetic: it is highly symbolic and overdetermined, evoking clusters of meaning.

⁴Exception: the children in the *Mary Poppins* stories. And the general principle may as well be stated here: I am presenting a story structure which exists in the abstract, yet is violated in one or the other point in each story. In relation to the perfect fantasy each story is like a web torn in a different spot in every instance and thus the pattern, i.e., the basic daydream, can be reconstructed by bringing them side by side and comparing them.

⁵In the discussion in London, 1956, Dr. B. Lantos pointed to their similarity with the inhabitants of the Garden Eden whose serene life flowed along without strife, murder, or sexuality.

232

⁶The Pogo characters of Walt Kelly, which use the childish form of the comic strip to amuse adults and to bootleg some biting social and political criticism, also are animal masks, also one of a kind and nondescript in their sex and age.

⁷Suppression is the conscious attempt to forget something, while repression refers to the unconscious mechanism. I am using negation and denial in a parallel fashion.

## REFERENCES

JUVENILES AND NOVELS

Andersen, H. C. (1835), *The Little Mermaid.*
Anonymous (about 1900), *Bad Boy's Diary.*
Barrie, J. M. (1906), *Peter Pan.*
Bishop, C. H. (1938), *The Five Chinese Brothers.*
Brontë, C. (1847), *Jane Eyre.*
Burnett, F. H. (1886), *Little Lord Fauntleroy.*
Busch, W. (1865), *Max und Moritz.*
Collodi, C. (1880), *The Adventures of Pinocchio.*
Crompton, R. (1922), *Just William.**
de Brunhoff, J. (1933), *Babar, the Elephant.**
Dickens, C. (1850), *David Copperfield.*
Ets, M. (1947), *Oley, the Sea Monster.*
Flack, M. (1933), *The Story about Ping.*
Grahame, K. (1908), *The Wind in the Willows.*
Kästner, E. (1929), *Emil and the Detectives.*
Lofting, H. (1920), *The Story of Dr. Doolittle.**
Milne, A. A. (1926), *Winnie—the Pooh.**
Potter, B. (1902), *The Tale of Peter Rabbit.**
Rey, A. H. (1941), *Curious George.**
Rigby, D. (1947), *Moustachio.*
Ruskin, J. (1851), *The King of the Golden River.*
Salten, F. (1926), *Bambi.*
Steinbeck, J. (1937), *The Red Pony.*
Stevenson, R. L. (1883), *Treasure Island.*

Thoma, L. (n.d.), *Lausbubengeschichten*.

Travers, P. (1934), *Mary Poppins*.*

Twain, M. (1871), *The Adventures of Tom Sawyer*.

—— (1882), *The Prince and the Pauper*.

*First volume of a series.

PSYCHOANALYTIC AND GENERAL

Abraham, K. (1923), Two Contributions to the Study of Symbols. *Clinical Papers and Essays on Psychoanalysis*. New York: Basic Books, 1955.

Balint, A. (1935), Die Bedeutung des Märchens für das Seelenleben des Kindes. *Ztschr. psa. Päd.*, IX.

Burlingham, D. (1945), The Fantasy of Having a Twin. *This Annual*, I.

—— (1952), *Twins*. New York: International Universities Press.

Buxbaum, E. (1941), The Role of Detective Stories in a Child's Analysis. *Psa. Quart.*, X.

Fraiberg, S. (1954), Tales of the Discovery of the Secret Treasure. *This Annual*, IX.

Freud, A. (1936), Chapter VI: Denial in Phantasy. *The Ego and the Mechanisms of Defense*, New York: International Universities Press, 1946.

—— (1953), On Losing and Getting Lost. Presented at the International Psychoanalytical Congress, London.

Freud, S. (1908), The Relation of the Poet to Day-Dreaming. *Collected Papers*, IV. London: Hogarth Press, 1925.

—— (1909), Analysis of a Phobia in a Five-Year-Old Boy. *Collected Papers*, III. London: Hogarth Press, 1925.

—— (1909b), Family Romances, *Collected Papers*, V. London: Hogarth Press, 1950.

Friedlaender, K. (1942), Children's Books and Their Function in Latency and Prepuberty, *Am. Imago*, III.

Green, P. (1959), *Kenneth Grahame: A Biography*. Cleveland: World Publishing Company, 1959.

Greenacre, P. (1955), *Swift and Carroll*, New York: International Universities Press.

Hoffer, W. (1931), Kind und Märchen, *Ztschr. psa. Päd.*, V.

Kris, E. & Kaplan, A. (1948), Aesthetic Ambiguity. In *Psychoanalytic Explorations in Art*. New York: Inrernational Universities Press, 1952.

Kris, M. (1932), Ein Märchenstoff in einer Kinderanalyse. *Ztschr. psa. Päd.*, VI.

Orwell, G. (1939), Boys' Weeklies, In *A Collection of Essays by George Orwell*, New York: Doubleday, 1954.

Peller, L. (1958a), Reading and Daydreaming in Latency, Boy-Girl Difference. *J. Am. Psa. Assn.*, VI.

—— (1958b), The Fantasy of the Night Parents. Presented at Hampstead Clinic, London.

Róheim, G. (1940), The Dragon and the Hero. *Am. Imago*, I.

# 3.

# READING AND DAYDREAMS IN LATENCY, BOY-GIRL DIFFERENCES

The three- to four-year-old child who wishes to be a great general, a doctor or a mother can without delay *become* that person, possibly supporting his magical thinking (denial in fantasy) with some token, a soldier's cap, a doctor's bag or a doll. He plays with abandon, without self-consciousness. With the beginning of latency this avenue does not become blocked entirely, but it grows narrower. Latency brings several changes: now the playing child adds realistic features to his play, his imagination carries him further and thus his play changes in two dimensions, becoming more realistic and yet more imaginative. But fantasy and reality do not float into one another all the time, as they did in the earlier years. The acting out of fantasies becomes labeled "make-believe play," with a clearly marked beginning and end. Fantasies more and more replace role play. Within a short time the psychological household grows far more complicated and daydreams become an essential release. Finding his own daydream woven into a story multiplies the release—the child can enjoy his own, his personal fantasy without feelings of guilt, shame, reproach. (This function of "the poet's" work is of course not latency-specific: we watch a play or read a novel in order to reap the same benefits.) Yet the fantasy which originally guided his attention toward the story usually remains the child's secret.

In child analysis the child acts out or relates his fantasies.

Sometimes we may gain access to fantasy material through his choice of a story or a joke he tells us. Margarete Ruben (10) has a good example in her analysis of Jackie: "At that time Jackie brought a funny cartoon into the session which was more expressive than Jackie would ever have dared to verbalize. It showed a sequence which represented a man sitting and reading, highly amused about the content of his book; in the second picture he wants his wife to participate in his pleasure and gives her the book to read, but she refuses and goes on knitting rapidly. Because of her reaction, the couple gets into a fight and the wife kills her husband with the knitting needles. Then she picks up the book which has fallen to the floor, sits down and is greatly amused by the story. Jackie's mother is an ardent and excellent knitter." Here the mere choice of a cartoon provides insight into the child's conflict.

For the disturbed child, daydreaming often becomes an expression of his disturbance. Either the intensity of his fantasies isolate him from reality (they are not the cause, but they take the place of friends, of school and play interests); or the child's daydreams are inhibited and he cannot enjoy stories that take him to new adventures. Tedd, an eight-year-old, who came for help because of sleeping disturbance and general anxiety, was an excellent student, came from a family which appreciated books. Unintentionally I may have tried to convey my interest in stories to him. By chance I learned that he had read his school reader a second and a third time. But he did not read anything else, he could not derive pleasure from reading that brought suspense.*

*There are other reasons which limit the neurotic child's reading enjoyment. Dr. Nelly Tibout, in personal communication, told me: "An adult patient of mine remembered in analysis her inability as a little girl to read any book in which the child enjoyed something that she, the reader, could not have herself." This was a good example of a disturbed child's inability to enjoy ready-made daydreams as offered in stories.

237

Until a short time ago stories read or listened to were the main outside source of the child's fantasy material. Recently TV has wrought a tremendous change, but contrary to the opinion of some, TV has not made books obsolete. You may be surprised, as I was, to learn that three to four times as many books of fiction are published annually per child as per adult.**

The child's need for fictional characters and plots is so great that he will often imbibe anything that comes his way, and most books for children are on a very low literary level. Yet in the torrent of trash one finds also books which bring delight not only to children but to the adult, stories that keep their appeal for three, four and even more generations. Translations into several languages testify to their wide and universal appeal—a circumstance which reflects the universal appeal of the daydream they contain.

It is very interesting that many of the books which have become favorites were written for an audience of *one* or of a well-defined *few*. The author who writes to please a child he knows and loves, or to keep in touch with the beloved child whose presence he misses, succeeds in re-creating childish dreams so fully that his tale becomes a favorite of all children. The desire to capture the interest of a child who is physically present (or for whose presence he is longing) unlocks for the author the gates to his own childhood fantasies and enables him to write a story appealing to millions. This is but a specific instance—in a way, it is a confirmation of Freud's general formula of the poet's creative activity: "a powerful recent experience awakens the memory of earlier, usually childhood experiences, creating a longing which is then discharged in the poet's writings"(4).

We may go one step further. The child tempts the adult to return to his own childhood fantasies. Yet the child's

*Calculated on the basis of Smith's statement.(11)

238

existence, his physical presence, makes the trip not only possible, it makes the trip safe. The child eagerly awaiting his story does not let the storyteller forget that he is an adult. He can abandon himself to the upsurging childhood memories as Odysseus listened to the Sirens' song—he is tied to reality. In technical language: there are well-defined limits to the regression into which he plunges.

As an example of books written this way one immediately thinks of the "Alice" books, recently the subject of a study by Greenacre(7). Other examples are: *The Rose and the Ring*, now over a century old. Thackeray in Rome, homesick around Christmas time, made the sketches and wrote the story for a group of English-speaking children he met in the boarding house where he lived. *Treasure Island's* map was drawn by Stevenson's stepson before Stevenson wrote the story for him. *The King of the Golden River* was written for Effie, the twelve-year-old, whom John Ruskin married ten years later. Helen Bannerman produced *Little Black Sambo's* story for her children who were in England while she had to stay with her husband in India. *Peter Pan* was written for five little boys, one of them named Peter, whom Barrie later adopted. During World War I Hugh Lofting found that he was losing contact with his children, as the most vivid descriptions of his war experiences aroused only lukewarm interest. But when he hit upon *Dr. Doolittle* and his crew of animals, his children looked forward to his letters. *The Wind in the Willows*, Edward Lear's *Nonsensebooks, Winnie—the Pooh* were all written for individual children. Dr. Hoffmann, a German pediatrician, invented a cautionary tale, later collected in the *Struwwelpeter* book, whenever he wanted to "cheer up" one of his child patients.

It seems that mostly men are moved by this desire to fascinate a child by writing a story for him or her. Perhaps women have other ways to express their tender feelings for

239

a child; perhaps the grownup woman's access to her childhood reveries is different. Her nostalgia for the days of youth finds a different expression. While women are prolific writers of juveniles, they write more often for the general, anonymous child audience, pretty much like literature for adults gets written.

At the core of every successful children's book there is a universal daydream. Recently I had occasion to report on this topic in London(8). Today I would like to discuss one type of fantasy, the tale of the hero. We may say the *oedipal hero* as the fantasy centers around oedipal wishes and their derivatives. Some fifteen years ago, Friedlaender (6) dealt with the functions of books and daydreams in latency and my presentation is based on her excellent study.

Here is the story's plot in a nutshell: The hero is an orphan or semi-orphan, often living with the parent (or a parent figure) of the opposite sex. (David Copperfield and Jim Hawkins of *Treasure Island* both live with a widowed mother. Remi, *Nobody's Boy*, lives with a peasant woman whom he believes to be his mother, until her husband's return from Paris shatters their peaceful home. Heidi lives with her grandfather, and Dorothy of *Wizard of Oz* with her uncle and aunt.) The story's hero is a bundle of abilities and virtues. He is kind, courageous, courteous, clever, clean and just. No wonder that the adults in the story accept him as one of them. The absence of his father helps. Jim Hawkins is the only boy sailing with the crew of the "Hispaniola" for the hidden treasure. Remi has been working under ground a few days only when an explosion takes the life of several miners. But it is Remi who helps save the men working near him. There are several or many father figures in each story and while some are kind and well-meaning, others have sinister plans against the group or community, and against the hero in particular. They succeed in fooling

240

everybody except our hero, who, after many episodes, unmasks them, thus gaining the triumph we, the reader, have wished him all the time.

In order to make my point I have outlined a simple, exaggerated version of the daydream. But this *is* the version which the hacks follow in the production of their potboilers. Stories presented with greater skill and on a higher literary level "violate" the daydream in one or more points. What is thereby detracted from direct gratification is more than returned in aesthetic pleasure.

Of other classics employing this daydream, I mention first Aldrich's *Story of a Bad Boy*, published in 1869, which is now being read by the fourth successive generation. Its author was a famous American newspaperman and the book is supposedly largely autobiographical. Tom, the hero, has many adventures and he also succeeds in uniting a couple who had been separated for decades. When Tom leaves New Orleans, his home town, to sail for Boston, sailor Ben becomes his special friend. Years later Ben shows up in Boston, their friendship is renewed, they have all kinds of illicit adventures and then, quite by chance, Ben turns out to be the long-lost husband of Kitty, the grandfather's faithful old cook. I consider this part of the plot a remote elaboration of and defense against oedipal wishes.

Second, there are to be mentioned *Coral Island*, and *Emil and the Detectives* and *Great Northern*. The last two are realistic stories, quite plausible in every detail. Yet they provide equally good support for the daydream as the roving fantasy tales. The villain is a respected father figure. Convincing the others of his wickedness is as hard or even harder than defying him. Fortunately the hero's shrewdness matches his persistence.

We will now consider what constitutes the element of gratification in these American, British, French and German stories. The hero is an orphan and this solves his

241

oedipal conflicts with finality and without guilt. Indeed, listening to this kind of story we are led to believe that anybody who gets anywhere in the world is an orphan. The Horatio Alger characters are, and so is Dick Whittington, thrice Lord Mayor of London. If he had not been an orphan, he never would have been the wretched kitchen boy who had nothing but his beloved cat and thus sent it to the savage king. All the other members of the rich merchant's household sent more reasonable gifts, but it was the cat that hit the jackpot for its owner. (We note that Dick does to his cat what his parents had unintentionally done to him.) It seems that only Little Black Sambo lives with both his parents and eats his pancakes with them, a togetherness sadly missed by Mrs. Bannerman in India. Her own children were far away in England getting their education there. Thus an author's own daydream may shine through his story. But, back to our reading child. The hero measures his strength successfully against the story's father figures. Friedlaender makes this explicit and also points to the pleasure of discovering quite by chance long-sought relatives or old friends in strangers. The latter is a further development of the family romance.

The stories have also other themes and characteristics which appeal to and gratify the young reader's wishes. The very young child is able to love and to hate the same person. But the strengthening of secondary-process thinking in the latency child puts a stop to this. In the stories the conflict of ambivalence is solved by the introduction of several father figures. The hero—and the reader with him—can distribute his feelings of like and dislike, admiration and ridicule, between them. Sometimes it seems to me that an author "sliced" the father image almost more often than necessary. Pinocchio has three in the very first pages: the carpenter who finds the piece of wood which talks back when he starts sawing it, the puppeteer who actually carves and paints the new puppet, and the constable who puts him into jail when his running away causes a minor uproar. Or look at the abundance of good and bad, courage and cowardice, cleverness and gullibility in the characters of *Treasure Island*.

Needless to say that stories here repeat on a larger scale the latency child's everyday life experience. As he enters school, camp, club and community, many father images become heirs to the one father figure of his early home. Even a boy who is but a year or two older than he may impress or frighten a child. The problem of authority crosses forever his path and the hero's calm and fearless way of meeting those who are in power makes the young reader feel good.

There are no siblings in the story who can compete with the hero; if there are any at all, they look up to him for leadership and protection and thus rather add to his glory.* And, although the hero is such a superman, he still enjoys the advantages of boyhood. He runs faster than any grownup, he may deftly trip a man and, being small, can hide easily, like Jim Hawkins in the apple barrel, and, unseen, overhear their evil plans. Without Jim's secret listening, every one of the story's good people would have been murdered by Long John Silver's men. Eavesdropping with a noble purpose must please the latency child who is conscious of the secrets the adults are guarding.

The hero's adventures may arouse the reader's envy, but the high-pitched, last-minute escape from danger, the travels and the hero's independence also saturate the boy's need for them. He feels better about staying within familiar environs.

It has been pointed out that the hero's high ethics appease the strict superego of latency years. Parents selecting a story for their son, librarians putting a book on the most

*This point was made by Dr. A. Royon in a personal communication.

accessible shelf, do so with the hope that the young reader will emulate the hero. Of course he often does. Yet sometimes when the boy has been vicariously glowing in the hero's high morals, it seems easier to dispense with these virtues in his own life. Having admired the hero's fearless honesty, a little bit of cheating in his own life seems unimportant. He is satisfied to have the hero be moral. This reminds us of the various mechanisms of projection and altruistic surrender, which come into play when the child's rigid moral code clashes painfully with his wishes.

Neither the sadistic and masochistic elements woven into these as into many other stories, nor the frequent animal fantasies will be discussed here. Instead we will go to the hero story's counterpart, to the *story of the Heroine*. This type is similar in many features; for instance, the heroine too is an orphan, she too is the personification of many virtues. But the girl's story usually stays nearer home. There are fewer adventures; instead the story often acquires color by the introduction of fairy-tale elements.

But there is one aspect well worth our interest: there are certain regular features in many girl's stories—elements which come up in the story but are *not* woven into a coherent daydream. To name the most frequent ones: *secrets* play an important part, and these secrets usually concern the heroine personally, her body. Secrets figure prominently in boy's stories too, but there they concern the entire group. They are more objective in nature. Then there is the *encounter* between the heroine and the man. It comes unexpectedly to her or to both; usually they are alone, with the heroine scantily dressed, often in her nightgown, or she is in bed. As I am trying to describe this to you, it sounds like a scene which is slightly risqué, but the story integrates the encounter into the web of the narrative, making it plausible and discouraging any frivolous thought. Another recurrent element is a *handicap* from which the heroine suffers

244

and is cured (or a temporary one is acquired) or some bodily change takes place. Finally, the heroine is asleep during a crucial part of the story, or *unconscious* or dizzy. It is quite evident what these elements spell out if they were linked with one another: it would be an erotic scene, an anticipation of the female role in the bridal chamber. In early latency this fantasy, though exciting, is too anxiety-loaded, hence its elements pop up but remain *membra disiecta*. Sometimes it is the heroine's male partner who is incapacitated and the encounter brings his salvation. (The beautiful prince would drown without the little mermaid's timely arrival.)

We may take the story of *Heidi* to show how the aforementioned elements are woven into a plot. The book, published in the 1870's, tells of the adventures of a little Swiss girl, the embodiment of carefree innocence. Hardly has Heidi mastered the rudiments of reading when she begins to read the Bible to her grandfather, who years ago stopped attending the village church and became a recluse and finally an outcast. Where the villagers and the minister have for many years failed (to bring him back to religion), Heidi succeeds in a matter of weeks. Here we see the daydream of the child who dares to approach and eventually to tame an old man, held in awe and avoided by everybody else (Anna Freud).

Heidi, visiting Clara, the rich paralyzed girl in Frankfurt, feels terribly homesick, but keeps her heartache a secret. When Clara's father returns from a business trip, the servants tell him that the house has been haunted by a spirit roaming through the halls every midnight. Mr. Sesemann laughs off the tale, yet invites his friend, the doctor, and the two men decide to stay up in the living room with a bottle of good wine and two loaded guns on the table. Sure enough, the noise starts shortly after midnight. The doctor, loaded gun in hand, proceeds cautiously toward the queer figure descending the stairs and just about to open the heavy door toward the street. The ghost turns out to be Heidi in her nightgown, sleepwalking and trembling with cold and fright. The doctor gathers the shivering child in his arms, carries her upstairs, tucks her into bed and sees to it that she is promptly sent home to Switzerland.

Later in the story, Clara visits Heidi. As she sits one afternoon on the lovely green mountainside, Peter, the mischievous and now jealous boy-goatherd, pushes her wheelchair over the cliffs. And this—plus the good mountain air, the sleeping in the hay loft and the simple wholesome food—helps Clara to discover that she is not paralyzed and can walk! This story has the figure of the heroine split into two: there are two little girls of approximately the same age, but differing and thus supplementing each other in all other aspects. Heidi is the far more important one. To her happens the sleepwalking and the encounter and she guards her personal secret, while the miraculous cure comes to Clara. Story and plot are constructed in such a way that the elements of a feminine erotic fantasy are there, yet the story which introduces them also isolates them from one another, the narrative actually interferes with the daydream and makes the coherent, the completed fantasy impossible. Usually the overtly told story permits and veils the daydream, but here it is the story's function to start the daydream and then quickly to interrupt it, so that it remains fragmented. This function cannot be revealed by reading an individual tale. It is the recurrence of these elements and the recurrence of this constellation in many girl's stories which support my thesis.

Besides *Heidi* I would mention: *Madeline*, Burnett's *Little Princess* and *Secret Garden, Enchanted Eve, The Wizard of Oz, The Little Mermaid, Jane Eyre*'s first chapter. In this selection quite a number of countries are represented. These are masterfully told stories, not stories offering pat solutions to

246

crude pressures. Thus each tale changes the basic plot and creates a unique variation. In the stories mentioned the allusive elements remain unconnected, except in one: *Madeline* tells the story of a little girl's appendectomy with such prosaic details that in this case the elements can be integrated into a fantasy without arousing erotic anxiety. We may say that the story is told on two levels; all our conscious attention is held by the highly believable account of Madeline's adventures.

Interestingly enough in stories read by even younger girls, the feminine fantasy is presented coherently and on the conscious level, namely in fairy tales. For instance, in Sleeping Beauty, in Snowwhite and in Cinderella, the encounter with the Prince is followed by the heroine's awakening or her liberation, or cure and promptly by a splendid marriage. But the events in a fairy tale have a faraway quality, the reader looks at them through a window, they do not happen in her own world.

I will merely enumerate other types of girl's reading. There are books for teenage girls, describing in a romanticized yet pedestrian way all the boy-girl situations and problems which "may arise." They are read almost invariably by girls younger than the heroine. The book jacket is not a bit bashful in the announcement of the information (the precedents, so to say) contained in the book, all ready to be put to good use. The little girl's sexual anxiety has shifted into social anxiety; if she knows how others behave, if she can act in conformity with others—then she can indulge in the anticipation of her feminine role.

Not all the favorite books of girls support feminine daydreams. In recent years another type of book has become tremendously popular in our country: its heroine is a girl detective, for instance, "Nancy Drew," only daughter of a widowed lawyer. The formula of these and similar hacks is simple. Nancy is a girl in name, in her dress and in a few meager details. Otherwise she is for all intents and purposes a boy. For instance, even after Nancy has notified the police where the robbers are heading with their loot, even then she will hop into her shiny blue roadster, speed after them, hide in a dark barn or in a deserted roadhouse to meet them. The thought that she may be left locked up and starved to death or thrown out of a moving van flashes through her mind, but never the fear of rape. Or when a highly desirable young man turns up, Nancy saves his life, discovers that he is the long-sought heir to a fabulous fortune, yet Nancy, the detective, is very pleased to see him marry her best friend. These stories know how to arouse the reader's excitement and how to support the daydream which at this time has not yet disappeared: Maybe I can be a boy! One minor detail reveals the precariousness of this fantasy. Nancy carries not only a loaded pistol with her, she never forgets her flashlight nor her reserve batteries!

These two groups of books appeal to girls only and comparable books for boys are almost nonexistent. Once he has outgrown children's fare the boy goes to adult books, to biography, adventure and detective stories—books that may be for unsophisticated adults, but the fact remains there is no literature appealing specifically to the boy of prepuberty age. In other words, there is no group of books dealing with the adventures of fifteen-year-old boys and read mainly by twelve-year-olds. But there are many such books for girls.

Besides all these types of books, girls also read boys' books, but not vice versa. Here we may point to the girl's bisexual identification in latency, mentioned by Greenacre(7).

*Comment*

I have used this literary excursion for two purposes: to point out the functions and gratifications of fiction in latency and prepuberty, and to indicate the different constellations of drives and defenses for boys and girls.

To summarize: the difference existing between the two sexes at the beginning of latency is well known. In the course of normal development the girl dissolves her oedipal attachment slowly and seldom completely, while the boy has to do this rather abruptly. Berta Bornstein (1) described regression to the pregenital level as a defense often found at the beginning of latency. In the course of normal development this regression is more typical of the boy than of the girl. The girl, as a defense against penis envy, often wants to stress the difference between her and the boy. At this age the boy makes a display of being wild, dirty, unwilling to learn in school, while the girl becomes visibly neat, obedient, in short "good" and often righteous to boot. I see here one of the reasons why, all through elementary school, girls are as a group the far better students; the girl tries harder to do what the adult expects of her. The other reason for the girl's eagerness to learn may be the last flicker of her hope to obtain from the teacher what the mother failed to give her. By becoming a good student in school she still hopes to catch up with the boy. Here then is a startling fact—penis envy *and* the defense against penis envy may both find expression in the same manifest behavior in early latency.

In the later years of latency, boys and girls anticipate in their daydreams their adult roles. In the boy's daydreams aggressive and ambitious elements prevail and these can reach consciousness. The girl partly shares the boy's daydreams, partly her fantasies center around erotic elements. These may be so anxiety-arousing that they remain barred from consciousness. Or, the anxiety awakened by anticipating her adult feminine role may be deflected into social anxiety, creating the wish to know how other girls behave.

## Conclusion

The instinctual pressures seem to be more stringent for the boy at the beginning of latency and for the girl in the latter half of it. This may account for the well-known fact that girls between five and nine surpass boys in their school achievements.

So far in psychoanalytic literature the sex-specific differences of the preoedipal, the oedipal and the puberty period have attracted more attention than those of the latency phase. I would venture the statement that boys and girls in latency years are in certain aspects of their behavior as different from one another as men and women ever will be, and this in spite of the fact that important facets of sexuality tend to be quiescent during these years.

## REFERENCES

JUVENILES AND NOVELS

Aldrich, T. B. *The Story of a Bad Boy*, 1869.
Andersen, H. C. *The Little Mermaid*, 1835.
Ballantyme, R. M. *The Coral Island*, 1858.
Bannerman, H. *Little Black Sambo*, 1899.
Barrie, J. M. *Peter Pan*, 1906.
Baum, F. *The Wonderful Wizard of Oz*, 1900.
Bemelmans, L. *Madeline*, 1939.
Brontë, C. *Jane Eyre*, 1847.
Burnett, F. E. H. *Little Princess*, n.d.
Burnett, F. E. H. *Secret Garden*, 1911.
Carroll, L. *Alice in Wonderland*, 1865.
Carroll, L. *Through the Looking Glass*, 1872.
Collodi, Lorenzini C. *The Adventures of Pinocchio*, 1880.
Grahame, K. *The Wind in the Willows*, 1908.
Hoffmann, H. *Struwwelpeter*, 1845.
Kaestner, E. *Emil and the Detectives*, 1929.
Keene, C. *Nancy Drew Mystery Stories*.

Lear, E. *The Book of Nonsense*, 1846.
Ley, M. *The Enchanted Eve*, 1946.
Lofting, H. *The Story of Dr. Dolittle*, 1920.
Milne, A. A. *Winnie—the Pooh*, 1926.
Ransome, A. *Great Northern?* 1947.
Ruskin, J. *The King of the Golden River*, 1851.
Spyri, J. *Heidi*, 1891.
Stevenson, R. L. *Treasure Island*, 1883.
Thackeray, W. M. *The Rose and the Ring*, 1855.

PSYCHOANALYTIC AND GENERAL

1. Bornstein, B. On latency. *The Psychoanalytic Study of the Child*, 6:279-285. New York: International Universities Press, 1951.
2. Deutsch, H. *The Psychology of Women*. New York: Grune & Stratton, 1944.
3. Freud, A. *The Ego and the Mechanisms of Defense*. New York: International Universities Press, 1946.
4. Freud, S. The relation of the poet to day-dreaming (1908). *Collected Papers, 4*:173-183. London: Hogarth Press, 1925.
5. Freud, S. Family romances (1909). *Collected Papers, 5*:74-78. London: Hogarth Press, 1950.
6. Friedlaender, K. Children's books and their function in latency and prepuberty. *Am. Imago, 3*:129-150, 1942.
7. Greenacre, P. *Swift and Carroll*. New York: International Universities Press, 1955.
8. Peller, L. Children's daydreams and favorite books. Unpublished lecture Hampstead Clinic, London, 1956.
9. Rank, O. *The Myth of the Birth of the Hero*. New York: Nervous and Mental Disease Publishing Co., 1913.
10. Ruben, M. Delinquency—a defense against loss of reality. *The Psychoanalytic Study of the Child, 12*:335-355. New York: International Universities Press, 1957.
11. Smith, L. *The Unreluctant Years*. Chicago: American Library Association, 1953.

# 4.

# FREUD'S CONTRIBUTION TO LANGUAGE THEORY

From the eighteenth century until recently the dominant view of language as presented in textbooks of psychology was that its origin and main function lay in its being an instrument of social control, man's main vehicle of communication. Human language was seen as a further development, a "higher" branch of animal communication but not categorically different from it. Karl Bühler (1934) stressed the fact that a study of the child's acquisition of language will yield the most valuable clues to mankind's acquisition of it.

Recently other views, some old, some new, have come to the fore. Language is seen as a requisite for conceptualized thought (Cassirer, 1944); the structure and vocabulary of specific language types are considered of primary importance in shaping the thinking of an ethnic group (Whorf, 1956); language is regarded as a vocal actualization of man's tendency to see realities symbolically (Sapir, 1933). Communication is one of the basic functions of language.

It is, of course, generally known that the term "symbol" has a specific meaning in psychoanalysis. It refers to the affect-loaded, partly unconscious, *primordial* symbols that are central to our understanding of mental disorders and of creative thought, dreams, parapraxes, jokes, etc. Freud, Ferenczi, Jones, O. Rank, Sachs, Silberer, and others all used it in this way. However, in general usage and in language theory "symbol" has a very broad meaning: a symbol is primarily a conceptual tool. It represents, brings to the mind, something that is a "mere idea" and as such has no other physical properties, or something that transcends the sensory data given here and now.

A superficial study of Freud may leave the impression that he ignored the existence of symbols in that broad sense, i.e., of *cognitive* symbols. Nothing could be further from the truth. Freud's "verbal sign" ("word remnant") obviously has a symbolic function; it is a symbol in the general sense. Many everyday symbols carry an affective charge in addition to their cognitive significance. Many primordial symbols are universally ("naturally") understood. They transcend the understanding of language.

Freud's early study of the functions of consciousness led him to views about language which, to the best of my knowledge, anticipated those of later thinkers. His references are brief, indeed fragmentary, yet they hit upon essentials. They are unknown for a number of reasons, one of them being that they are cast in different terms.

Therefore, I shall briefly comment on Freudian terms and on some key linguistic concepts before I come to my main topic. Many of Freud's propositions departed radically from those generally accepted, yet he hardly ever entered into polemics.[1] Instead he simply avoided terms which implied assumptions he regarded as no longer tenable. For instance, the term "libidinal object" was introduced by him in order to undo the contemporary belief that sexual strivings of necessity attach themselves to a person of appropriate age and opposite sex. A "libidinal object" may very well be such a person, but it can also be somebody of the same sex; it can be oneself, a body part, a thing or—an idea. Furthermore, while a "beloved person" is generally treated in about the same way throughout the relationship, the libidinal object is—during the successive phases of individual development or during life's vicissitudes—experienced and treated in radically different ways.

For the new science of psychoanalysis, Freud sought to avoid such terms as *Geist, Seele* (mind, soul) and instead introduced the neutral "mental apparatus."[2] He shunned expressions like "reasoning" (judging, meditating, cogitating) and spoke simply of "mental acts." The deliberate simplicity of this terminology is obvious. We have a muscular apparatus carrying out muscular acts, and we have a mental apparatus carrying out mental acts.[3] And of mental acts there are *two* basic types. Again striving for the least pretentious terms, Freud introduced *numerals* to denote them. He spoke of mental acts (functions, processes) which are either on the *primary* or on the *secondary* level. These terms are not content oriented. Not being definitive, they do not hamper further modifications of the concepts. (The irony is that today the terms primary and secondary are far from being simple.) Primary processes are called so for two reasons: they come earlier and they are more primitive (1900). They are governed by affects, while secondary processes also take cognizance of reality.

In linguistics we speak of *signs, signals*, and *symbols*. I shall use "sign" as the umbrella concept, comprising both signals and symbols. In our daily life we seldom wait for the full impact of an event but respond to its signals. To give simple examples: dark clouds signal rain; when a car slows down on the highway, red lights shine up in its tail fins. Here we have one *natural* and one *artificial* (conventional) signal. Both inform us about impending events and tell us how to act, to behave, now or in the very near future. Higher animals, too, respond to a wide variety of signals. A grazing deer sniffs the air or stands motionless to detect the faintest rustle of leaves "signaling" a hunter. Obviously animals may surpass us in the detection of particular signals and in the speed of their motor response. Although animals also respond to artificial signals, the other kind of signs, namely, symbols, are not part of their world, of their *Umwelt* (self-world) in Jakob von Uexküll's sense (1934). A symbol represents something that transcends the physical data given to us *hic et nunc*. It may represent—and thus make manageable (or permit us to make public)—something that has no other sensory qualities. Here I have referred primarily to a symbol in the general sense, to a conceptual symbol.

A symbol in the psychoanalytic sense refers to an image carrying an affect that in the deepest strata belongs to something else. According to Ferenczi (1912): "Only such things (or ideas) are symbols in the sense of psycho-analysis as are invested in consciousness with a logically inexplicable and unfounded affect . . . which . . . they owe . . . to *unconscious* identification with another thing (or idea), to which the surplus of affect really belongs" (p. 277).

Psychoanalytic (or *primordial* symbols, as I propose to call them) and conceptual symbols may be far apart, but they are not categorically different. I have introduced (1962) yet another term, *protosymbol*, to refer to the young child's not differentiating clearly between symbol and symbolized. Many times his interest goes to things which he seemingly confuses with body parts, functions, products, or persons. A transitional object, for instance, is something that stands midway between a protosymbol and a psychoanalytic symbol. The intense affect that the infant directs toward it belongs in its fullness to his mother and to his own body self. Hence, it is typical for the child to lose the transitional object when his relationship to his mother is profoundly shaken.

Freud's comments about language can be found in his earliest and latest writings (1891, 1895, 1900, 1911, 1913, 1915, 1923, 1933, 1939, 1940). In a way, all references to primary and secondary processes deal implicitly with the functions of language. Freud's brief scattered comments on the relationships between thought processes, consciousness, and verbal signs (language) should be culled from his work so that they can be related to one another and to the more recent studies in the field. Hartmann's comment (1956) about the long latency of many Freudian ideas comes to mind. The different terminology partly explains the delay, but another reason is probably more important: Freud's later work assigns to consciousness a position of secondary importance, while his comments on language seem to stress the fact that consciousness plays—via language—a decisive role in shaping mental acts.[4] Yet this supposed contradiction is hardly an actual one. By clarifying the specific functions that consciousness performs, we obviously also deepen our insight into the consequences of its absence. Here are several of Freud's main references to language in their chronological order.

In two remarkable passages, Freud outlined, in 1900, the functioning of the mental apparatus in its relation to language:

> ... [this apparatus] is capable in waking life of receiving excitations from two directions. In the first place, it can receive excitations from the periphery of the whole apparatus, the perceptual system; and in addition to this, it can receive excitations of pleasure [*Lust*] and unpleasure [*Unlust*], which prove to be almost the only psychical quality attaching to transpositions of energy in the inside of the apparatus. All other processes in the $\psi$-systems, including the *Pcs.*, are lacking in any psychical quality and so cannot be objects of consciousness, except in so far as they bring pleasure or unpleasure to perception. We are thus driven to conclude that *these releases of pleasure and unpleasure automatically regulate the course of cathectic processes.* But, in order to make

more delicately adjusted performances possible, it later became necessary to make the course of ideas less dependent upon the presence or absence of unpleasure. For this purpose the *Pcs.* system needed to have qualities of its own which could attract consciousness; and it seems highly probably that it obtained them by linking the preconscious processes with the mnemic system of linguistic symbols, a system which was not without quality. By means of the qualities of that system, consciousness, which had hitherto been a sense organ for perceptions alone, also became a sense organ for a portion of our thought-processes. Now, therefore, there are, as it were, *two* sensory surfaces, one directed towards perception and the other towards the preconscious thought-processes [p. 574].

The new surface (the new organ of perception) has a highly specific function: it registers those thought processes that are coupled with verbal signs.

The second passage deals with the same facts, but the emphasis and the metaphors are altered. Freud speaks of the creation of a new series of qualities or attributes leading to "a new process of regulation which constitutes the superiority of men over animals" (p. 617). He states the reasons why this new series of qualities arose. On the one hand, mental functions as such have no sensory properties (i.e., they cannot be heard, seen, or touched); on the other hand, affects accompanying thought must be kept within narrow limits lest they disturb its course. How, then, can mental processes reach consciousness? He answers: by becoming linked with word memories, with verbal signs.[5]

I have some comments on these passages. To state in 1900 that human beings had something that animals did not possess, not even to a lesser degree, must have taken considerable courage. This was, after all, the century in

257

which the concept of discontinuity between man and beast had been most forcibly and spectacularly challenged.

The problem of the *origin* of language has long been an arena for speculation. Freud might have felt that the tools for tackling this problem of human evolution were not yet at hand, or that its solution was not mandatory at this juncture, and thus he went straight to the *function* which language serves, bridging the gap in our knowledge with a bluntly teleological phrase: "it later became necessary" (p. 574).

He returned to problems of thinking and language in 1911. The explanatory concept of fluid and bound cathexis was amplified and thinking was defined as a kind of trial action, requiring expenditure of less energy than would actions of our striated muscles. He also expanded his earlier idea: those mental processes that deal not with mere pictorial representations (memory images) of sensory data, ikons in today's terminology, but with *relations* between them were originally unconscious. Only by becoming linked with verbal signs did they obtain qualities which then could reach consciousness.

Once again I recommend comparing my version with a verbatim translation of the same paragraph. To describe the process of thinking as a kind of trial action is in line with Freud's endeavor to use the least pretentious terms and similes. Moreover, this simile is very fruitful. Not only does a trial action require less energy; it is characteristic that everything that occurs in a trial action can be reversed, undone.[6] That an action executed merely in "thought" is not final can of course also be a tremendous danger. For creatures living in the midst of constant emergencies, it would be more often than not a severe, potentially fatal drawback. Those who are not surrounded by predators, however, become free to explore a wider range of possibilities. They can—without anxiety—try many more com-

258

binations: whatever has been "done" in thought can be undone. In this and in some other respects I consider play to be the prestage or matrix of thought. In play, too, almost every move can be reversed.

In "The Unconscious" (1915), Freud discussed the functions of language more extensively than in any of his earlier or later studies. He examines the peculiarities of schizophrenic language and thought and amplifies what he said earlier about primary and secondary processes. Nonanalytic psychology distinguishes between the simple and rather concrete thought processes of animals and the "higher" mental acts of man, and some writers have seen in Freud's distinction between primary and secondary processes a parallel to these two forms of thought. This view I cannot share. Both processes as characterized in psychoanalysis are quite distant from the mental processes of animals; both rely on symbols, although on different kinds of symbols: the role of primordial symbols for primary processes is similar to the role of conceptual symbols for secondary processes.

In the same study Freud introduces another topic: the conscious representation of an object can be regarded as consisting of the representation of a thing (*Sachvorstellung*) to which has been added the representation of the word. It is the joining of these two—thing and word—that creates the representation of the object. In short: thing representation plus word representation equals object presentation. This may seem to be a novel and difficult idea, but only because we often use "thing" and "object" as synonyms, which they are not. Actually, it is a restatement of Freud's earlier views: a mental function which carries no affect can reach our awareness only by becoming linked with a verbal sign. This addition of a verbal sign constitutes a hypercathexis: "It is these hypercathexes, we may suppose, that bring about a higher psychical organization and make it

259

possible for the primary process to be succeeded by the secondary process . . ." (p. 202).

In 1900, Freud had differentiated between the act of mentally *representing* something (*vorstellen*) and the act of *relating* such representations. Now he indicates the importance of relations:[7] they and not the images of sensory data constitute the decisive part of our thought processes.[8]

He returned to this topic in 1923. In addition to verbal signs, indeed, prior to them, there exist visual memory traces which can be linked by thought processes. Some people seem to have a preference for them. Yet, by and large, such images can bring to consciousness only the sensory *materials* of thought, not the relations between them. Visual or other sensory expressions for relations do not exist. Thus thinking in images produces at best a very incomplete awareness. It remains closer to unconscious processes than does thinking in verbal signs. No doubt, it is both ontogenetically and phylogenetically older.[9]

Freud then deals with the question: how can something be remembered? How can it once again become conscious? This is his reply: "it dawns upon us like a new discovery that only something which has once been a *Cs.* perception can become conscious, and that anything arising from within (apart from feelings) that seeks to become conscious must try to transform itself into external perceptions: this becomes possible by means of memory-traces" (p. 20).

No doubt, experiences of the preverbal phase exert a far-reaching influence upon our character, and actual experience in analysis shows that the earliest preverbal memories tend to reappear in dreams, symptoms, moods, and affects, but seldom and only with great difficulty can they be cast into verbal form. They remain forever shadow-like, unconvincing. Of course, events that occurred in the child's preverbal phase may have been later recounted to him by a parent or a relative and the child may confuse the memory of the anecdote he was told with the actual experience. We also need to remember that the verbal phase starts with the understanding of language, not with its use. Between the two there may be quite a time gap.

Freud's statement (1923) may refer to the complete and distinct clarity with which verbal signs endow our experience. In the foregoing studies he had based the need for verbal signs upon two different factors. Verbal signs are introduced in order (a) to *replace* affects, or (b) to bestow sensory attributes upon thought *relations*, thereby enabling them to reach consciousness. And later, he added that relations—not imagery of *any* kind—are the characteristic of thinking.

However, Freud not only elaborated his earlier views and added to them, he also revised one point. In 1915, Freud had declared verbal signs to be indispensable for thinking on the secondary level, but in his last work (1940) he modified his earlier view: "It would not be correct, however, to think that connection with the mnemic residues of speech is a necessary precondition of the preconscious state. On the contrary, that state is independent of a connection with them, though the presence of that connection makes it safe to infer the preconscious nature of a process" (p. 162).

This revision cuts deep.[10] Verbal signs remain a reliable indication that a process takes place on the secondary level, but they are no longer regarded as indispensable. The formation of an idea and putting this idea into inner language are not *one* but *two* distinct, processes. We may assume that secondary processes have a widely varying admixture of verbal signs, which may be faint or distinct, auditory, visual, or kinesthetic. In Freud's formulation: "The preconscious state, characterized on the one hand by having access to consciousness and on the other hand by its connection with the speech-residues, is nevertheless something peculiar, the nature of which is *not exhausted by these two*

261

*characteristics*" (p.162; my italics). But if the presence of verbal signs is not mandatory, we are left with the question: what *is* the essential feature of thought processes on the secondary level? Freud stated the question but left it unanswered. In his writings Freud discussed primary processes extensively, but he referred only occasionally to processes on the secondary level. Would it nevertheless be possible to pinpoint *the essential features* of secondary processes by first enumerating the characteristics of primary processes and then stating their direct opposite? While such a procedure may not necessarily yield correct results, it is worth attempting.

In the *New Introductory Lectures* (1933), Freud tells us quite forcefully that primary mental acts lack the framework of time and space which philosophers regard as the essential prerequisite for all thought. That the dimension of time has no validity for the processes in the unconscious had been stated by him repeatedly before. In 1900 and again in 1915 he had pointed out that primary acts are basically isolated from one another. They enjoy a high degree of mutual independence. It is this isolation that results, among other things, in the fact—so bizarre to our conscious thinking—that incompatible opposites may stand side by side without disturbing each other. In still other contexts, we are told that for primary processes external reality is nonexistent; they know only inner reality. In a footnote added to "The Unconscious" Strachey states: "Mentions of the 'timelessness' of the unconscious will be found scattered throughout Freud's writings" (p. 187).

By the direct and complete reversal of these findings, we arrive at the following characteristic of *secondary* mental processes: they take place in a *framework of time and space*— and, we may add—of *causality*. They follow the laws of grammar, syntax, and logic. Secondary mental processes relate to external reality. Secondary mental acts are *coherent*. And here we realize that we are back on very familiar

262

ground: the ego's synthetic or organizing function reigns for secondary processes (Nunberg, 1930).

By this indirect procedure, we may, after all, have struck upon the distinctive feature of secondary mental acts: they occur within a stable multiple framework *the conception of which is predicated upon language*. It is for this reason that they can be so easily cast into verbal signs. And verbal signs, i.e., words, enable us to make mental acts public, to project them into the future or to retrace them step by step, to compare them with physical reality and with the thoughts of others, to distinguish the possible from the actual.[11]

When Freud first mentions verbal signs he refers primarily to the fact that they endow mental processes with attributes, i.e., sensory attributes which render then "perceivable." This is similar to the way in which a thyroid metastasis becomes perceptible to the Geiger counter: i.e., by becoming linked with a *substance* that registers with the electronic device. Or, in order to study certain features of the blood circulation, we inject methylene blue into the arteries of a rabbit. In either case the added substance does not change the process we are observing; it merely temporarily links this process with something that can register with our senses. But verbal signs have a different function: they change the basic character of mental acts. Or more correctly: the addition of verbal signs is indicative of a basic change. Freud's later formulation (1915) makes this quite clear: "becoming conscious is no mere act of perception, but is probably also a *hypercathexis*, a further advance in the psychical organization" (p. 194).[12]

A person's mental acts can take place on the secondary level only insofar as he recognizes and accepts the framework of *time, space*, and *causality*. The laws of ordered (disciplined) thinking are predicated upon this framework. These laws in turn can be conceived and integrated only by someone who has developed the "second surface of perception." In sum: for conceptual thought verbal signs must be

263

*available* to the mental apparatus. By no means do they have to accompany each step of a mental act. Words are not tags added to precreated images; they may serve as labels, but that is not their principal function.

Freud commented on the role of language only in relation to our thought processes; he did not deal with communication. However, in today's discussion this essential function of language cannot be left out. Animals living in groups communicate with one another effectively, with the help of signals, employing various sense modalities—hearing, sight, smell, and touch. Some even have coded signals—that is, signals with a standardized meaning (see, e.g., the studies on communication among bees and ants by von Frisch [1927] and Schneirla [1946]).

Human beings also communicate with one another by means outside the realm of symbolic language. Just what comes under the heading "communication"? Spitz (1957) tells us: "We will call communication any perceivable change of behavior, be it intentional or not, directed or not, with the help of which one or several persons can influence the perception, the feelings, the emotions, the thoughts or the actions of one or several persons, be that influence intended or not" (p. 3).

In the worthy attempt to avoid a narrow definition (i.e., "communication equals language"), Spitz seems to have gone too far. I consider it communication when the mood, affect, or thought of one person reaches another person, influencing his thought or affect. A communication may be conscious or not, addressed (directed) or not, current (face to face) or recorded (mediated over spatial or temporal distance).[13]

The foremost means of direct communication are speech, facial and body expression, gesture, pantomime.

264

Vocalization of any kind and tactual contacts can also serve communication. Recorded (i.e., mediated) communication can use various sensory modalities. Usually there is a *sender* and a *receiver*. However, a broad definition should also include those marginal instances in which there is only a sender or only a receiver; e.g., the recording of a thought without making it public (making it potentially public) or the erroneous assumption that the behavior of another person expresses an affect or thought. There is only a sender in the former case, while there is only a receiver in the latter. In addition, there is self-communication, the case in which sender and receiver are one and the same person.

Spitz's definition does not cover all these instances, but it includes other interactions which I do not consider communication. Another person's action, his "perceivable change of behavior" may influence my behavior in a mechanical way, i.e., without conveying any affect or thought of his. For instance, in a crowd somebody pushes me and I am perfectly aware that he did not do it deliberately and is unaware of it. In this case his behavior does influence my actions, and it may indeed cause strong feelings—yet he did not communicate with me. Spitz's definition minimizes the human element. The defunct author of a book, or of an orally transmitted song or riddle, or of a sculpture or a painting, still communicates with us. Indeed, human existence is unthinkable without this kind of communication.[14]

A disturbed mother may take care of her baby in a competent way—she goes through the processes of feeding, cleaning, dressing—without any attempt to communicate with the infant. There is plenty of "perceivable changes of behavior" on her part; yet there is no communication. Spitz himself has contributed excellent studies of this phenomenon and its dire consequences. Direct communication relies mostly "on changes of behavior"; yet these are not indispensable, while the knowledge that "the other" has feeling and thought is. The patient who remains silent for a few minutes communicates something else to us than when he prolongs the silence for a longer time, and the same is, of course, true for the person who stares at us for a short time or a long period. The *absence* of a change of behavior can indeed be communicative.

Loewenstein (1956) says about unconscious communication: "Certainly we do not underestimate the importance of the immediate understanding of the unconscious between two people, of the intuitive grasping of non-verbal forms of emotional expressions" (p. 466).

One more point: there is little doubt that for most of us communication with others is needed not only for social give and take, but to preserve the integrity of secondary-process thinking. Recent studies on sensory deprivation have shown that hallucination takes over when there is no sensory input (Heron et al., 1953; Lilly, 1961). It is safe to assume that even with sensory input but without communication with anyone, secondary processes are likely to deteriorate. Restriction of self-communication (no pen and paper) will accelerate the decay. Defoe's Robinson Crusoe starts a diary before he takes care of other urgent needs.

Today the conceptual organization of experience is considered to be the primary function of language. Freud's views on language were in sharp contrast to those dominant in his own time; that may explain why they were ignored. Today they are unknown partly on account of the terms he used. This is a loss because his hypotheses about primordial symbols and instinctual drives, about consciousness and language are relevant to modern linguistics. The ability to use conceptual symbols is preceded by and can scarcely be seen as independent of the propensity to understand symbols and to form them in the psychoanalytic sense (primordial symbols). The acquisition of language activates the

266

child's latent ability to bestow conceptual order on his experience. This development changes the child's whole existence; it is by no means restricted to his intellectual growth. Anna Freud (1936) has expressed this forcefully and lucidly: "We recall that in psychoanalytic metapsychology, the association of affects and drive processes with verbal signs is stated to be the first and most important step in the direction of the mastery of instinctual drives. . . . The attempt to take hold of the drive processes by linking them with verbal signs which can be dealt with in consciousness is one of the most general, earliest and most necessary accomplishments of the human ego. We regard it as an indispensable component of the ego, not as one among its activities" (p. 178; my translation).

In other words, the ego does not gradually learn to use symbolic language; symbolic language is one of its constituents. In a recent study A. Katan (1961) indicated that emotionally disturbed children whose ability to express their feelings was severely limited could be helped by fostering this ability.

An animal has instincts and can be taught to restrain them by a system of reward and punishments. These may be either gross or subtle; in any case, they are external agents. A human being is not only differently endowed; he also goes through phases that are radically different from the phases of animal development. Rewards and punishments play their part, but they are not the *essential agents of the child's changes*. It is the acquisition of symbolic language that makes possible the metamorphosis of the manifestations of drives and the burgeoning of human mental life. Language brings a tremendous enrichment to all inner life, to the affects we experience as well as to our thought processes. The acquisition of language is in turn predicated upon earlier emotional developments. All cognitive growth is based upon earlier steps in the sphere of affects. The following points may have been expressed before; however, for me, they represent new facets, arrived at by combining recent findings about language with those indicated by Freud. Academic psychology stresses how much language widens our knowledge of the external world. Now we add that language deepens greatly our awareness and knowledge of our inner world and that the two developments are interdependent. The tool of language enables us to take a position of distance from our own physical and mental acts. Of course, the clarity of self-awareness differs greatly for different people and for the same person at different times. Language gives us both a distance from and a new intimacy with our own selves. Because language permits us to make mental processes public it also enables us to keep them private. And the defense mechanism of repression is predicated upon language.

Language enables us to "step out of our skin," to see ourselves as it were from the outside. Thus it is language that makes it possible for us to put ourselves into somebody else's place. The infant comes to differentiate between self and nonself in a gradual way. With the acquisition of language this distinction becomes far more clear-cut. This view in turn implies that there are strata of the personality for which this distinction is not valid.

Once the child has entered the language world, his store of information about the world around him grows by leaps and bounds—not because the acuity of his sensory organs or his memory span increases so much but because language makes possible the conceptual organization of what he sees and hears.

Freud stressed that initially we tend to *deny the existence* of something we do not like. Later we become able to conceive of its existence, even though it gives us displeasure. There are other somewhat similar developments. The young child acts as if things that he cannot perceive at the moment, upon which he cannot act with his sensory or motor apparatus, have *ceased to exist* (Piaget, 1957). By developing an attitude of trust in his mother and by practical experience the child gradually learns that something that is absent or hidden *can* return. He begins to live in a world where there is *object constancy* (Hartmann, 1952). This decisive step in the child's object relations and in his cognitive growth is predicated upon antecedent emotional development. But it is language that makes this step far more reliable and distinct: if something is not here now, we may nevertheless be in a position to know—through the coordinate system of verbal signs—how far away in space and time it is. We may even establish if, how, and when it will be here again. In Freud's terminology: the mental representation of a sensory datum—the thing representation—now has the hypercathexis of the word representation.[15]

The developments which issue in early object constancy do not depend upon language. On the other hand—and this is my proposition—the oedipal situation is unattainable without language. The genital arousal, the awakening of possessiveness, of jealousy and hostility, are, of course, not language bound; but the oedipal fantasies and ambitions, the broad spectrum of oedipal wishes are.

Gradually we come to realize how decisively language influences the expression of drives and is influenced by them. One more comment: language appears as the most distinctive human achievement. Yet this does not imply that the gulf between the preverbal human infant and the offspring of the other primates is smaller than the gulf between the human adult and the adults of the other primates (Peller, 1962).

According to Kris (1950), formulations in terms which permit differentiations in degrees, in shading, are preferable to formulations in terms of extremes. Yet in presenting che functioning of the mental apparatus the concept of two types of mental activities seems indispensable. It is a theoretical rather than a practical distinction because both types take part in most mental activities. Even in dreams and in the manifestations of neurosis secondary processes are not absent. Moreover, the decision which type an act belongs to is at times very difficult.

Freud's insight into the functions of language came in these steps: first he realized that language, "verbal signs," endowed mental acts with qualities that made it possible to perceive them, to make them public and manipulate them. Later he postulated that language had a far greater scope— it made possible, indeed, it brought into being "a higher psychic organization" which from then on could partly replace the earlier organization. Finally, he postulated that this did not imply the linkage of every mental act with a verbal sign.

Recent theoretical formulations (Hartmann, 1953; Arlow and Brenner, 1964; Beres, 1957) stress that the structural point of view adds far more to the understanding of dynamics than the descriptive fact of consciousness or its absence. It seems that by a completely different route, emphasizing very different aspects of mental processes, I have come to a similar finding: verbal signs are the decisive acquisition of mankind not because they aggrandize the potential territory of consciousness but because they make possible a radically different organization of our mental apparatus.

I am well aware of the incompleteness and the shortcomings of my presentation. Today's formulations have a good chance of appearing crude and trivial tomorrow. Perhaps we are still bypassing essentials, but that should not be a reason to hold back what we can state. Language does two things of very unequal consequence: it labels sensory data and by this adding of another physical property—i.e., the name—makes them more definite and stable. And language is our main tool in the construction of a symbolically organized universe. Words are both—signals as well as symbolizers. In the former capacity they are additions to something pre-existent. In the latter capacity they take part in the creation of what they symbolize.[16]

And one more speculative thought. Freud (1900) asserts that unconscious wishes are always active (p. 577). In another context (p. 567) he says that nothing but a wish can set our mental apparatus at work. And in still another place (p. 537) he states that all psychical activity starting either from outer or inner stimuli ends in innervations. I suggest this reformulation: *our mental apparatus is active all the time.* Most of this activity is unconscious. An arising wish gives it direction, effectiveness, and may bring it to consciousness. Only a part of our mental activity becomes conscious and *only a part* of either kind (conscious or unconscious) leads into acts that are open to sensory inspection: to talking, doing, or intentional perceiving. Another part remains without visible, palpable results. This brings me to my last point.

The function of language which interested Freud was the added consciousness (awareness) it could bestow on mental acts. From here we can go on a short excursion into theoretical biology. It is customary to differentiate between lower and higher phyla by the early absence and the later growing ability to learn by experience. Instinctive acts of, say, insects were formerly viewed as absolutely rigid; today students of animal behavior concede that there is a limited plasticity. A spider follows a sequence of acts in catching its prey; a moth has a certain chain of acts in finding and preparing a place where it will deposit its eggs, disguise the spot, etc. If the experimenter interrupts this sequence and then permits the animal to return to it, the insect will not continue from where it left off—it will start again from the beginning. This

271

can be repeated until the animal gives up altogether. In contrast, the members of the higher phyla are said to "learn," i.e., to observe environmental conditions and to adapt their behavior to them. Feedback modifies their behavior. They learn from previous experience.

I would like to express the same facts with a slightly changed emphasis. The awareness of lower animals of the effects which their own actions have upon the environment is very limited. This may account for the narrow limits within which they can change their actions. In contrast, the higher animals are able to see, hear, feel or smell *what their actions* do to the environment and to modify them accordingly. The ability of higher animals to learn, to profit by experience, is a function of their ability to observe the impact of their own acts upon their environment.

Man's specific asset is his ability to "observe" the impact of his motor acts *and* of his mental acts as well. We can say that the source of his superior power to modify his environment derives from his ability to evaluate, to gauge, to change his doings *before* they have any visible effects. We arrive at this paradox: man is capable of carrying out complex acts which are—for the time being or forever—*completely inconsequential for his physical environment*. This ability is the matrix of his power to modify his physical environment profoundly, to construct and destroy on a far greater scale than any other animal.

## NOTES

[1]Dr. L. Jekels once told me that Freud also advised his disciples not to waste time and energy in polemics.

[2]Here I am at variance with Arlow and Brenner (1964). According to them, "mental apparatus" refers to a particular group of processes, to a part of the contents of the mind, mind being the more inclusive term.

³"*Psychischer Apparat*" in German. However, "psychic" carries other connotations in English. The customary "mental" neglects affects. The abbreviation "psy" may be the most appropriate usage. However, in this study I shall use the customary term.

⁴Edelheit (1964) states: "I should like to speak of the ego as a vocal-auditory organization—both a generator of vocal utterances (speech) and, reciprocally, a differentiated structure whose features are critically determined by vocal utterances and its derivatives."

⁵My summary of these and subsequent statements is considerably simplified and the original text should be consulted.

⁶A similar thought has been expressed by Craik (1952): "If the organism carries a 'small-scale model' of external reality and of its own possible actions in its head, it is able to try out various alternatives, conclude with the best of them, react to future situations before they arise" (p. 61).

⁷"Relations" refer to any and all connections, functions between representations of things; relations establish facts, abstractions, groupings, generalizations.

⁸"But most of our interests center upon events, rather than upon things in static spatial relations. Causal connections, activities, time, and change are what we want most of all to conceive and communicate. And to this end pictures are poorly suited. We resort, therefore, to the more powerful, supple, and adaptable symbolism of language. . . . The trick of naming relations instead of illustrating them gives language a tremendous scope; one word can thus take care of a situation that would require a whole sheet of drawings to depict it." This quotation is from S. Langer (1942, pp. 71-72), on whose clear distinctions I have drawn to a large extent.

⁹Of course, some formal relations can be crudely indicated by images (this happens in dreams), and motor activities can be pantomimed.

¹⁰Without it we might find ourselves thrown back to a position resembling the theories of J. S. Mill who postulated an identity between correct thought and correct language. Students of psychoanalysis and language conceptualize the relations between language and thought in different ways. Balkányi (1964) distin-

guishes verbalization—putting something into inner language—
from the process of speech.

11"The psychic concatenation, or the establishing of the unity of
context, is due to the synthetic function of the ego; we are thus
faced with a general principle that may well deserve to be re-
emphasized" (Kris, 1950, p. 308).

12"Freud found that in the transition from the unconscious to
the preconscious state, a cathexis of verbal presentations is added
to the thing-cathexis . . . [and later] the fixing of verbal symbols
is in the development of the child linked with concept formation
and represents one main road toward objectivation" (Hartmann,
1951, pp. 149-150).

13"Communication is a complex phenomenon that appears in
different forms wherever there is social structure whether in
human or animal society. In human beings communication is
supplemented by language and speech and becomes the more
subtle and delicate an instrument" (Beres, 1957, p. 421).

14As a definition of "social interaction" the statement by Spitz
may be more acceptable. The *Columbia Encyclopedia* (1950) gives
this definition of communication: "the transfer of thoughts and
messages, as contrasted with transportation, the transfer of goods
and persons. The basic forms of communication are by signs
(sight) and by sounds (hearing). The reduction of communication
to writing was a fundamental step in the evolution of society for,
besides being useful in situations where speech is not possible, it
permits the preservation of communication, or records, from the
past."

15"Indeed, the use of language permits human beings to give
actuality even to events that are remote in time and space, and yet
to distinguish them from those which exist here and now" (Low-
enstein, 1956, p. 466).

16Hartmann (1953), discussing the disturbances of language in
schizophrenia, also refers to the general functions of language.
Language provides signals for communication (a function which
is not restricted to humans), while symbolic language is "designa-
tory." He continues: "I am speaking of words meaning something, pointing to something, stating something—that function

by which . . . language, besides adding verbal to thing representation, is also that function by which the former is made to signify the latter (p. 189).

## REFERENCES

Arlow, J. A. & Brenner, C. (1964), *Psychoanalytic Concepts and the Structural Theory*. New York: International Universities Press.

Balkányi, C. (1964), On Verbalization. *Int. J. Psa.*, 45:64-74.

Beres, D. (1957), Communication in Psychoanalysis and in the Creative Process: A Parallel. *J. Amer. Psa. Assn.*, 5:408-423.

Bühler, K. (1934), *Sprachtheorie*. Jena: Fischer.

Cassirer, E. (1944), *Essay on Man*. New Haven: Yale University Press.

Craik, K. J. W. (1952), *The Nature of Explanation*. Cambridge: University Press.

Edelheit, H. (1964), Speech and Psychic Structure: The Vocal-Auditory Organization of the Ego. Unpublished manuscript.

Ferenczi, S. (1912), The Ontogenesis of Symbols. *Sex in Psychoanalysis*. New York: Basic Books, 1950, pp. 276-281.

Freud, A. (1936), *The Ego and the Mechanisms of Defense*. New York: International Universities Press, 1946.

Freud, S. (1891), *On Aphasia*. New York: International Universities Press, 1953.

—— (1895), Project for a Scientific Psychology. *Origins of Psychoanalysis*. New York: Basic Books, 1954, pp. 347-445.

—— (1900), The Interpretation of Dreams. *Standard Edition*, 4 & 5. London: Hogarth Press, 1953.

—— (1911), Formulations on the Two Principles of Mental Functioning. *Standard Edition*, 12:213-226. London: Hogarth Press, 1958.

—— (1913), Totem and Taboo. *Standard Edition*, 13:1-161. London: Hogarth Press, 1955.

—— (1915), The Unconscious. *Standard Edition*, 14:159-215. London: Hogarth Press, 1957.

—— (1923), The Ego and the Id. *Standard Edition*, 19:3-66. London: Hogarth Press, 1961.

—— (1933), New Introductory Lectures on Psycho-Analysis. *Standard Edition*, 22:3-182. London: Hogarth Press, 1964.

—— (1939), Moses and Monotheism. *Standard Edition*, 23:3-137. London: Hogarth Press, 1964.

—— (1940), An Outline of Psycho-Analysis. *Standard Edition*, 23:141-207. London: Hogarth Press, 1964.

Hartmann, H. (1951), Technical Implications of Ego Psychology. *Essays on Ego Psychology*. New York: International Universities Press, 1964, pp. 142-154.

—— (1952), The Mutual Influences in the Development of Ego and Id. *This Annual*, 7:9-30.

—— (1953), Contribution to the Metapsychology of Schizophrenia. *Essays on Ego Psychology*. New York: International Universities Press, 1964, pp. 182-206.

—— (1956), The Development of the Ego Concept in Freud's Work. *Int. J. Psa.*, 37:425-438.

Heron, W., Bexton, W. H., & Hebb, D. O. (1953), Cognitive Effects of a Decreased Variation to the Sensory Environment. *Amer. Psychologist*, 8:366-372.

Katan, A. (1961), Some Thoughts about the Role of Verbalization in Early Childhood. *This Annual*, 16:184-188.

Kris, E. (1950), On Preconscious Mental Processes. *Psychoanalytic Explorations in Art*. New York: International Universities Press, 1952, pp. 303-318.

Langer, S. K. (1942), *Philosophy in a New Key*. Cambridge: Harvard University Press; New York: Mentor Books, 1951.

Lilly, J. C. (1961), Symposium on Sensory Deprivation. In: *Sensory Deprivation*. Cambridge: Harvard Univ. Press.

Loewenstein, R. M. (1956), Some Remarks on the Role of Speech in Psycho-Analytic Technique. *Int. J. Psa.*, 37:460-468.

Nunberg, H. (1930), The Synthetic Function of the Ego. *Practice and Theory of Psychoanalysis*. New York: International Universities Press, 1960, pp. 120-136.

Peller, L. E. (1962), Language and Development. In: *Early Childhood Education*, ed. P. B. Neubauer. Springfield: Thomas, 1965.

Piaget, J. (1957), The Child and Modern Physics. *Sci. American*, 196:46-51.

Sapir, E. (1933), *Selected Writings of Edward Sapir in Language, Culture, and Personality*. Berkeley: University of California Press, 1964.

Schneirla, T. C. (1946), Ant Learning as a Problem in Comparative Psychology. In: *Twentieth Century Psychology*, ed. P. Harriman. New York: Philosophical Library, pp. 276-305.

Spitz, R. A. (1957), *No and Yes*. New York: International Universities Press.

von Frisch, K. (1927), *Aus dem Leben der Bienen*. Berlin: Springer.

von Uexküll, J. (1934), A Stroll through the World of Animals and Men. In: *Instinctive Behavior*, ed. & tr. C. H. Schiller. New York: International Universities Press, 1957, pp. 5-80.

Whorf, B. L. (1956), *Language, Thought and Reality*. New York: Wiley & M.I.T. Press.

# 5.

# FROM "AFFECTIVE AND COGNITIVE DEVELOPMENT OF THE CHILD"

The acquisition of language changes the child's entire way of life, his cognitive as well as his emotional responses. Academic psychology stresses the fact that language tremendously broadens the world that the child lives in, while Freud pointed (in 1900, and again in 1915) to the burgeoning of the inner world. Discursive language makes it possible for the child to "tag" mental functions and acts, and thus to become aware of them, to observe them and to "manipulate" them. Language is a powerful tool; it enlarges the radius, not only of our actions, but of our perceptions as well. It increases, indeed it multiplies the perceptible data of both the outer and the inner world, and makes possible mental processes on the secondary level—or, in today's parlance, conceptualized thought.

For a simile, think of a pavilion with solid walls in which there are peepholes. If you cut large windows in the walls, the insider can look *out* better than before; and, because it is now light inside, he can get a better idea of what is *in* the pavilion. The pre-language child's self-awareness is limited to qualities of pleasure and displeasure; his memory stores only these in conjunction with experiences of sensory qualities. With the acquisition of language, memory becomes language-organized, and the child acquires "a sharp distinction between conscious and unconscious mental acts" (Freud).

Through this increase and stabilization of self-observation he becomes more critical of himself—with the result that certain pleasures become unacceptable to him. The strength of the defenses that he builds against them must be geared to the intensity of the gratification they have afforded him. The word-representations connected with them are barred from consciousness; they are repressed. Oblivion swallows an interest, a fantasy, which but recently was intensely pleasurable. We speak of childhood amnesia. It is known that specific aggressive or sexual impulses disappear; but I am equally impressed by the oblivion which almost overnight may cover a memory or a skill that was obviously not neutral but highly emotionally loaded.

A five-year-old who had come to this country about 18 months earlier chanced to see a picture of herself playing in the Vienna Stadtpark. The mother, seeing the child's puzzled and displeased expression, repeated, "That's you, and that's Hansi your friend. Surely you remember the dress with the dots and the red belt. It's too small for you now, but I still have it upstairs." But the child's detached, indeed estranged look did not change, and she stood her ground. "That's not me," she said firmly. In the literature, cases are reported in which a young child, upon returning with the parents from a foreign country (to the parents' home country), speaks the foreign tongue fluently, yet forgets it completely within a few months. Wm. Stern quotes the case of a boy who had stayed from age 0.9 to 3.0 with his parents in Sumatra. Although he had been exposed to his parents' German, he did not speak it but only Malayan, which he had picked up from the servants. Upon his return to Germany he began to speak both languages, never mixing them. At age 3.3, there was a "sudden switch": he stopped speaking Malayan and within a short time "completely forgot" it. In such cases we could speak of simply "forgetting," but the extent and the pace of the phenomenon indicates that repression has had its share in it. (This kind of sudden and complete oblivion is characteristic of the oedipal phase).

The tool of discursive language allows for the kind of self-observation and of memory organization that make possible repression. In all normal development, amnesia occurs during the oedipal phase, setting a precedent for all later repression. The immature ego needs repression in order to deal with impulses and interests that are not in keeping with the image of the new highly cathected ideal. The more mature ego will rely on negation by judgment, but may return to repression if it is hard pressed. Repression is the characteristic defense of the oedipal phase. Now we can pinpoint the essential difference between later repression and childhood amnesia—the sudden and complete forgetting of something where the ideas and impulses, forgotten and buried for the conscious mind, continue to shape a person's thoughts and feelings.

# Section V.

# Thoughts on Adoption

# Editor's Comments

> Behold, when it is transplanted, will it thrive? Will it not
> utterly wither when the east wind strikes it—wither away
> on the bed where it grew?
>
> Ezekiel xvii, 10

Though the problems of adoption may seem somewhat
off the beaten track to those not personally involved, they
are not a matter of just a few: The Department of Health,
Education and Welfare has estimated that there are about
five million adoptees in this country. The subject did not
fail to attract Lili Peller's daring and inquisitive mind.

In this Section we reprint her two papers on the problem,
written in 1961 and 1962. They brought considerable criticism at the time of publication, centering on her emphasis
not to talk too early about adoption or constantly to repeat
the fact to the child, but to watch for clues. Questions about
adoption are as hard for many parents to handle as questions of death—they touch our own unresolved concerns.

Today the point of view of forward-looking adoption
agencies is a lot closer to Peller's thinking than it was a
decade and a half ago.

I would like to illustrate her suggestion that group meet-
ings of mothers of adopted children would bring positive
results by my experience in leading several groups of
mothers of pre-schoolers. They met under the sponsorship

283

of a social agency—not connected with adoption (and I not being a social worker)—eight evenings, once a week, finishing with the women bringing the fathers along to the last meeting. There were ten to fifteen mothers in each group. The parents' feelings about adoption so strongly influence their children's development that some of their concerns struck me:

1. A four-year-old expressed her distress at being repeatedly told that he was a "chosen baby" by saying, "But I want to have come out of your own tummy, Mommy."

2. Anxiety of parents when in an emergency room they were asked about familial diseases and could not give any information.

3. Guilt feelings of two mothers who became pregnant nine and ten months after having adopted, one feeling closer to the adopted child than to her own.

4. Worries about behavior to be expected in puberty—though the girls were at most five years old at the time—since most of these children had been born to young mothers out of wedlock.

Lili Peller's papers deal with the problems of the young child and his parents about adoption. A large number of publications since then include broader issues—e.g., J. Goldstein, A. Freud, and A. Solnit, *Beyond the Best Interests of the Child* (New York: Free Press, 1973)—or they relate to the special identity conflict adoptees face both as adolescents and as adults—see, e.g., A. D. Sorosky et al., "Identity Conflicts in Adoptees," *American Journal of Orthopsychiatry*, January, 1975.

The problems of being adopted indeed don't end in childhood. A group called Life History Study Center is an organization composed of adopted men and women "in search of their natural parents." Their book, *The Adopted Break Silence*, issued by the Center, is based on the response to an ad in the *Saturday Review*. Forty adults voiced their thoughts, mostly concerns, about their identities. The book was "compiled and written" by Jean Paton who since then has published *Orphan Voyage* (New York: Vantage, 1968). A similar group, ALMA (Adoptees Liberty Movement Association) was formed in 1971. It seems reasonable to expect the current wave of interest in "roots" to give these movements additional impetus.

The trend of the last decade to redefine the right to privacy as well as the right of access to information and to bring both under the purview of our judicial system has raised legal questions that were unheard of when Lili Peller wrote her papers. An outstanding example is the deadlock that results when an adoptee succeeds in identifying his or her natural mother but she does not want to reveal herself and to have any contact with her now adult child. The background picture provided by Peller's papers may help to guide the parties toward an equitable solution.

A brief episode sheds light on the depth of the feelings involved. As told to me by the father, this was the reaction of his adopted daughter when she first saw her new-born baby: "This is the first blood relative I ever had."

# 1.

# ABOUT "TELLING THE CHILD" OF HIS ADOPTION

The majority of the leading adoption agencies request the adoptive mother to tell the child at the earliest possible age that he or she is an adopted, a chosen child. The sources I consulted consider two to four the correct age. The adoption must be brought up repeatedly whether the child is willing to hear about it or not, so that the adoptive parents are sure the child is "facing the fact" and has ample opportunity "to work it through." This practice appears to me incompatible with our psychoanalytic knowledge of the young child's needs and questionable on the basis of clinical experience.

In recent years adoptive procedures have greatly improved. Adoptions are handled with real insight into the child's and the parents' difficulties, but telling the child repeatedly about his adoption and alluding to the subject time and again is in direct opposition to our knowledge about forces dominating the young child's life. If such advice is followed literally, it can do considerable harm and exacerbate a child's disturbance if there is one. I am going to quote from case histories and hope you will add your own experiences culled from the analyses or therapy of adopted children.

Adoptive agencies give their clients clear-cut instructions what to say, when and how to say it and what words to use. I must say right away that I have no such definite advice to offer, nor do I consider this our task. Instead I suggest a study of the general issues involved. The problems of the adopted child are more complex, yet basically the same as those which all children and all parents have to face.

My main thesis is that we may be able to convey to an adult factual information which is emotionally highly charged, provided we have skill, empathy and time; the same task becomes very difficult when we deal with an adolescent or a latency child and completely impossible with a young child. Whatever we say is drawn into the whirlpool of the child's sexual and sadistic fantasies or will be promptly denied, pushed aside. The child is too enmeshed in his own fantasies, his powerful wishes and anxieties. Gross distortion, denial or oblivion is the fate of *all* he hears or sees that *comes close to his vulnerable areas and to his own conflicts.* Information about adoption is bound to suffer the same fate.

A young child lives in his conscious and unconscious fantasies. You may object, "But my child asks such intelligent and down-to-earth questions." No doubt in certain respects a child is a great realist and a good observer. Freud spoke of the "radiant intelligence" of the young child contrasting it with the school child whose intelligence may be blunted by having absorbed so many of our conventional lies. The young child does ask questions about sober, realistic facts but the answers he receives, the facts he observes, are invariably woven into his own fantasies. A two-year-old was told that a baby was growing inside his mother's tummy. She had hardly finished the sentence when the boy put his palms on his belly, shook his head and solemnly said: "No, it's growing in mine." A three-year-old, when told by his adoptive father that he had grown "inside another lady," said with great determination, "No." He countered later attempts to tell him again by walking away, muttering "stupid lady," "don't want to hear"—yet the father was

287

relentless in his attempts to carry out what he considered his duty.

The repeated allusions to the child's adoption can achieve mainly one thing: convey to the child that he really is a stranger in the family. That's by no means what the parent says, but that's what the child hears. A step-parent who comes into a child's life when the child is three or five or even older will be rightfully pleased and happy when the child seems to have forgotten that he is not his biological parent. Why should adoptive parents have a different goal?

Our intention is *not to misinform* the child. However, this should not lead us to ignore his powerful fantasies and wishes. If the parents have worked through their own conflicts and the family situation is a happy one, then all the talk about adoption will be more or less harmless, because the young child has this great capacity to deny what does not suit him. If he feels threatened by something and helpless at the same time, he can resort to massive denial. If there are conflicts in the family, the uneasy reminders and the talk about the adoption aggravates them. This is especially true of parents who are themselves in or near the field of psychiatry or social work and are conscientious in carrying out instructions.

It is our impression that a greater proportion of adopted children need help with emotional problems. This is not due to the adopted child's inferior heredity, but to the adoptive parents' greater anxiety. The popularization of many of our recent insights has unfortunately increased the feeling of inadequacy for many parents. Popularization cannot be prevented but should be supplemented by competent guidance. The difficulties of the adoptive family could be alleviated or solved by long-term psychoanalytic guidance. Much of it could be provided in a group situation, which would give parents the assurance of not being unique and also reduce expenses. The adoptive parents' anxiety would be relieved and much could be learned about adoptive families.

Children have been reared by other than their biological parents since time immemorial, yet today the situation of the adopted child is radically different. In other societies family ties and parental obligations were taken more lightly. Less than one hundred years ago there were many more orphans in our own society. In addition, children who had one or both parents were not infrequently brought up by relatives or friends of the parents. Today this situation is still common among some groups, for example Negroes. In contrast, the middle class white parents who are on the waiting list of adoptive agencies or of doctors for several years are a "child hungry" group. For the latter group it seems right to make "a clean break," that is, not to let biological and adoptive parents meet. Yet it is this break which, in conjunction with today's great emphasis on family ties and on good or bad heredity, frequently inaccurately judged, creates new anxieties and new problems.

Ours is a society where the Hansel and Gretel story cannot be told to children because any mention of cruelty or of the desertion of little helpless children is considered traumatizing. Yet it is well nigh impossible to tell a child the story of his adoption without providing unintentionally the element for a fantasy of desertion and rejection. Another resultant fantasy is that he has been "kidnapped," which creates a longing for the human being from whom he has been forcibly separated. From analysis we know that a young child may simultaneously indulge in several fantasies incompatible with one another.

The adoptive agency today provides the adoptive mother for her very difficult task with the words to use ("chosen baby," "the lady inside whom you grew," etc.). The agency advises that adoption be mentioned only when child and parent are warm and close together and admonishes the parent to be cheerful and relaxed about it. We know that the young child lives in a world far removed from our own and under the spell of primitive, crude and often cruel fantasies. A mother expected to give enlightenment about the facts of life needs to know well the psychic world in which the young child lives and which has far more reality for him than the sober biological facts she tells him. I am not discussing now how much a child should be told but indicating the soil on which any information falls.*

The very young child believes that wishes—good and evil wishes—are the reason for anything that happens or has happened to him. His mind harbors a host of gross misconceptions about pregnancy, birth, sexual differences, about sexual matters between the parents, etc. Pain, sickness and accidents are seen as the result of evil wishes, death as a deliberate killing or as a voluntary heartless desertion or as a punishment for the child. Very, very slowly and with many setbacks, he comes to accept the causal laws of the world of adults.

A young child asks about his origin in a direct or a very indirect way. When he is told about his adoption without having asked, then this information may be either completely meaningless and hence quickly repressed, or it conjures up these archaic fantasies and becomes entangled in them. As analysts we all had the experience of working with a child who is groping to understand sexual matters or conflicts between adults or events of sickness and death. You are familiar with our psychoanalytic rules: we put into words what he is ready to understand. We explain and set

*A study (3) presented at the March 1961 meeting of the American Orthopsychiatric Association illustrates this consideration: The adoptive mother's explanation that she wanted a little baby but none would grow in her was interpreted by the child that his adoptive mother had been injured and was defective. This is another reminder not to try to explain to a young child things which are way beyond his grasp.

things into their proper context where his fantastic misconceptions have been the cause of great anxiety. As analysts we are very careful to follow his pace, not to rush him and not to impose our reasoning. In spite of this he may suddenly drop the matter with us, though he is still beset by worries or by curiosity and talks more than freely with other children. I know parents who have answered fully and repeatedly all a child's questions in sexual matters. Years later the child reproached them bitterly for never telling him anything until other people laughed about his ignorance.

When "Little Hans" was not little any more but in his late teens, he visited Freud (1). In the conversation it appeared that he had no memory of what he had gone through at the age of four and five. His severe phobia of horses, his inability to leave the house, his other anxieties, his jealousy and his sexual fantasies, the interpretations given to him—all had been swallowed by oblivion.

Mrs. Bornstein tells of a boy whom she had helped at the age of four-and-one-half years, overcome an inhibition to urinate. When he appeared a few years later in analysis, he accused her of having forbade him to masturbate, to touch his penis. She did not remember anything of the sort. However, in the analysis a dream in which a rusty coil appeared, an element to which the child did not associate, struck a familiar note to her and caused her to look up her notes of the previous treatment. She then recognized the incident. On a walk they had taken together, he had picked up a rusty coil of wire, to which she said, "Oh, leave it, it is so dirty." His conflict about masturbation was at that time very active and her casual warning became enmeshed into this conflict and assumed a different, a fateful meaning.

Emotionally charged material will be assimilated into the young child's dominant fantasies or it will be denied or forgotten and replaced by cover memories. If human beings were more reliable and unbiased as chroniclers of their

291

life history, years of analysis would not be needed to piece things together. We know that many a child forms the fantasy that he is not the parents' child. His "real" parents are important people from whom he was separated through tragic events or kidnapping. This fantasy, released by some trifle, by an undeserved punishment, or a preference of a sister or brother, is actually engendered by the child's need to loosen his oedipal attachment to his parents. Many of the favorite children's tales deal with this "family romance" in one or the other disguise.

The family romance comes at a time when the dissolution of the oedipal ties is the central developmental task. Both fantasies are indispensable stages of normal development. The family romance destroys the oedipal fantasy when the child is ready for that step. But coming back to the adopted child, insistent references to his adoption interfere with the full flowering of the oedipal fantasy. This fantasy with its strong positive and negative affects cannot take its normal course when the child is repeatedly told that "he grew inside another lady." The oedipal attachment is predicated on feeling uniquely close to the parent and to consider him tops in everything, in power, wisdom and love. Of course, a child at times gets angry with his parent and sees him as mean and unloving. But such storms blow over and the basic fantasy remains. The oedipal child's thinking is largely governed by primary process thinking, by wishes and fears, inconsistent with one another and incompatible with reality. The introduction of another lady or another set of parents confuses him far more than the baby pond and the stork!

Speaking of the adopted baby as "chosen" is an unfortunate innovation. To the child the new term is either irrelevant or grossly misleading—he does not know what to do with it. Neither in our culture, nor officially in any other, are the good home and loving parent bestowed upon an infant who is "chosen," while others are left unchosen.* That would be frightening indeed. The term is dishonest and the underlying idea is contrary to all our ideas of charity. In defense of the term, it might be said that it tries to convey to the child that his coming to this set of parents was not an accident. They wanted him and no other child would do and now "he has mummy and daddy for ever and ever." Sooner or later he hears that the parents chose one another. But they are grown-ups and they know what to do, while the child in spite of his fantasies of omnipotence realizes his helplessness. He who has been chosen on account of certain virtues, while others were rejected, could in turn be rejected if he disappointed his parents. Even without introducing the concept of having been chosen, the child who has been told about his adoption often does not feel secure. It is my impression that the adolescent revolt is often faint or even absent in adopted children. Learning difficulties may take its place. The latter channel for the youngster's hostility is less dangerous: it is not his fault if he is not bright. There is a strong tendency in many adopted children to hold on to their adoptive parents, their home, their family name.

His sexual ideas are still vague and confused. Being inside somebody's body has obviously a sexual connotation for him and taxes his reasoning and his imagination as any parent knows who has given this information. "How did I eat when I was inside you?" "But how did you put your hands inside to make my hands and feet?" Or he comes back a few days later. "But you forgot—a baby could not breathe if it were inside." In other words, he takes our

*Kornitzer (2). ". . . The fact to get home is that (1) the parents were lonely till they had the child, and the child made them very happy, (2) the child had no parents until they arrived and wanted him, and (3) the child was chosen among a number because he was the one the parents loved best . . ."

293

simplified statement of facts for a fanciful invented tale.

To illustrate a few of the difficulties that may be encountered in a child who was repeatedly told about his adoption, I will relate the case of Michael, a seven-year-old boy of superior intelligence. He was truant, uncooperative in school and a severe behavior problem at home. In his fits of rage he deliberately smashed lamps, windows, furniture. He stole money from his parents. He had been told about his adoption when three-and-one-half years old and, according to one version, he had been a placid baby and his trouble started thereafter. (As it happens, the parents' reports were not quite consistent.) He was unable to stay in nursery school and was different from other children. An older brother and sister, not adopted, were well adjusted and good students and Michael was closer to them than to his parents. His fits of destructiveness provoked by the slightest disappointment (delay of a meal through a telephone conversation) seemed acts of revenge. The very well-intentioned and devoted parents repeated and repeated the story of his adoption to enable him to work it through, and in doing so, gave more details than they intended. Michael learned the name of the city where he was born, that he was six weeks old when "chosen," and that his "new" parents paid hospital expenses for his real mother. (The parents knew as well as you and I that the last item should never have been divulged—but it happened.) Michael brought to his analytic sessions his sadistic fantasies of stores with lots of babies on the shelves where people come in to choose and buy them. Having his children, lots of stuffed animals, lined up on a shelf was his long drawn-out evening ritual. He talked with them and one by one they went "under water," under his bedcovers to fondle his penis. He was obsessed with buying candy, toys and food— often things he had at home and for which he had little use. By no means do I claim that all his problems stem from the fact that he was insistently told about his adoption. But details of his difficulties, as well as specific interests of his clearly point in this direction. He lived for the day when he'd find his mother and get even with her for deserting him. In the meantime, he punished his adoptive parents for kidnapping him.

He related well to me—obviously expecting that I would help him to escape and to find his mother. He never took money from me, although I deliberately left money around, nor from anyone else. In his early days here he did not talk, only pointed to things and had a broad smile when I understood him. He walked with small shoving steps as if his feet were tied together, "baby steps" he called them later. When he played and talked more fully, he would sometimes mutter: "I want to go back to *her*," quite out of context and without looking at me. At home once an outburst had started, it was impossible to stop him—except when a stranger knocked at the door. Then he "turned it off" and was all smile and meekness. If his parents punished him, this was new evidence of their heartlessness; if they tried to ignore his rage to placate him, he took this as helplessness and an admission of their guilt in "kidnapping" him. His outbursts continued, but gradually he became able to stop himself and was very contrite afterwards. After a bad scene he cried, "Why did you buy such a bad boy?" But references to his adoption also came on perfectly peaceful days. Once, as he was chatting about something, his father commented jokingly, "I know my Michael boy," and he retorted, "Yes, all my life, except the first six weeks." This was years after this fact had been mentioned to him. His behavior, his talk, his fantasies, even his realistic interests—all indicated what was on his mind. After his stealing stopped (or rather became a rare exception) interest in money shifted to collecting pennies, boiling and polishing them, etc. When his father bought a new car he commented, "Did you pay more for the car than you paid for me?"

We looked together at a book giving sexual information and showing also a picture of twins. "Oh she had two," Michael said, although there was no picture of the mother. "When the mother gets stabbed, will the baby get hurt?" was another question. Another time he came: "I've seen two cats go up and down (hand motion) you know, making a baby. When some of the seed does not go inside, but drops down, will it be adopted?"

Michael, as well as other adopted children to whom the story of their adoption has been repeated from earliest time on, is severely disturbed in the sense of his own identity. Currently authorities want a child to be told very early about his adoption, perhaps even before he can talk. "Whisper in his ear, 'my adopted son—my adopted daughter,' so that adopted becomes a term of endearment" and later discussion can build on "this early glowing feeling about adoption." The adoptive parents are told to "find natural opportunities to reopen the subject of adoption when their child does not do so for himself for a very long period."

I consider this early and repeated telling as confusing and destructive. Parents need not be obsessed by the idea that somebody else might tell him. Here as in other areas heavyhanded prevention can do more harm than what we are trying to prevent could do. Never, never should information be repeated without the child's wish to hear it again. Perhaps the following consideration can help. Telling the *child* about his adoption; telling those other people who are very close to him and should know it; and the mother's facing the facts—these are three distinct and separate tasks. That a child is adopted is a very *intimate, personal piece of sexual information* and there is no more need to make it public than other private affairs of the family. Thus there is no reason to send out announcements or to celebrate "adoption day" in later years. Usually there are some people who know about the adoption. The child should know about it as he reaches the age where he can reason or rather, when his ability to reason can confront an emotionally charged issue without being smashed. Being familiar with a child and his family will help to find the age and the way that seems right, but the present dogmatic attitude closes the door to our learning. The parents should avoid saying anything they will have to take back later. But this is not always possible. The present practice of some states to issue birth certificates which do not indicate that the child was born to another mother is laudable.

The very young child lives in a world of fantasies and his reasoning is dominated by wishes, irrational fears, fantasies, misunderstandings. Facts of reality which come his way and are likely to provoke anxiety or curiosity or make him excited should be explained to the extent that he can understand them. But when he rejects our words and clings to his fantasies or to denial, we should not insist and repeat. For instance he should be told about a death in the close family, about an impending hospitalization or separation. But when he responds to our information by clinging the harder to his fantasies, we had better leave him alone. In spite of his denial, he somehow took in what we said but needs time to mull it over and to give up his own fantasies.

The young child is not an asexual creature, as was assumed formerly, and adoption is a sexual topic, not just a piece of family history. Matters of sex, of life and death may be the cause of great excitement or resentment towards the parent, and some sexual observation or information is bound to be thoroughly misunderstood. For instance, a boy may consider the birth of a young sibling as an act of treason on the mother's part, or a little girl may ascribe her lack of a penis to the mother's stinginess, a latency child may be deeply shocked by a parent's frivolous behavior (frivolous in the child's eyes). In the process of growing up, these traumata are mastered. Only when there are other disturbances, then the above mentioned events may become the starting point of serious trouble. The adopted child has to resolve one more problem, but basically his lot is not different from that of others. A young child whose biological family ties have been broken can be helped only if we replace them with social family ties which are as absolute as those which he lost.

I have no ready prescription about what should be said to the child. As consultants our role is to go along with the mother, to listen to her and to increase her awareness of the child's comments and questions about all the facts of life. Missed opportunities and wrong answers do not matter as long as she does not feel guilty or anxious. But if we provide formulas, then the mother who is anxious will use them with desperate rigidity and be unperceptive to the child's negative response. Some observers would then say: "The mother used our advice to express her own hostility." But this does not absolve us, if it was our advice she used.

We still have to learn when, what and how we can tell a child about his origin, without impairing his oedipal attachment and without feeding his own cruel archaic fantasies. The clash of love and conventions, of hypocrisy and guilt which leads a mother to give up her child is absolutely beyond a child's grasp. The adoptive parent has a difficult stand and may need psychoanalytic support to face it and to weather the mistakes he inevitably will make. All of us have a great deal to learn and we may gain more insight into the development of all children from following closely the development of adoptive families.

# REFERENCES

1. Freud, S. (1922), Postscript to the Analysis of a Phobia in a five-year-old boy. *Standard Edition, 10*, 148-149. London: Hogarth Press, 1955.
2. Kornitzer, M. *Adoption in the Modern World.* New York: Philosophical Library, 1952.
3. Livermore, J. Some identification problems in adopted children. Presented at the meeting of the American Orthopsychiatric Association, March 1961.

# 2.

# FURTHER COMMENTS ON ADOPTION

Workers in progressive agencies in child welfare fields—adoption, foster-care, family care—have absorbed a great deal of psychoanalytic knowledge and make good use of it (3, 4). A young child's stable tie to his mothering person is considered of central importance and today adoptions are handled accordingly. Workers in agencies—psychiatrists as well as social workers—see a large number of children, while therapists see a selection. This leads them towards stressing different needs. "Telling the child about his adoption" is a case in point. I am aware that other aspects of adoption have a far greater bearing upon its eventual success. But it is the issue of "telling" which in recent years has been the subject of controversy. When I presented my point of view (12) in 1961, I was unaware that M. D. Schechter (13) had already in 1960 advised the postponement of the knowledge of the child's adoptive status until after the resolution of the Oedipal conflict.

My previous presentation centered on the following issues: (1) the young child's involvement in archaic fantasies leads to gross distortion of any emotionally stirring information. An account of the child's adoption and of the events leading up to it is no exception. (2) I objected to the method which was used, i.e. to prescribing the specific words to be used and to raising the issue of adoption irrespective of the young child's desire to hear about it. I am

300

convinced that this approach is inadequate and that it closes the door to our learning more about how adopted child and adoptive parent feel.

Parents who adopt a child may need guidance, psychoanalytic help, or group discussions with other adoptive parents whose children are of the same age or older. Or their wish to be "just like other parents" may outweigh any other consideration, and they may want to be left alone. The adoptive agency's tact in this matter makes it easier for those who initially refuse help to come back later. The temptation to exert parental authority over the parents is greater in this field than in other areas of social work.

An older child of three or four who is placed for adoption and whom the social worker visits not only to supervise the home but also to enable the child "to keep a tie with his past" may from one month to the next come to dislike her visits. We may infer that the child, having begun to like his new parents, has formed the fantasy that he has been with them ever since he can remember. The social worker's visit shatters this illusion. Today's practice of reporting the child's "ambivalence" in the next agency session and of continuing the visits for the customary period seems questionable. A "link with his past" is most important under certain conditions, e.g. a dingy doll or mother's scarf for the hospitalized young child. But a reminder of a confused, unhappy past is unwelcome and may be actually destructive for a child. If the agency considers a contact or supervision with the adoptive family indispensable, the mother can be asked to come to the agency with or without her child. This gives less supervision but it is easier for the child who experiences the social worker's visits to "his" home as an intrusion.

The more a social agency succeeds in not giving advice but in presenting the pros and cons of a procedure, the better. My preference is for *not* telling the young child

301

about the adoption, and the pros for this were discussed. Now, let us see the other side of the problem and enumerate the reasons which seem to favor telling the very young child about his adoption:

(a) Between the young child and his mother there exists a special understanding, almost a kind of telepathy. In revealing to him his adoption, the mother may tell him something that on one level he knew anyway. (b) Parents want to be relieved of their anxiety that an outsider will tell the child. (c) Some analysts are in favor of telling the child of his adoption whenever the child gives an opening directly or indirectly. They assume that harm is done only by the repeated insistence on talking adoption to a child who is loath to hear about it. I am inclined to agree with this. However, while an occasional reference to adoption may relieve the parent it is probably irrelevant for the child—as he will promptly forget about it. (d) Some workers assume that frequent references to the adoption help the mother to face her own feelings and to work them through. I cannot agree with this. As analysts we know that determined denial of an issue is compatible with intellectualizing about it. Frequent references to adoption will not be of assistance to the mother. Indeed, glib talk may substitute for and prevent the acceptance of a painful fact. The mothers who have come to my attention had been burdened, not helped, by the task of talking about the adoption. (e) Unless the parents know that they have to tell their child at an early date, they will shelve this difficult task indefinitely and then comes the great danger that an adolescent learns accidentally about his adoption, a shocking experience indeed. The adolescent is normally very critical of his parents and merciless with their shortcomings. Learning that they are not even his own parents but in addition have deceived him, may shatter the youngster's attachment to them and do even more harm. To this specific point we will come later.

302

Adoption is of great interest because it highlights so many of the universal problems of bringing up children. When and what a child should be told about his adoption is but *one aspect of the general problem*: *How much of the serious concerns of an adult* can a young child face? How intense should be exposure in childhood to the harsh sides of life?

These perplexities are of recent origin. They did not arise when life was tradition bound. I don't know whether we are facing more or fewer dangers than our ancestors. However, the main reason for the emergence of the quandary is our recently changed image of childhood. In pre-psychoanalytic days the child was seen as absorbed in his toys, uninterested in anything beyond his play unless forced to be, for instance, in school. Being a child meant being childish and unaware of what the grownups do in their world until it touched directly upon the child's concerns and pleasures.* Being innocent and helpless, the good, obedient child trusted his parents and accepted their decision. If he was brought to nursery school and mother said that teacher and school are nice, he accepted this, waved goodbye to his mother, and that was all. He stayed put. If he did not, he was naughty, disobedient, "spoilt." It was psychoanalytic reasoning that pointed out that anxiety is a young child's *normal* response to a new situation involving strangers. Confidence in his parents and gradual exposure to the new environment enable a child to accept new adults and to trust them.

The three- or five-year-old child who goes without hesitancy with a complete stranger when told by his mother to do so, does not show exemplary obedience but rather emo-

---

*Child psychologists outside the psychoanalytic school may take such a view even today. J. Church in a recent book (2) with many sound observations on young children nevertheless comments that although the young child may talk grandiosely of the future, "adult life and its concerns are still wholly remote and essentially meaningless . . ."

tional disturbance or choking fear. Simple as this insight is, it could come through psychoanalysis only. Formerly, we were unaware of the young child's gropings with primordial fantastic versions of all the basic problems of the adult world. In this instance his specific problem is: Who is trustworthy? Because he is emotionally, intellectually and physically unequipped for finding the answer, he fails miserably unless he has parents whom he trusts and who stand by him. In the textbooks of child psychology up to about 1930 the child's emotions receive scanty mention and are presented as shallow and unpredictable. This can be easily "corroborated" by observation: a child crying desperately about a serious loss can be made to laugh out loud while tears are still streaming down his face. An infant approached by a laughing or weeping adult will within minutes adopt the corresponding expression. These observations are correct but the conclusions based on them were utterly wrong. A child's emotions change quickly, indeed abruptly, but psychoanalysis taught us that they are as intense as ours (A. Freud). They may leave incisive memories. Here is one of the areas where direct observation turns out to be less trustworthy, indeed, less informative than recollections of long ago.

The child's intense emotions may generate grotesque misunderstandings. Invariably, he reacts far more strongly to our emotional state than to the information we are trying to impart. How much can and should we tell him about the death of a near relative, the loss of our job or fortune, the threat of an enemy attack, the prospect of moving to another town? He senses our anxiety regardless of our efforts to hide it. Therefore, we should tell him as promptly as possible what has happened to us. He is worse off if he senses our upset and does not know its reason. His imagination outdoes reality in the production of monsters and dangers.

304

But don't expect him to keep a secret for you. You ask an intelligent child of five or seven years to keep a secret and he may spill it within an hour. "Daddy is buying a washing machine for your birthday. It's a secret and you're not supposed to know about it. I shouldn't have told you—please forget it," is fairly typical.

A child should never be taken to a doctor, let alone to a hospital, or on a trip, unless he knows about it in advance. How long in advance will depend upon his age, his temperament, previous experience. Here is something that fortunately is becoming common practice. The general public is unaware that it is based on psychoanalytic insight. A child can take a painful or frightening experience provided he has been prepared for it. And in case he has suffered an unexpected shock, its traumatic effect can be lessened if we talk about it afterwards or play-act it with a younger child.

I suppose this insight is also behind the advice of the adoption agency to the parent: "Refer to your child's adoption whether he wants to talk about it or not." But there are flaws in this reasoning. For the child who was adopted as a baby, adoption is not the memory of a personal experience. Moreover, parents are not therapists.

Whenever we communicate something to a child we communicate first of all our emotion—our joy or anxiety, despair or enthusiasm. The content, the meaning of what we say registers only to the extent that the emotional impact left room for it. It is quite possible that the cruel fantasies which I have reported would not have corrupted the child's emotional life had the adult who informed the child not been in the grip of his own anxiety or bitterness.

It is hard and almost impossible for a young child to understand adult sexuality. It is outright impossible for him to understand death, or that a person can go away and part with a child for a sober, practical reason.* Death for biological reasons is inconceivable. We "learn in the analyses of adults who lost their mothers through death in infancy, that unconsciously they have never ceased to blame them for desertion" (7). If a person dies he has been punished and cursed by somebody, or he deserted his family willfully or he left in order to punish them. Death and punishment invariably go together for the young child. But death for him has also a benign side: it is reversible. The person who got killed can be resurrected. The person who willed to die can change his mind and come back to life. A child's fear of the doctor may be rooted in a conviction that is universal among primitives: the very fact that the doctor can cure an ailment implies that he can inflict it. Unless you propitiate him he may bring pain or disease upon you whenever the whim to do so strikes him. It is safer to keep away from the person who has the curing power.

The young child knows that some things are forbidden and others are allowed. While the infant gave in to any impulse, the two-year-old has more or less accepted our restrictions. He knows the difference between dirt and cleanliness, between cruelty and kindness. He may have learned modesty. In his everyday life he shows compassion, he curbs his destructive impulses. He also knows that some of our injunctions are far more stringent than others. And yet, he has no conscience, no universal principle that would guide his acts towards his fellow men. All this is well known, but here I want to point to one important consequence: because there is no conscience guiding him, he cannot conceive of others having one.

This explains why murder is nothing startling to a child.

*I have had the privilege of reading the manuscript of a forthcoming book by H. D. Kirk of McGill University, Montreal. (10) The author points out that the typical information "She gave you up because she loved you so much" can only cause confusion to a child.

A very disturbed thirteen-year-old boy, bizarre in his interests, a failure, and friendless in school, came to my office. His widowed mother was unable to discipline him, to live with him. His quaint little games and manipulations, compulsive features and verbal stereotypes dominated his early analysis. At the age of seven he had been sent to camp. On the day after he left town his father, until then in perfect health, died of a heart attack. The boy was not informed and when his mother came on the regular visiting day, she found a casual excuse for his father's absence in order not to disturb the boy's "good time." Only after he returned from camp at the end of the summer did he learn what had happened. In his analysis it gradually emerged that he had never doubted that his father's death was his mother's doing. Fortunately, she did not know that he knew, for if he were careless and she found out, she might bump him off, too. Of course this one string of events does not account for the boy's pathological development, but contributed to it. We are less surprised that a seven-year-old could form such a fantasy, than that a boy of almost fourteen had never brought this fabric of memory and fantasy to his conscious mind and had never revised his abominable fantasy.

I am also thinking of a five-year-old who in every analytic session killed his father and mother and did so for weeks and months. He had been adopted as a young infant and this had been discussed with him in the usual way: his father and mother wanted a baby very much and could not grow one and the mother, who had borne him, had died. My interpretation, which came rather late, was received in such a way that there could be little doubt: he had fantasized that his adoptive parents, in order to get the baby they wanted so much, had killed the lady who had borne him. In his play he got even with them or perhaps it is more correct to say that he merely identified with them. Any young child in an analytic session may subject dolls representing parental

307

figures to cruel punishment and kill one or both. But in the case of this boy there was a compulsive repetitive sameness to the play, and great excitement leading to masturbation. I have since gone through very similar play scenes with other adoptive children. My little patient had also been diagnosed as accident prone. He actually sought situations of grave danger. This too, I have met in other adopted children who had been told that their mother or parents had died. Some workers are in favor of pronouncing the parents dead in any case; they seem unaware of the problems this may cause.

These experiences remind us that adoption today usually refers to one special type of adoption, posing a special problem. A child who is brought up and adopted by relatives because his mother died or who lost one parent and has a stepfather or stepmother suffered, no doubt, a severe loss. But the child who was given up by his birth mother and who, through the intervention of strangers, came to other strangers who never had seen or talked to her, faces an additional puzzle. Photographs of other relatives and of friends, even of some who live far away and whom the child has never met are on the wall, but his mother's face is not among them. Their names are mentioned at times, but not her name. To an older child we can explain what a social agency is, what a judge, a court and legal procedure imply. We might even attempt to point out how wise and necessary it is to respect people's privacy. He goes to school, has looked into other families, knows people outside his family. But the child in his second, third or fourth year of life has had no experience which could give him the frame, the background, for the story of his legal adoption.

The situation is different again when the family adopts a second child and the older one comes to know through his own concrete experiences some of the things that are done in an adoption. For him it is not a fanciful tale but a series of

308

realistic events. In recent years agencies have given two children to one family more often than formerly and thus this situation has become more frequent.

Today we see the oedipal constellation as well as castration anxiety as phases and phase-specific trends of development not as indication of pathology. We can spell out their content and their ramifications more and more as our observations of children yield the material. The essence of the oedipal situation is the child's beginning awareness that his parents are persons, that they have intense emotions, wishes and pleasures of their own. With the ardor, selfishness and irrationality which characterize his desires, he craves and fantasizes for himself all that they do, possess and experience. Horseplay, sexual excitement, physical closeness and tenderness, great power, and good riddance through murder are part of it. His own wishes are also projected on the others. They try to do to him what he wishes upon them.

Castration anxiety belongs to the most archaic strata of our mind and it is more alien and even less acceptable to our conscious thinking than the oedipal affects. Its core is the fear of genital castration and of physical mutilation. But I also want to spell out its broader meaning, namely: a child carefully protected from life's harshness, from hunger, cold and enemies, nevertheless develops at a certain age fantasies in which those who love him and care for him are capable of the most brutish assaults upon him. If we get a glimpse of such a monstrous fantasy in a young child we might surmise that he has watched scenes of brutality or that he has sensed the desire for cruelty in those who are his protectors, or that he is in the grip of rage about something that has happened to him and projects his fury onto others. But to the best of our knowledge he may not have gone through any of these tribulations. If he feels that his parents are loving and trustworthy, these archaic fears remain

309

vague, fleeting, and inconsequential. Yet a joke, a misunderstanding, or a sense of guilt over some minor misbehavior may awaken them. Even a young latency child may be grotesquely unaware of the most elementary restrictions which we observe in dealing with others.

Here is an observation which highlights this: "Katrina, eight years, saw the doctor before the students' anatomy lecture with a big book under her arms. She wanted to open the book, found a picture of a cross-section of a human body and seemed to look at it with interest and understanding. But before the doctor actually went into the staff-room she asked her: 'And whom are you going to cut open today?' In her imagination about the goings-on in the closed staff-room, she had turned the theoretical lecture into a horrible operation with one of the students as the doctor's victim" (6).

In his early work (1905) Freud (8) stated that the first sexual problem arousing the child's curiosity was: where do children come from? And he added why this problem comes before others: the child is aware that the newcomer curtails the amount of love he receives. His self-interest spurs his inquisitiveness. Later (1925) Freud changed his formulation (9). The child ponders about the difference between boys and girls *before* other sexual matters make him inquisitive. In the intervening years Freud had introduced the concept of narcissism, and was aware of the young child's precarious pride in his body. The young child compares himself and others. He is a relentless, anxious and easily mistaken observer. Exuberant narcissism is characteristic for childhood. The talk about his adoption shakes his self-esteem, his pride. He is told that he as well as his parents could not achieve what everybody else achieved. It's only a fantasy which we take away from him, but a fantasy may be more important than many tangible possessions.

In my former study (12) I enumerated and dealt with some of the fantasies which make it so hard for him to listen soberly to the information about his adoption. But it is not the child only for whom fantasies are relevant. The adult who has a closer tie to reality, nevertheless needs them. When the adoptive mother (5) bathes and feeds the child or scolds him and is outraged by his behavior, it is good if she can forget that another mother gave birth to her child. No doubt, a nurse or a nursery school teacher gets at times fed up with her little charges—yet she is in a completely different position and this gives her another outlook. Teaching nursery school or nursing is her vocation. She may be dedicated to it—still her emotional anchorage is not in it. Freud speaks of the sexual overestimation which a lover shows for his love object and which the woman in the typical case shows for her child. We can supplement this by the observation that today probably both parents overinvest in the child. They have to, to make all the big and the small daily sacrifices that a child requires.

The parents have been instructed to repeat the adoption story. They sense the child's efforts to evade hearing about it. So they train themselves to be very perceptive and not to miss any opening for bringing it up or at least hinting at it. The adoption is on their mind all the time. Here I would like to quote what a successful adoptive father of two said the other day: "You must completely forget about the adoption if you want to live your life with your children and it must be on your mind all along." I suppose you cannot forget something about which you have to be diplomatic all the time. Having children gratifies the parents' narcissism and fullfills the cycle of their oedipal wishes. The needs of adoptive parents are the same as those of other parents (14).

For a very young child the physiological facts of birth and of pregnancy and their difference from food intake, diges-

311

tion and excretion are difficult, indeed well nigh impossible to grasp, irrespective of whether the information comes from another child, or from a well-meaning adult. Support by the child's own observation may help or may only increase his anxiety and thus his confusion. If the story of his adoption is added to the rest the child does not get enlightened but confused. That has been my experience. Freud recommended honesty in dealing with sexual matters. He pointed out that the young child's successful sexual research is the doorway to investigations in broader fields. If the child's early efforts to "know" lead him into tangles of failures and guilt, he will lack the spirit of enterprise in other fields. In our endeavors to be radically honest with the adopted child we expose him to more than he can take, and the ensuing anxiety may discourage future quests in any area as much as evasive, dishonest, mocking or threatening answers of the adult. Obviously there is more than one way to impair the child's desire to know about things. Today, progressive agencies advise parents to make references to adoption *before* the child asks (or is likely to ask) about sexual matters. I still have not met one child under eight who had been enlightened in this way and did not have the grossest misconceptions about the events and about the persons involved in his birth and his adoption. Perhaps this does not prove that it cannot be done, but only that it is difficult. Incidentally, I think that birth-parent and birth-mother are better terms, than "natural" mother or "biological" or "original" parent or "the lady in whose tummy you grew," let alone the slip "your real mother." The adoptive parents who love and provide for their child are certainly doing something natural and biological.

My various experiences in the field of adoption have brought home one point: we need to learn far more about adults who went through an adoptive childhood, about mothers who part with the child they have borne, about adoptive parents. Today quite a few adopted children are referred for analytic help. The material which accrues from analytic intervention should be collected and used.

An analyst may gain a child's trust and confidential material as well as fantasies and dreams come into the session. Sometimes a child brings his worries and painful experiences that he keeps from all other adults and yet does not mention his adoption and the analyst waits and waits for him to do so. A teenager may bring a lot of smutty stories which he would never discuss with his parents and the analyst is pleased at this sign of confidence, and yet nothing happens. It has been my experience that silence about the adoption acts as a plug. Fantasies that carry strong emotions, masturbation fantasies will not come into the analysis until adoption has been discussed. My usual practice is to let the child know quite early that his parents spoke to me about the important past events of his life. In this way I deprive myself of an important sign of his confidence, but clear the way for analytic work, for uncovering anxieties, fantasies and misunderstandings which are at the roots of his present difficulties. From analysis we know that the fact of being adopted is of tremendous importance to a child, and invariably foments a number of intense fantasies. The child may imagine that he has been the subject of a conspiracy, that there is a thick web of lies around him, that his mother deserted him because he is damaged and no good, that his adoptive parents kidnapped him, secretly paid ransom for him, changed him, hid him, murdered his parents. The adopted child's "prehistoric" fantasies must be worked through.

The authors of a pamphlet (11) for adopted teenagers pose the question: What is it that makes people a family? and rejects the answer "People are a family if they are related." They continue: "The first adoption in your family

313

took place when your parents—once complete strangers—
came to love each other and decided to marry." By telling to
the teenager only one part of the truth the author makes a
statement that is dishonest and confusing. Husband and
wife are indeed not related by blood but have a different
intimate relationship, one which has no parallel in the relationship to their children. There are too many sugar-coated
statements in the popular literature on adoption. Together
with this mock honesty comes a tendency to deny or demote
genital sexuality.

It is my conviction that adoption should be discussed with
the child after his social orbit has widened, *after* he has met
other children and their parents, that is, in his early school
years. Probably all latency children toy with the idea that
these parents who care and provide for them and who say
NO to some of their most ardent wishes are not their real
parents. They indulge in the fantasy of the "family romance." It has been said that the adopted child in his
fantasies reverses the family romance: he longs to see his
real parents. But such a statement misjudges the nature of
fantasy. Both sets of children put others into the place of
their parents. Both sets of children fantasize about people
whom they do not know. The only difference is that the
adopted child's fantasy is supported by reality.

In any case, the family romance is an essential aspect of
latency. The school child has emotional ties outside his
family, he may have a best friend, admire a teacher, etc.
Other developments have gone on in his life. He compares
himself with a wider range of people. He also has found out
that a special or a painful situation is easier to take if it is
shared with others.

It seems that in these years a child can learn about his
adoption with less upset than earlier or later in his life. The
adoptive parents are certainly the ones to give the first
information. It might be a help to child and parent to have

314

an outsider familiar to the child, psychoanalytically trained and in a position of authority, say, a judge, a minister, a social worker or teacher, confirm and broaden it. I am thinking of a number of sessions for each child which could lead up to group sessions for those who want them. Only practical experience can prove or disprove the value of my suggestion. I see in it these advantages. Today at least half of all the adoptions are carried through outside social agencies, they are so-called independent adoptions. The conferences I am suggesting would embrace all children. Thus we will have a safeguard that a youngster will not learn about his adoption for the first time during adolescence—a shocking experience indeed. In talks with a well qualified outsider the child could lodge his complaint that people who had their own interest at heart, manipulated him and acted as it pleased them. The child can be in a group with others who are in the same boat. Finally in psychoanalysis we think that an injunction should be revoked by the person who gave it. In the adoptive child's past a power outside and beyond the family has made weighty decisions for him, therefore, the same agency (or its successor) should reappear and act again, this time with and not entirely for the child. I am thinking of youngsters ten to thirteen years of age. At present they can reach the people who handed them over only by insisting on doing so and often only by brushing their parents aside. As a growing child acquires the ability to understand institutions of society, he should have direct communications with a representative of the law which so decisively shaped his life. Needless to say that the function I am suggesting requires a person of unusual sensitivity, experience and training. His not being a family member is essential. Every adolescent knows that he needs his parents, yet he also distances himself from them. My suggestion supports and formalizes the identical tendencies for the adopted child. It also adds a human dimension to

315

what the orphans' court does for an orphan today. Let me repeat that these are suggestions for further study, not for immediate action.

The literature often mentions the danger that a child might be told about his adoption by an irate grandparent or by some outsider. Another very real danger needs to be considered. To a couple expecting a baby, relatives and friends of the family usually give their approval, and their support increases after the baby is born. In contrast, relatives, especially grandparents, often do not approve of adoption. It takes time to change their attitude, even to a luke-warm acceptance. There is still another issue. In my work with adoptive parents I have been surprised by the frequency of snide remarks they get from neighbors, friends, from parents of their children's schoolmates. What sanctions have the adoptive parents broken to deserve malicious comments? They are probably intended for the child's birth-mother, but the adoptive parents have to cope with them. Because these attitudes exist, it is so important that the rapport between parent and agency remains sincere and unclouded by dishonesty.

In certain population groups (Jewish and Protestants) more couples apply for children than there are children available for adoption. The agency facing the very difficult task of spotting less fit parents as *early* as possible asks searching questions. But the parents' friends have prepared them for this and coached them. "Will you find it difficult to tell the child that he or she was adopted?" is one of the crucial questions and a well-advised parent knows the answer. Thus a burden of dishonesty is added to one aspect of adoption that can never be easy, even under favorable conditions. This is unfortunate as the parent still needs the agency after the initial task—bringing child and parents together—has been fulfilled. He looks to the agency not as a censoring superparent but as somebody who wholeheartedly approves of the institution of adoption. Adoption moves a child from an insecure home to a well qualified one and thus practices preventive child psychiatry (1).

The very young child's world differs in essential points from ours. For instance: he knows one kind of physical intimacy only. It is the developmental task of the oedipal phase to accept the existence of two kinds of family relationships which are mutually exclusive: the *filial/parental* and the *marital*. Although this is a highly realistic adjustment the child's fantasies are an indispensable help in reaching it. In his fantasies he takes the role of the adult sexual partner and competitor of his parents. A broad spectrum of gratifications and frustrations, of play activities and sexual investigations assist him. Persistent interference with his fantasies adds to the dilemmas of this stormy phase. We try to avoid traumatic events or to lessen their impact if they have happened. The account of the child's adoption and the reasons for it will never be easy, but the older child is emotionally and intellectually better equipped to cope with it.

## NOTES

[1]Bernard, V. W. Application of psychoanalytic concepts to adoption agency practices. In: *Psychoanalysis and Social Work*, Heiman, M. (Ed.). New York: International Universities Press, 1953.

[2]Church, J. *Language and the Discovery of Reality*. New York: Random House, 1961.

[3]Clothier, F. Adoptive procedure and the community. *Mental Hygiene*, 25:196-209, 1941.

[4]—Placing the child for adoption. *Mental Hygiene*, 26:257-274, 1942.

[5]Deutsch, H. *The Psychology of Women*, Volume II. New York:

Grune and Stratton, 1945. Chapter II, "Adoptive Mothers," pp. 393-433.

6Freud, A. and Burlingham, D. *Infants Without Families*. New York: International Universities Press, 1944.

7Freud, A. *Safeguarding the Emotional Health of Our Children*. New York: Child Welfare League of America, Inc., 1955.

8.Freud, S. Three essays on the theory of sexuality (1905). *Standard Edition*, 7:125-245, London: The Hogarth Press, 1957.

9—Some psychological consequences of the anatomical distinction between the sexes (1925). *Standard Edition*, 19:243-258, London: The Hogarth Press, 1961.

10Kirk, H. D. Six Lectures on Adoption. Adoption Research Project, McGill University School of Social Work. (in press)

11LeShan, E. J. and Rabinow, M. *So You Are Adopted!* New Rochelle, N. Y.: The Guidance Center.

12Peller, L. About "telling the child" of his adoption. *Bull. Phila. Assoc. Psychoanal.*, 11:145-154, 1961.

13Schechter, M. D. Observations on adopted children. *A.M.A. Arch. Gen. Psychiat.*, 3:21-32, 1960.

14Toussieng, P. W. Thoughts regarding the etiology of psychological difficulties in adopted children. *Child Welfare*, 41:59-65, 1962.

# INDEX OF NAMES

Names of authors that are not mentioned in the text are not indexed, but can be found in the bibliographical sections (References, Notes) on pp. 54, 88, 106-107, 191-193, 233-235, 250-251, 275-277, 317-318.

Abraham, K. 231
Aldrich, C. K. 43
Aldrich, T. B. 241
Alger, H. 242
Alpert, A. 103
Arlow, J. A. 270, 272

Baldwin, M. 129-131
Balkányi, C. 273
Bally, G. 133
Bannerman, H. 239, 242
Barrie, J. M. 239
Beres, D. 270, 274
Bergler, E. 169
Bernfeld, S. 89
Bernstein, B. 142, 158, 249, 291
Bettelheim, B. 206
Birch, C. 197
Blatz, W. 40
Brenner, C. 270, 272
Brunswick, R. M. 96, 171, 173, 181

Buehler, K. xv, 131, 163, 169, 252
Burlingham, D. 58, 102, 166, 170, 176, 219, 220
Burnett, F. F. H. 246
Busch, W. 219
Buxbaum, E. 212

Carr, S. 132
Carroll, L. 126
Cassirer, E. 252
Chomsky, N. 206
Church, J. 303
Conant, J. B. 109
Copernicus, N. 123
Craik, K. J. W. 273
Crompton, R. 219

Darwin, C. xv, 123, 131, 175
Defoe, D. 266
De Vries, H. 59
Dewey, J. 47, 84, 87, 111

Edelheit, H. 273
Ekstein, R. x, 40
Erikson, E. H. xvii, 114, 126, 133
Ezekiel, 283

Fenichel, O. 48-51
Ferenczi, S. 252, 255
Fraiberg, S. 100
Freud, A. x, xiv, xviii, 52, 58, 96, 102, 140, 144, 155-156, 166, 170, 215, 217, 267, 284, 304
Freud, S. ix, x, xv, 49, 89-92, 104, 105, 124, 133-136, 149, 164, 170, 173-174, 180-183, 190, 197, 207, 212, 217-218, 229, 238, 252-274, 278, 287, 291, 310-312
Friedlander, K. 217-218, 220, 240
Frisch, K. v. 264
Froebel, F. 47

Gesell, A. 40, 73
Goethe, J. W. 164, 184
Goldstein, J. 284
Grahame, K. 224, 227
Greenacre, P. 175, 239
Groos, K. 61, 128-129, 168-169, 175

Hall, S. 45, 132
Harrison, P. A. xxiii
Hartmann, H. 90-92, 101, 143, 256, 269-270, 274
Hendrick, I. 133, 166

Heron, W. 266
Herron, R. H. 126
Hesse, H. 121
Hilgard, E. 195
Hoffmann, H. 239
Huizinga, J. 201

Jekels, L. 169, 272
Jones, E. 252

Kafka, F. xiv
Kaila, E. 65
Kaplan, A. 232
Katan, A. 267
Keliher, A. 77
Kelly, W. 233
Kirk, H. D. 306
Koehler, W. 196
Kornitzer, M. 293
Kris, E. 62, 93, 141, 180, 182, 232, 269, 274
Krown, S. 103

Lamarck, J. B. 50
Langer, S. K. 273
Lantos, B. 232
Lazarus, M. 129, 133
Lear, E. 239
Lilly, J. C. 266
Lindstrom, M. 62
Loewenstein, R. M. 266, 274
Lofting, H. 227, 239

Marx, K. 123
McKinnon, R. xxii
Mill, J. S. 273
Millar, S. 126
Milne, A. A. 79, 227

Montessori, M. ix, x, xiv, xv, xvii, xviii, xxii, 3, 16, 39, 59
Moore, A. C. 70
Mumford, L. 19
Murphy, L. B. 77-78, 82-83, 126

Nunberg, H. 143, 263

Oedipus 46, 217
Orwell, G. 222
Otto, B. 103

Paton, J. 285
Peller, S. xix
Pestalozzi, H. 47
Piaget, J. 55, 62-63, 169, 181, 190, 269
Piers, M. W. 126
Plank, R. xxii

Rank, O. 252
Rilke, R. M. xiv
Róheim, G. 231
Rosen, V. H. 205
Royon, A. 243
Ruben, M. 237
Rush, B. 41
Ruskin, J. 216, 239

Sachs, H. 252
Sapir, E. 252
Schechter, M. D. 300

Schiller, F. v. 128, 196
Schiller, P. H. 196-197
Schneirla, T. C. 264
Schuster, F. 4, 5, 8
Silberer, H. 252
Smith, I. 238
Solnit, A. 284
Sorosky, A. D. 284
Spencer, H. 128-129
Spitz, R. 65, 264-265, 274
Steinbeck, J. 220
Stern, W. 279
Stevenson, R. L. 239
Strachey, L. 262
Sullivan, L. 19
Sutton-Smith, B. 126

Tarzan 175
Thackeray, W. M. 239
Thoma, L. 219
Tibout, N. 237
Twain, M. 220

Uexküll, J. 255

Waelder, R. 93, 98, 133-134, 141
Weisz, E. ii, 17
Whorf, B. I. 252
Whitehead, A. N. 48
Winnicott, D. W. 64
Winter, F. 211
Wundt, W. 131